THE DRAKE GUIDE TO
GILBERT AND SULLIVAN

THE
DRAKE GUIDE TO
Gilbert and Sullivan

MICHAEL HARDWICK

DRAKE PUBLISHERS INC NEW YORK

PUBLISHED IN 1973 BY
DRAKE PUBLISHERS INC
381 PARK AVENUE SOUTH
NEW YORK, N.Y. 10016

Amateur groups presenting any of the Gilbert and
Sullivan works are at liberty to quote the plot
summaries contained in this volume, in whole or
in part, in their programmes provided acknowledgment
is made to the title, author and publisher.

Library of Congress Cataloging in Publication Data
Hardwick, John Michael Drinkrow, 1924–
  The Drake Guide to Gilbert and Sullivan.
      Bibliography: p.
    1. Operas—Stories, plots, etc.
  2. Gilbert, Sir William Schwenck, 1836–1911.
3. Sullivan, Sir Arthur Seymour, 1842–1900. I. Title.
MT.100S.9747H3   1973   782.8'1'0924   73–3150

ISBN 0-87749-461-4

Printed in Great Britain

Contents

Introduction

THE scheme of this work is straightforward. It comprises a series of self-contained, yet also interlocking, sections which I hope will provide both pleasurable browsing and a quick and complete reference service.

A biographical section describes the backgrounds of W. S. Gilbert, Arthur Sullivan and Richard D'Oyly Carte before and after the years of their tripartite collaboration. The development and decline of their partnership is outlined in the accounts of the creation and first presentation of each opera, which precedes their plot summaries.

There follows a 'Who's Who' listing of the 200-odd named characters in the works, most of them accompanied by a line of quotation.

Each plot summary is followed by a generous selection of quotations from the work. Inevitably, this is a subjective choice, but I have tried also to anticipate what enthusiasts will expect to find included. Where a song is a universal favourite, I have usually printed it in full. There are also quotations within the plot summaries. The index of songs from each work – first line and, in many cases, a supporting line or lines by which the song might be more readily recognized – adds further still to the body of quotation, but I have tried to avoid repetition between the sections. Short of reproducing the complete Gilbert and Sullivan texts, I think there is enough here for all but the most esoteric needs.

The 'Gilbertian Glossary' embraces archaic terms and some still in use which might puzzle overseas readers. More might have been added, perhaps, for the benefit of the latter, but I have generally included only words and terms which would not be found in a simple modern English dictionary.

The discography carries its own introductory note. I am grateful for advice in its compilation from Mr Peter Parker, whose father, Mr Stanley H. Parker, was secretary and treasurer to the D'Oyly Carte Opera Company from 1913 until his death in 1960; and to Mrs Elizabeth Dunford, in charge of the record department of Messrs Goulden and Curry, booksellers and record dealers, of Royal Tunbridge Wells, Kent.

Mr Colin Prestige, honorary editor of *The Gilbert & Sullivan Journal* has kindly scrutinized the greater part of the manuscript, corrected errors, and supplied additional details, especially of first American performances. The dates shown for these are of first ever production, whether authorized or pirated.

I am obliged to Mr Albert A. Truelove, the present secretary and treasurer of the D'Oyly Carte Opera Company, for assistance, and to the Company for kindly supplying the selected bibliography in this volume.

The bibliography of Gilbert and Sullivan and their works is vast and almost entirely out of print, but the small selection of works to which I have found myself turning most often to verify details has consisted of *The D'Oyly Carte Opera Company in Gilbert and Sullivan Operas* by Cyril Rollins and R. John Witts (Michael Joseph, London); *The Gilbert and Sullivan Book* by Leslie Baily (first published by Cassell, London, and reprinted by Spring Books, London); *A Picture History of Gilbert and Sullivan* by Raymond Mander and Joe Mitchenson (Vista Books, London); and, of course, the texts of the works themselves, which are published in handy forms in several editions, of varying accuracy; though none includes *Thespis*, which can be found in the fourth series of *Original Plays by W. S. Gilbert* (Chatto & Windus, London). Keen students of the texts will have found discrepancies between editions, and, further, between those in printed form and those on records; no definitive text has ever been published. But every one of my quotations has passed through the hands of the D'Oyly Carte Opera Company, whose amendments I have incorporated; so that the quotations here may be regarded as the 'authorized versions'.

My final acknowledgement is to my wife, who introduced me to Gilbert and Sullivan in the first place and has given me her consultation and assistance throughout the preparation of this book.

MICHAEL HARDWICK

Gilbert, Sullivan, and D'Oyly Carte

SCHWENCK is not a euphonious name. It certainly was not to William Schwenck Gilbert, who had acquired it from his god-mother, and he insisted on being known professionally as W. S. Gilbert. In any case, the Victorian literary and theatrical worlds were not ones in which, like today, Christian-name terms were reached almost upon first meeting. Throughout their collabora-tion, Gilbert was Gilbert, Sullivan was Sullivan.

Gilbert was born on 18 November, 1836 in London, at 17 Southampton Street, Strand. His father, William Gilbert, was a retired Royal Navy surgeon; his mother, formerly Anne Morris, was a Scottish doctor's daughter. William Gilbert had literary leanings – he passed his retirement in writing now-forgotten novels and other works – and his son grew interested enough in the theatre while at Great Ealing School to apply to the actor-manager Charles Kean for a job, at the age of 15. Kean told him to go back to school.

He went on to King's College from Ealing, with Oxford as the ultimate goal; but the Crimean War broke out in 1854, when he was 17, and by the following year he was studying eagerly for the examination for a direct commission into the Royal Artillery. Before he could sit the examination, in 1856, the war ended and the intake of artillery officers ceased. With a University of London Bachelor of Arts degree to support his application, Gilbert got an assistant clerkship in the Education Department of the Privy Council Office: 'in which ill-organized and ill-governed office,' he wrote later, 'I spent four uncomfort-able years.' An unexpected legacy rescued him. He laid it out in three parts: 'With £100 I paid my call to the Bar (I had previously entered myself as a student at the Inner Temple), with another £100 I obtained access to a conveyancer's chambers; and with the third £100 I furnished a set of chambers of my own, and began life afresh as a barrister-at-law.'

The lure of a uniform had not ceased. He joined the Militia and served for many years as an officer. If fate had not had other plans for him, he might have spent his life as a full-time lawyer and part-time soldier, with perhaps a little writing in addition. But his few years as a barrister were almost totally unfruitful. Perhaps he had too much sense of irony to take his profession seriously: he could even portray the military man as – though magnificent – vain and unimaginative.

His home life was not especially happy. His father was hot-tempered and quarrelled increasingly with his wife, until they compromised by living apart, she in London and he in Salisbury. Gilbert's restlessness and discontentment manifested itself, not in disillusioned gloom, but in humour. He was blessed with that incomparable asset, a sense of the ridiculous in all things, which makes molehills out of mountains.

He had discovered a talent for caricature, and since his schooldays had been toying with light verse. In 1861, while he was still studying law, the magazine *Fun* was founded. Gilbert read a few issues and determined to try his hand. 'With much labour I turned out an article three-quarters of a column long, and sent it to the editor, together with a half-page drawing on wood. A day or two later the printer of the paper called upon me with a request to contribute a column of "copy" and a half-page drawing every week for the term of my natural life.'

He doubted that he could think up even one more piece; but he tried and, to his surprise, succeeded. These were the first of hundreds of contributions to the magazine, among them the charming and amusing series of comic poems, illustrated by himself, which came to be reprinted many times in book form as *The Bab Ballads* and *More Bab Ballads*, later purged by Gilbert into *Fifty Bab Ballads*, retaining only those which he considered the best. The name 'Bab', by which he signed the illustrations, had been his pet name as a child.

Fun was a rival to the older-established *Punch* and attracted a wide variety of readers. Other editors noticed Gilbert and commissioned articles and poems. More importantly, in the long run, he was spotted by Thomas William Robertson (1829–71), the dramatist and producer whose refreshingly realistic works and methods of staging them were just then beginning to revolutionize English theatre out of its conventions of exaggeration and bombast. Several times Robertson urged Gilbert to write a piece for the stage. The eventual result, on the strength of a request by the lessee of the St James's Theatre for a short Christmas play, to be written inside a fortnight, was *Dulcamara, or The Little Duck and the Great Quack*, a burlesque on *L'Elisir d'Amore*, which opened on 29 December, 1866. It earned him only £30; but the experiment had been agreeable, and proved successful enough to float him into the mainstream of his literary career. Having given up the Bar to live as a writer, he now married an Army officer's daughter, Lucy Turner, pretty, 17 and eleven years his junior – she would always be 'Kitten' to him – and turned his attention increasingly towards the theatre.

The pantomime he wrote for the Lyceum Theatre for the following Christmas earned him twice as much as its predecessor, but it was still very far removed from what would follow in later years. He did not try to emulate Robertson and transform existing conventions, but was happy to throw in his lot with them, writing pieces whose style was readily acceptable to their audiences. He absorbed many technical lessons, learned what was good and bad about contemporary writing, acting and staging, and was able to try the effect of touches of his own, while working out a profitable apprenticeship.

Another explorer in the world of theatre at about this time was a man six years Gilbert's junior, but already his senior in achievement and public recognition: Arthur Seymour Sullivan. He, too, was sensitive all his life about his name, or rather his initials.

Sullivan had been born on 13 May, 1842 in the unfashionable south London working-class district of Lambeth. His father, Thomas Sullivan, was a musician of Irish descent, at that time playing the clarinet in a theatre orchestra in the evenings and copying music and teaching by day. His mother, who had been Mary Clementina Coghlan, was also Irish, of Italian descent. Their home, at 8 Bolwell Terrace, resounded with music and it was obvious before Arthur Sullivan was out of infanthood that music would be his life's work. When he was 3, his father was appointed bandmaster at the Royal Military College, Sandhurst. For one who hoped no son of his would follow him into the precarious profession of music, he made the naïve mistake of letting Arthur attend his band practices. To the astonishment of the military musicians, the child moved from one instrument to another, trying them all. By the time he was 5, he could play most of the instruments to be found in a military band.

His voice was good enough to get him into the Chapel Royal at the age of 12. This implied a general and musical education at the Chapel's school and a place in the choir. He was one of those model pupils whose industry match their talents. He became head boy of the small establishment and principal boy soloist at the royal services and ceremonies which the choir existed to serve. After one of these occasions he was given half a sovereign by the Prince Consort, foreshadowing the royal patronage he would enjoy throughout his life. He was 12 when his own first anthem was performed. Then in 1856, aged 14, he became the first winner of the Mendelssohn Scholarship to the Royal Academy of Music, instituted by the 'Swedish nightingale', Jenny Lind, and her husband, Otto Goldschmidt, in memory of the composer whose songs she interpreted supremely. Sullivan was, in short, a musical prodigy. While still in his teens he could play any instrument, sing superbly, compose on the grand scale for both orchestra and voices, and conduct well enough to be told by his masters in Leipzig – where his specially extended scholarship took him after two years at the Academy in London – that he was born to it.

Arthur Sullivan's first major composition was incidental music to Shakespeare's *The Tempest*. He began it in Leipzig, finished it in London, and heard it performed for the first time at the Crystal Palace on 5 April, 1862 through the agency of his new friend George Grove, later Sir George Grove and author of the great musical dictionary which bears his name, who was then secretary of the Crystal Palace Company. Sullivan declared later of that concert, 'It is no exaggeration to say that I woke up the next morning and found myself famous.' He was not quite 20.

One of the many appointments which came his way after this sensational public début was organist to the Royal Italian Opera in London in 1864. Close acquaintance with the theatre fascinated him. He wrote a ballet, *L'Ile Enchantée*, his first composition specifically for the stage, and it was performed at Covent Garden that year. Pure music kept him busy for the next few years – he was by now one of the most sought-after composers and conductors in the kingdom – but in 1866 he was approached by the dramatist Francis Cowley Burnand (1836–1917), with the proposal that he should set to music a farce which Burnand was getting up to entertain a party at his home. Sullivan agreed. Burnand adapted the comic play *Box and Cox* by J. Maddison Morton into the libretto of *Cox and Box*, Sullivan set it to music, and after its private performance it was presented publicly at a special matinée at the Adelphi Theatre on 11 May, 1867; but it was not until 29 March, 1869 that it was presented on the full scale at the Royal Gallery of Illustration, Regent Street, by the impresario German Reed, who in 1867 had commissioned Sullivan's first substantial comic opera work, *The Contrabandista*, again to a libretto by Burnand.

The Contrabandista had been successful artistically but not commercially, and had run only briefly. By contrast, *Cox and Box* achieved some 300 performances and lives on today in the repertoire of the D'Oyly Carte Company in a version pruned of most of its original dialogue and much of the music, and is generally presented as a curtain-raiser to *Pirates of Penzance*. Although it exists as something of an interloper amongst the

Savoy operas, having no connection with W. S. Gilbert, it is historically interesting to note that it shared the bill at the Royal Gallery of Illustration with a one-act sketch by Gilbert, *No Cards*. This was the first time their names appeared in anything like juxtaposition, and it brought the two men together one day late in 1869 when they were introduced by Frederic Clay, another contributor of music to German Reed's popular and respectable entertainments.

The first encounter between the two took no more momentous form than an amiable exchange. Next year, though, German Reed invited Sullivan to provide music for a one-act comedy Gilbert was writing for him. Sullivan declined. His head was full of serious music – religious and secular – and there may have been some hesitation in him to lend his now illustrious name to a kind of work which would appear unseemly to many of the people who had admitted him into their august social circles. Nevertheless, it was not many more months before the two men were at work together on the first of their fourteen joint works, *Thespis*.

The history of each of the Gilbert and Sullivan works is told briefly at the head of its plot summary elsewhere in this book. The rise, decline, and eventual decay of the relationship is reflected in that narrative, so that it is perhaps enough to add here a little about the lives and other works of the partners between the years 1871–96 through which their collaboration lasted, and afterwards.

Arthur Sullivan has often been quoted as a classic case of the artist who cannot recognize his true genius when it stares him in the face, and strives in vain to materialize it elsewhere. This is not quite accurate. Without doubt, it is as the partner of W. S. Gilbert that his name will live, and there is no question that his music for their operas is his most individual and enduringly admirable. Yet he had every reason to suppose that his serious works would be his true monument. They were tremendously acclaimed and universally admired. The oratorios *The Light of the World* (1873), *The Martyr of Antioch* (1880), and *The Golden*

Legend (1886), were seen as major achievements, worthy of a Mendelssohn at least. It was a barren period in the history of English music; and such grandiose works on exalted themes were exactly attuned to the needs of the provincial festivals at which they were presented. It is little wonder, though, that they have not survived. His grand opera *Ivanhoe*, which was to have enabled Richard D'Oyly Carte to 'establish English opera' at his specially built Royal English Opera House, Shaftesbury Avenue (now the Palace Theatre), seemed to have achieved its aim: its first performance was given an ecstatic reception and achieved a record run for any serious indigenous opera up to that time. Yet its only surviving remnant is the comic song 'Ho, jolly Jenkin!' In fact Sullivan without Gilbert, in terms of works that have lived and seem likely to go on doing so, can be credited with little more than *Cox and Box*, the overture *Di Ballo*, a number of hymns, including 'Onward, Christian Soldiers!', and that most widely sung of all ballads, 'The Lost Chord'. Yet it is worth repeating that in his time he was England's chief musical ornament, respected by his colleagues, admired by a vast public, received on equal terms in the highest society, which did not often extend its patronage to interlopers of so lowly a background as Sullivan's; and he was on the friendliest terms with the Royal Family. He was knighted in 1883, and when he died on 22 November, 1900, aged only 58, he was buried in St Paul's Cathedral. A nation notorious for its grudging recognition of its artists never did more for one of them than it did for Arthur Sullivan.

He was charming and easy-going, revelling in the social whirl, to which he would return thankfully after each frenzied bout of composition. Almost all his work with Gilbert was accomplished in frantic haste, and often in spite of crippling attacks of a kidney complaint which troubled him throughout his adult years and several times came close to killing him. He remained a bachelor, though a number of women figured in his life to degrees which have never been explicitly revealed. The principal among them was the beautiful and gracious Mary Ronalds, an American-born singer living in London apart from her husband and moving in the highest society. She was as close to the Royal Family as Sullivan was, but their relationship, which lasted from 1877 until his death, was quietly accepted. Their mutual friend the Prince of Wales, later King Edward VII, remarked of Mrs Ronalds, 'I would travel the length of my kingdom to hear Mrs Ronalds sing "The Lost Chord".' When she died in 1916, aged 77, the manuscript of this song was buried with her at Brompton Cemetery.

A curious feature of the Gilbert and Sullivan partnership is that their names are always printed and spoken in that order. This is virtually unique. Almost every other opera – serious or light, English or foreign – is credited principally to the composer of the score, while the librettist is given subsidiary mention, and is seldom remembered even by fervent admirers of the music. *Thespis*, their first work, bore the credit 'Written by W. S. Gilbert. Music composed by Arthur Sullivan'. The advance billing for their next piece, *Trial by Jury*, omitted Gilbert's name entirely and the first-night programme read 'Music by A. Sullivan. The Book by W. S. Gilbert'. Thenceforward, though, it was Gilbert and Sullivan all the way.

The question of who was deferring to whom in the creation of their works was an increasing irritant in their relationship. Sullivan was unquestionably the more famous in his own right: he had been dead nearly seven years, and their partnership had been ended eleven years, before a knighthood was bestowed on Gilbert. Yet W. S. Gilbert, *solus*, was far from unknown to the public. His pieces in *Fun* and other periodicals often appeared anonymously, or by 'Bab'; but from the apprenticeship as a playwright in the German Reed days there had developed a successful career as dramatist with such pieces as *The Palace of Truth* (1870), *The Wicked World* (1873), *Sweethearts* (1874), *Tom Cobb* (1875), *Dan'l Druce, Blacksmith* (1876) and *Engaged* (1877). In 1871, the year of his first collaboration with Sullivan, he had five plays of his own produced in London, as well as a new German Reed entertainment, *A Sensation Novel*. One of the five plays, *Pygmalion and Galatea*, made him some £40,000 over the years. Although it is the only one of his several dozen plays that is ever revived, Gilbert, like Sullivan, was a success in his own right, in his own time – though not on Sullivan's scale.

He was the antithesis of Sullivan in character and habits, which made for an ideal artistic collaboration but not for personal friendship. Their relationship blew hot and cold: cordial at best, icily formal at worst. There was no question of shared travels or other pleasures. Gilbert's life was as rigidly proper as Sullivan's was indolently bohemian. For all his mockery of the Establishment he enjoyed the dignity of being an officer, a magistrate, and Deputy Lieutenant of the County of Middlesex. He remained married to the same wife and preferred to live in large homes, representative of his wealth, dignity and success.

As a worker he was as thorough in his habits as Sullivan was erratic. All their operas were directed by Gilbert in the most meticulous fashion, following months of thought and note-making, and weeks of planning with the aid of sketches and models. He knew exactly what he wanted, and invariably got it; and woe betide any member of his company who tried to argue him down or slip in unrehearsed business. Fortunately, Gilbert's demands were exactly the right ones. He insisted that the works be performed 'straight', not burlesqued in any way. The humour was already there in the words and situations; and, as any modern producer who has tried to improve on Gilbert and Sullivan by 'sending it up' has discovered, there is little room for improvement of the originals. By deliberately casting a virtual non-singer, George Grossmith, as J. Wellington Wells in *The Sorcerer* created the tradition, followed highly effectively in all the works, of bringing the principal 'comedian' into special focus amongst a cast of singers. Once established as members of the Gilbert and Sullivan company, players tended to stay with it for long periods, so that the ways of moving and speaking ordered by Gilbert became established tradition, to be handed on exact to newcomers. Inevitably, like most people who believe in their own infallibility and have the power to get their own way, Gilbert did not enjoy Sullivan's popularity as a person. The witticisms which sprang so readily to his lips in conversation were too often razor-edged, and the cuts they inflicted hurt. He was admired, but not loved.

After the final break with Sullivan, Gilbert continued to write plays of his own and to collaborate with others, but with little success. He was wealthy enough to rest on his laurels as a country gentleman at his last home, Grim's Dyke, near Harrow. He died there of heart failure on 29 May, 1911 after helping a woman who had got into difficulties in the ornamental lake in his grounds, in which it had been his custom to take an almost daily bathe. He was 74. His ashes are buried at Stanmore, near Grim's Dyke.

The man to whom much of the success of the Gilbert and Sullivan works is owed, both initially and in terms of their endurance, was Richard D'Oyly Carte. He was born in the heart of theatrical London, in Soho, on 3 May, 1844 the son of a flautist who was also a partner in a firm making musical instruments. He began composing vocal works while young, but had the shrewdness to recognize that there could be more furtherance in managing the careers of other artists than in struggling along with one of his own. He opened a small office at Charing Cross in 1870 as a concert entrepreneur and agent for singers, instrumentalists and lecturers. He was almost instantly successful, and only seven years were to pass before he would find it worthwhile to lease the Opéra-Comique as a base for a series of Gilbert and Sullivan seasons.

A dispute with fellow directors in 1878 determined Carte to throw in his lot with Gilbert and Sullivan as a triumvirate to exploit their works to the full on both sides of the Atlantic and, in due course, in many other countries. With the success of the enterprise assured, he decided to replace the by then inadequate Opéra-Comique with a brand new theatre of his own. It opened in 1881, with its entrance on the Thames Embankment, but was rebuilt in 1929 and its entrance is now in Savoy Court, near the Savoy Hotel, also built by Carte. The Savoy Theatre was the first in England to be lit by electricity, and to organize its patrons into queues. It also gave the name 'the Savoy Operas' to the Gilbert and Sullivan works, and the term Savoyard came to be used of anyone who appeared there in them.

Richard D'Oyly Carte made a fortune out of Gilbert and Sullivan, but it may also be fairly said that he made a fortune for them. In less capable hands the partnership might have gone fatally off course in quite early days, and would almost certainly have broken up long before it did. Carte's stance between the two jealous principals was an uneasy and often embarrassing one, but his blend of firmness and diplomacy usually triumphed. Generally, he tended to sympathize more with the plaintive Sullivan than with the irascible Gilbert, and a touching last memory is of him dragging himself from what would soon be his own death-bed in Adelphi Theatre to see Sullivan's funeral cortège pass along the Embankment. He died on 3 April, 1901 in his fifty-seventh year.

The former actress Helen Lenoir, who had been Carte's in-dispensable assistant for many years and had become his second wife in 1888, took over his affairs at his death and in 1906 mounted the first major series of revivals of the Gilbert and Sullivan works after Sullivan's death, produced by Gilbert himself, and followed it with another in 1908–9. That the works would survive permanently was by then apparent; and there has always been a Carte to administer them. Helen D'Oyly Carte died in 1913 and was succeeded as head of the company by her stepson, Rupert. At Rupert's death in 1948, only one D'Oyly Carte remained, Rupert's daughter Bridget, and since then she has controlled the D'Oyly Carte Opera Company's immensely diversified affairs.

Under copyright law, an artist's works pass into public domain fifty years after his death, or after first publication, whichever is later. Sullivan's music became public property in 1950, but Gilbert's lyrics did not until 1961, so that it is only from that date that any company has been free to present the joint works in any way it pleases. The principal professional company remains the D'Oyly Carte, now administered by a Trust of which Miss Bridget D'Oyly Carte is head. The expected spate of newly styled productions by others did not eventuate. The Sadler's Wells Opera presented *Iolanthe* and *Pinafore*; but in general, wherever Gilbert and Sullivan works are performed, it is in much the original form. This is the way the majority of their vast and constantly regenerating public in Britain and many other parts of the world prefers to enjoy them: the tradition surrounding them has become a major dimension.

The Characters

ADA: A graduate of the woman's university, and its bandmistress. *Please you, ma'am, the band do not feel well, and can't come out today.* (*Ida*)

ALHAMBRA DEL BOLERO, DON: Grand Inquisitor of Venice, abductor of the infant heir to the throne of Barataria. *I stole the Prince, and I brought him here, And left him gaily prattling With a highly respectable gondolier, Who promised the Royal babe to rear, And teach him the trade of a timoneer With his own beloved bratling.* (*Gondoliers*)

ANGELINA: Plaintiff in a Breach of Promise case. *Oh never, never, never, since I joined the human race, Saw I so exquisitely fair a face.* (Judge, *Trial*)

ANGELA, LADY: One of the twenty love-sick maidens, ultimately married to Major Murgatroyd. *If you have never loved, you have never known true happiness.* (*Patience*)

ANNIBALE: A gondolier. (*Gondoliers*)

ANTONIO: A gondolier. (*Gondoliers*)

APOLLO: The Sun God. *I've a great mind to show myself in London this winter, they'll be very glad to see me.* (*Thespis*)

ARAC, GURON and SCYNTHIUS: King Gama's three warrior sons, brothers of Princess Ida. *We are warriors three, Sons of Gama, Rex. Like most sons are we, Masculine in sex.* (*Ida*)

BARRE, SIR BAILEY, Q.C., M.P.: An eminent English lawyer, one of the Flowers of Progress imported by Princess Zara. *All preconceived ideas on any subject I can scout, And demonstrate beyond all possibility of doubt, That whether you're an honest man or whether you're a thief Depends on whose solicitor has given me my brief.* (*Utopia*)

BECKET, BOB: Carpenter's Mate. (*Pinafore*)

BERTHA: A member of Ernest Dummkopf's theatrical company. (*Grand Duke*)

BLANCHE, LADY: Mother of Melissa. Eldest member of the woman's university, where she is Professor of Abstract Science and jealous to replace Princess Ida as principal. *I bide my time. I once was Some One – and the Was Will Be. The Present as we speak becomes the Past, the Past repeats itself, and so is Future! This sounds involved. It's not. It's right enough.* (*Ida*)

BLUSHINGTON, MR: An English County Councillor, one of the Flowers of Progress imported by Princess Zara. *All streets and squares he'll purify Within your city walls, And keep meanwhile a modest eye On wicked music halls.* (Zara, *Utopia*)

BOATSWAIN of H.M.S. *Pinafore.*

BOBSTAY, BILL. Boatswain's Mate of H.M.S. *Pinafore.*

BUNTHORNE, REGINALD: Owner of Castle Bunthorne; a fleshly young poet. A leading figure in the aesthetic movement, he really hankers after philistinism and Patience. *There is more innocent fun within me than a casual spectator would imagine. You have never seen me frolicsome. Be a good girl – a very good girl – and one day you shall. If you are fond of touch-and-go jocularity – this is the shop for it.* (*Patience*)

BUTTERCUP, LITTLE: A Portsmouth bumboat woman named Mrs Cripps. Formerly foster-mother to Captain Corcoran and Ralph Rackstraw. *Aye, Little Buttercup – and well called – for you're the rosiest, the roundest, and the reddest beauty in all Spithead.* (Boatswain, *Pinafore*)

BYFLEET, SIR MARTIN: See COLFAX, RICHARD. (*Yeomen*)

CALVERLEY, COLONEL: Senior officer of the 35th Dragoon Guards. He marries Lady Saphir. *When I first put this uniform on, I said, as I looked in the glass, 'It's one to a million That any civilian My figure and form will surpass.'* (*Patience*)

CALYNX: Vice-Chamberlain of Utopia; an admirer of all things English. *They say that in England the conversation of the very meanest is a coruscation of impromptu epigram.* (*Utopia*)

CARRUTHERS, DAME: Housekeeper of the Tower of London and successful pursuer of Sergeant Meryll. *Rapture, rapture.*

When love's votary, Flushed with capture, Seeks the notary. (*Yeomen*)

CASILDA: Daughter of the Duke and Duchess of Plaza-Toro and Queen of Barataria, having been married by proxy at the age of six months to the heir to the throne. In love with Luiz. *Sir, you will find in this young lady a combination of excellences which you would search for in vain in any young lady who had not the good fortune to be my daughter.* (Duke, *Gondoliers*)

CELIA: A fairy. (*Iolanthe*)

CHLOE: A graduate of the woman's university. (*Ida*)

CHOLMONDELEY, SIR RICHARD: Lieutenant of the Tower of London, in whose custody Colonel Fairfax lies. *Sir, I greet you with all good-will; and I thank you for the zealous care with which you have guarded me from the pestilent dangers which threaten human life outside. In this happy little community, Death, when he comes, doth so in punctual and businesslike fashion; and, like a courtly gentleman, giveth due notice of his advent, that one may not be taken unawares.* (Fairfax, *Yeomen*)

CITIZENS, FIRST and SECOND: (*Yeomen*)

COLFAX, RICHARD: A fellow prisoner of Sir Martin Byfleet, Colonel Fairfax, Warren, the preacher-poet, and others, in the Tower of London. All are fictitious characters, and only Fairfax appears. *A dozen poor prisoners . . . all packed into one small cell, not six feet square.* (Dame Carruthers, *Yeomen*)

CORCORAN, R.N., CAPTAIN: Commander of H.M.S. *Pinafore*. Foster-son of Mrs Cripps and father of Josephine. *A better captain don't walk the deck, your honour.* (Rackstraw, *Pinafore*) Though reduced to Able Seaman by the end of *Pinafore*, he reappears in *Utopia Limited* as Captain Sir Edward Corcoran, K.C.B., one of the Flowers of Progress imported from England by Princess Zara. *Though we're no longer hearts of oak, Yet we can steer and we can stoke, And, thanks to coal, and thanks to coke, We never run a ship ashore.*

CORCORAN, JOSEPHINE: Daughter of Captain Corcoran. Wooed by Sir Joseph Porter and won by Ralph Rackstraw. *The fairest flower that ever blossomed on ancestral timber.* (Captain Corcoran, *Pinafore*)

COUNSEL FOR THE PLAINTIFF: Angelina's counsel in the Breach of Promise action. *With a sense of deep emotion, I approach this painful case.* (*Trial*)

CRIPPS, MRS: See BUTTERCUP, LITTLE. (*Pinafore*)

CYMON: A young Thespian who assumes the functions of Time on Olympus. *Father Time – rather young at present but even Time must have a beginning. In course of time, Time will grow older.* (Thespis, *Thespis*)

CYRIL: Courtier friend of Hilarion and Florian. He infiltrates the woman's university with them and eventually marries Lady Psyche. *A hundred girls! A hundred ecstasies!* (*Ida*)

DALY, DR: Vicar of Ploverleigh and former tutor to Alexis Pointdextre. He sighs for love, but only at length recognizes Constance Partlet's love for him, by which time she is temporarily infatuated with the Notary. *I will be no man's rival. I shall quit the country at once – and bury my sorrow in the congenial gloom of a Colonial Bishopric.* (*Sorcerer*)

DAPHNE: The Thespian who assumes the role of Calliope, the Muse of Fame, on Olympus.

NICEMIS: *Daphne would flirt with anybody.*

SPARKEION: *Anybody would flirt with Daphne. She is quite as pretty as you and has twice as much back-hair.* (*Thespis*)

DAUNTLESS, RICHARD (DICK): Man-of-war's man and foster-brother of Robin Oakapple. He marries Zorah. *Admit that Dick is not a steady character, and that when he's excited he uses language that would make your hair curl. . . . But look at his good qualities. He's as nimble as a pony, and his hornpipe is the talk of the Fleet!* (Robin, *Ruddigore*)

DEADEYE, DICK: Able Seaman aboard H.M.S. *Pinafore*. *From such a face as mine the noblest sentiments sound like the black utterances of a depraved imagination. It is human nature – I am resigned.* (*Pinafore*)

DIANA: Elderly Goddess of the Moon. *Ugh! How cold the nights are! I don't know how it is, but I seem to feel the night air a great deal more than I used to.* (*Thespis*)

DRAMALEIGH, LORD: A British Lord Chamberlain, one of the Flowers of Progress imported to Utopia by Princess Zara. *Court reputations I revise, And presentations scrutinize, New plays I read with jealous eyes, And purify the Stage.* (*Utopia*)

DUMMKOPF, ERNEST: Manager of the Speisesaal theatrical company. In love with Julia Jellicoe and would-be usurper of the Grand Duke's title. *Oh, the man who can rule a theatrical crew, Each member a genius (and some of them two), And manage and humour them, little and great, Can govern this tuppenny State!* (*Grand Duke*)

DUNSTABLE, DUKE OF: Lieutenant in the Dragoon Guards. He marries Lady Jane. *I am as cheerful as a poor devil can be expected to be who has the misfortune to be a duke, with a thousand a day!* (*Patience*)

EDWIN: Defendant in the Breach of Promise case, concerned to demonstrate that he is no loss to Angelina. *I smoke like a furnace – I'm always in liquor, A ruffian – a bully – a sot; I'm sure I should thrash her, perhaps I should kick her, I am such a very bad lot!* (*Trial*)

ELLA, LADY: One of the twenty love-sick maidens. Having failed to win Bunthorne's heart, she marries his solicitor. *Go, breaking heart, Go, dream of love requited; Go, foolish heart, Go, dream of lovers plighted; Go, madcap heart, Go, dream of never waking; And in thy dream Forget that thou art breaking.* (*Patience*)

ELSA: A member of Ernest Dummkopf's theatrical company. (*Grand Duke*)

FAIRFAX, COLONEL: Soldier and student of science and alchemy awaiting death in the Tower of London on charges of practising sorcery. Elsie Maynard is paid to become his bride. *He's the bravest, the handsomest, and the best young gentleman in England!* (Phoebe, *Yeomen*)

FIAMETTA: A Venetian contadina. (*Gondoliers*)

FITZBATTLEAXE, ARTHUR: Captain in the First Life Guards who commands Princess Zara's escort back to her country and is secretly betrothed to her. *When soldier seeks Utopian glades In charge of Youth and Beauty, Then pleasure merely masquerades As Regimental Duty!* (*Utopia*)

FLETA: A fairy. (*Iolanthe*)

FLORIAN. Brother of Lady Psyche and friend of Hilarion and Cyril, with whom he infiltrates the woman's university. *A woman's College! Maddest folly going! What can girls learn within its walls worth knowing? I'll lay a crown (the Princess shall decide it) I'll teach them twice as much in half an hour outside it.* (*Ida*)

FOREMAN OF THE JURY: *Oh, I was like that when a lad! A shocking young scamp of a rover. I behaved like a regular cad; But that sort of thing is all over. I'm now a respectable chap And shine with a virtue resplendent, And, therefore, I haven't a scrap of sympathy with the defendant!* (*Trial*)

FRANCESCO: A gondolier. (*Gondoliers*)

FREDERIC: Apprenticed a pirate by error, he is the matrimonial objective of Ruth, but falls in love with Mabel Stanley. *A keener hand at scuttling a Cunarder or cutting out a P. & O. never shipped a handspike.* (Pirate King, *Pirates*)

GAMA, KING: Neighbouring monarch of King Hildebrand. Father of Princess Ida and three sons, Arac, Guron and Scynthius.

> GAMA: *This leg is crooked – this foot is ill-designed –*
> *This shoulder wears a hump! Come, out with it!*
> *Look, here's my face! Now, am I not the worst*
> *Of Nature's blunders?*

> CYRIL: *Nature never errs.*
> *To those who know the workings of your mind,*
> *Your face and figure, sir, suggest a book*
> *Appropriately bound.*   (*Ida*)

GIANETTA: One of the contadine, sister of Tessa. She marries Marco Palmieri. *Though her charms are overrated, Still I own she's rather nice.* (Marco, *Gondoliers*)

GIORGIO: A gondolier. (*Gondoliers*)

GIULIA: A Venetian contadina. (*Gondoliers*)

GIUSEPPE: See PALMIERI. (*Gondoliers*)

GOLDBURY, MR: A company promoter; one of the Flowers of

Progress imported from England by Princess Zara. *Soon or late I always call For Stock Exchange quotation – No schemes too great and none too small For Companification!* (*Utopia*)

GOODHEART, ADAM: Faithful old retainer to Robin Oakapple, the secret of whose true identity he shares. *As I belong to that particular description of good old man to whom the truth is a refreshing novelty, let me call you by your own right title once more! Sir Ruthven Murgatroyd! Baronet! Of Ruddigore! Whew! It's like eight hours at the seaside.* (*Ruddigore*)

GRETCHEN: A member of Ernest Dummkopf's theatrical company. (*Grand Duke*)

GROSVENOR, ARCHIBALD: An idyllic poet known as 'Archibald the All-Right'; childhood sweetheart of Patience and ultimately her husband. *Gifted as I am with a beauty which probably has not its rival on earth, I am, nevertheless, utterly and completely miserable.* (*Patience*)

GURON: See ARAC. (*Ida*)

HANNAH, DAME: See TRUSTY, DAME HANNAH. (*Ruddigore*)

HASHBAZ, BEN: Court costumier to the Prince of Monte Carlo. (*Grand Duke*)

HEBE: First cousin to Sir Joseph Porter.

> HEBE: *Fear nothing – while I live I'll not desert you. I'll soothe and comfort your declining years.*
>
> SIR JOSEPH: *No, don't do that.*   (*Pinafore*)

HERALD: (*Grand Duke*)

HERCULES: Sir Marmaduke Pointdextre's major domo. (*Sorcerer*)

HILARION, PRINCE: Son of King Hildebrand, married to Princess Ida when she was 1 year old and he was 2. *I remember feeling much annoyed that she should weep at marrying with me. But then I thought, 'These brides are all alike. You cry at marrying me? How much more cause you'd have to cry if it were broken off!' These were my thoughts; I kept them to myself, for at that age I had not learnt to speak.* (*Ida*)

HILDEBRAND, KING: Father of Hilarion, he holds King Gama and his sons hostages for the life of his son, held by Princess Ida. *If you'd pooh-pooh this monarch's plan, Pooh-pooh it, But when he says he'll hang a man, He'll do it.* (Arac, Guron and Scynthius *Ida*)

IDA, PRINCESS: Daughter of King Gama and sister of Arac, Guron and Scynthius. Married to Hilarion at the age of 12 months, but become founder and principal of a woman's university and devoted to women's emancipation. *That he is fair, and strong, and tall, Is very evident to all, Yet I will die before I call Myself his wife!* (*Ida*)

INEZ: Mother of Giuseppe (or Marco) Palmieri, whom she had substituted in infancy for Liviz, heir to the Baratarian throne, whose nurse she was. *At present the wife of a highly respectable and old-established brigand, who carries on an extensive practice in the mountains around Cordova.* (Don Alhambra, *Gondoliers*)

IOLANTHE: Fairy wife of the Lord Chancellor and mother of Strephon, banished for marrying a mortal. *Iolanthe was the life and soul of Fairyland. Why, she wrote all our songs and arranged all our dances! We sing her songs and we trip her measures, but we don't enjoy ourselves!* (Leila, *Iolanthe*)

JANE, LADY: Eldest of the twenty love-sick maidens. She marries the Duke of Dunstable, having passed over Reginald Bunthorne. *Do not dally too long, Reginald, for my charms are ripe, Reginald, and already they are decaying. Better secure me ere I have gone too far!* (*Patience*)

JELLICOE, JULIA: English comedienne with Ernest Dummkopf's theatrical company, loved by Ernest Dummkopf. *The beautiful Julia, whose dramatic ability is so overwhelming that our audiences forgive even her strong English accent.* (Ernest, *Grand Duke*)

JUDGE: The jurist trying the Breach of Promise action. He attributes his rise to eminence to a judicious engagement to a rich attorney's ill-favoured daughter. *Though all my law is fudge, Yet I'll never, never budge, But I'll live and die a Judge!* (*Trial*)

JUPITER: Aged ruler of the gods on Mount Olympus. *You're so much out of repair. No, you don't come up to my idea of the part. Bless you, I've played you often.* (Thespis, *Thespis*)

KALYBA, PRINCESS: See NEKAYA and KALYBA. (*Utopia*)

KATE: Niece of Dame Carruthers. (*Yeomen*)

KATISHA: Nanki-Poo's elderly lover, inveigled into marrying Ko-Ko. *He did not love me, but he would have loved me in time. I am an acquired taste – only the educated palate can appreciate me. I was educating his palate when he left me. . . . It takes years to train a man to love me.* (*Mikado*)

KO-KO: A cheap tailor of Titipu, elevated to Lord High Executioner and ultimately married to Katisha. *Surely, never had a male Under such-like circumstances So adventurous a tale, Which may rank with most romances.* (*Mikado*)

KRAKENFELDT, BARONESS CAROLINE VON: Betrothed to the Grand Duke Rudolph. *An antique, I should say – of the early Merovingian period.* (Prince of Monte Carlo, *Grand Duke*)

LEILA: A fairy. (*Iolanthe*)

LISA: Soubrette of Ernest Dummkopf's theatrical company. She marries Ludwig, though not without preliminary discomposure. *I really cannot stand seeing my Ludwig married twice in one day to somebody else!* (*Grand Duke*)

LORD CHANCELLOR, THE: Suitor of Phyllis, but revealed to be the husband of Iolanthe and father of Strephon. *His Lordship is constitutionally as blithe as a bird – he trills upon the bench like a thing of song and gladness. . . . He is, perhaps, the only living instance of a judge whose decrees have received the honour of a double encore.* (Lord Mountararat, *Iolanthe*)

LUDWIG: Leading comedian of Ernest Dummkopf's theatrical company, betrothed to Lisa (whom he eventually marries), but required meanwhile to marry Julia Jellicoe upon being briefly elevated to the position of Grand Duke. *When an obscure comedian, whom the law backs, To sovereign rank is promptly elevated, He takes it with its incidental drawbacks! So Julia and I are duly mated.* (*Grand Duke*)

LUIZ: Private drummer and suite of the Duke and Duchess of Plaza-Toro, and sweetheart (actually, husband) of Casilda. He is eventually revealed to be the foster-son of Inez and, therefore, King of Barataria. *The Royal Prince was by the King entrusted To my fond care, ere I grew old and crusted. . . . I called* him 'son' with pardonable slyness – His name, Luiz! Behold his Royal Highness! (Inez, Gondoliers)

MAD MARGARET: Deranged former sweetheart of Sir Despard Murgatroyd, to whom he returns upon his reformation. *Aye! I love him – he loved me once. But that's all gone. Fisht! He gave me an Italian glance – thus – and made me his.* (Ruddigore)

MARCO. See PALMIERI. (Gondoliers)

MARS: The God of War. *A terribly famous conqueror, With sword upon his thigh.* (Timidon, Thespis)

MARTHA: A member of Ernest Dummkopf's theatrical company. (Grand Duke)

MAYBUD, ROSE: Dame Hannah's beautiful niece, loved diffidently by Robin Oakapple, but more enthusiastically by Richard Dauntless. *I'm – I'm took flat aback – I never see anything like you in all my born days. Parbuckle me, if you ain't the loveliest gal I've ever set eyes on. There – I can't say fairer than that, can I?* (Dauntless, Ruddigore)

MAYNARD, ELSIE: A strolling singer, travelling with her mother, Bridget Maynard, and Jack Point, her companion with whom she has an unspoken 'understanding' of betrothal. She marries the condemned Colonel Fairfax for a fee of 100 crowns. *Though tear and long-drawn sigh Ill fit a bride, No sadder wife than I The whole world wide.* (Yeomen)

MELENE: A Utopian maiden. (Utopia)

MELISSA: Lady Blanche's daughter. A young student in the woman's university, brought up in complete ignorance of men, but captivated by her first sight of one of them (Florian), whom she subsequently marries. *My natural instinct teaches me (And instinct is important, O!) You're everything you ought to be, And nothing that you oughtn't, O!* (Ida)

MENTONE, VISCOUNT: A supernumerary from the Theatre Monaco, engaged as a member of the Prince of Monte Carlo's suite.

HASHBAZ: *You're Viscount Mentone, ain't you?*

MENTONE: *Blest if I know. It's wrote here – yes, Viscount Mentone.* (Grand Duke)

MERCURY: Messenger of the gods, and Jupiter's deputy in their absence. *Now that you gods are too old for your work, you've made me the miserable drudge of Olympus – groom, valet, postman, butler, commissionaire, maid of all work, parish beadle, and original dustman.* (*Thespis*)

MERYLL, SERGEANT: A Yeoman of the Guard in the Tower of London. Father of Leonard and Phoebe and an old fellow-campaigner of Colonel Fairfax, who has twice saved his life. Reluctant suitor of Dame Carruthers. *Why, look ye, chuck – for many a month I've – I've thought to myself – ' There's snug love saving up in that middle-aged bosom for some one, and why not for thee – that's me – so take heart and tell her – that's thee – that thou – that's me – lovest her – thee – and – and – well, I'm a miserable old man, and I've done it – and that's me!* (*Yeomen*)

MERYLL, LEONARD: Son of Sergeant Meryll and brother of Phoebe. Appointed a Yeoman of the Guard for saving his regimental standard. *Leonard Meryll! Leonard Meryll! Dauntless he in time of peril! Man of power, Knighthood's flower, Welcome to the grim old Tower!* (*Yeomen*)

MERYLL, PHOEBE: Sergeant Meryll's daughter and sister to Leonard. 'Betrothed' to Wilfred Shadbolt. *Come – I am thy Phoebe – thy very own – and we will be wed in a year – or two – (or three, at the most. Yeomen*)

MIKADO, THE: Emperor of Japan; father of Nanki-Poo. *A more humane Mikado never Did in Japan exist, To nobody second, I'm certainly reckoned A true philanthropist.* (*Mikado*)

MONTE CARLO, PRINCE OF: Father of the Princess. *Confined for the last two years within the precincts of my palace by an obdurate bootmaker who held a warrant for my arrest, I devoted my enforced leisure to a study of the doctrine of chances . . . and this led to the discovery of a singularly fascinating little round game which I have called roulette.* (*Grand Duke*)

MONTE CARLO, PRINCESS OF: The Prince's daughter, betrothed in infancy to the Grand Duke Rudolph, to whom she is at length married. *You're an attractive little girl, you know, but you're as poor as a rat!* (Rudolph, *Grand Duke*)

c

MOUNTARARAT, GEORGE, EARL OF: Friend since boyhood of his fellow Earl, and rival for the hand of Phyllis, Lord Tolloller. *I don't want to say a word against brains – I've a great respect for brains – I often wish I had some myself.* (*Iolanthe*)

MURGATROYD, MAJOR: Officer of the Dragoon Guards. He wins Lady Angela by feigning conversion to the aesthetic brotherhood. *I don't know why, but I've an idea that this is not quite right.* (*Patience*)

MURGATROYD: Various past baronets of Ruddigore: Conrad, twelfth baronet; Desmond, sixteenth baronet; Gilbert, eighteenth baronet; Jasper, third baronet; Lionel, sixth baronet; Mervyn, twentieth baronet. (*Ruddigore*)

MURGATROYD, SIR DESPARD: Bad baronet of Ruddigore. Younger brother of Sir Ruthven. He marries Mad Margaret and joins her in conducting a National School. *Oh, why am I moody and sad? And why am I guiltily mad? Because I am thoroughly bad! You'll see it at once in my face.* (*Ruddigore*)

MURGATROYD, SIR RODERIC: Twenty-first baronet of Ruddigore, uncle of Sir Despard and Sir Ruthven, and spokesman for the ghosts of his line. Former fiancé of Dame Hannah.

ROBIN: *I recognize you now – you are the picture that hangs at the end of the gallery.*

SIR RODERIC: *In a bad light. I am.* (*Ruddigore*)

MURGATROYD, SIR RUPERT: First baronet of Ruddigore whose wicked ways brought down the curse upon his line. *Sir Rupert Murgatroyd His leisure and his riches He ruthlessly employed In persecuting witches.* (Dame Hannah, *Ruddigore*)

MURGATROYD, SIR RUTHVEN: See OAKAPPLE, ROBIN. (*Ruddigore*)

NANKI-POO: Son of the Mikado, posing as a wandering minstrel in order to find and woo Yum-Yum. *A wandering minstrel, who plays a wind instrument outside tea-houses, is hardly a fitting husband for the ward of a Lord High Executioner.* (Yum-Yum, *Mikado*)

NEKAYA and KALYBA, PRINCESSES: Daughters of King Paramount of Utopia and sisters of Princess Zara. Educated on English principles. *How fair! how modest! how discreet! How bashfully demure! See how they blush, as they've been taught ... How English and how pure.* (Chorus, *Utopia*)

NICEMIS: A Thespian who marries Sparkeion. She assumes the role of Diana on Olympus. *I am the moon, the lamp of night. I show a light – I show a light.* (*Thespis*)

NOTARY: Lawyer of the village of Ploverleigh, married to Mrs Partlet after being briefly pursued by her daughter, Constance, under the influence of the love-philtre. *He's dry and snuffy, deaf and slow, Ill-tempered, weak, and poorly! He's ugly and absurdly dressed, And sixty-seven nearly, He's everything that I detest, But if the truth must be confessed, I love him very dearly!* (Constance, *Sorcerer*)

OAKAPPLE, ROBIN: Incognito of Sir Ruthven Murgatroyd, elder brother of Sir Despard. Foster-brother of Richard Dauntless. A prosperous but shy farmer in love with Rose Maybud, whom he eventually marries. *He combines the manners of a Marquis with the morals of a Methodist.* (Dame Hannah, *Ruddigore*)

OLGA: A member of Ernest Dummkopf's theatrical company. (*Grand Duke*)

PALMIERI, GIUSEPPE and MARCO: Venetian gondoliers, married respectively to Tessa and Gianetta. One of them is the son of the late Baptisto Palmieri, the other of Inez; but which is which cannot be resolved. One of them is thought to be heir to the kingdom of Barataria, which they rule jointly for a time while the matter is sorted out. *We are called 'Your Majesty', we are allowed to buy ourselves magnificent clothes, our subjects frequently nod to us in the streets, the sentries always return our salutes, and we enjoy the inestimable privilege of heading the subscription lists to all the principal charities. In return for these advantages the least we can do is to make ourselves useful about the Palace.* (*Gondoliers*)

PARAMOUNT I, KING OF UTOPIA: Father of the Princesses Zara, Nekaya and Kalyba. Subsequently married to Lady Sophy. He models his rule upon English institutions. *We'll go down to Posterity renowned as the first sovereign in Christendom who registered his Crown and Country under the Joint Stock Company's Act of Sixty-Two!* (*Utopia*)

PARTLET, CONSTANCE: Mrs Partlet's 17-year-old daughter, in love with Dr Daly whom she marries after a brief and involuntary passion for the Notary. *Dear friends, take pity on my lot, My cup is not of nectar! I long have loved – as who would not? – Our kind and reverend rector. Long years ago my love began So sweetly – yet so sadly – But when I saw this plain old man, Away my old affection ran – I found I loved him madly.* (*Sorcerer*)

PARTLET, MRS ZORAH: Widowed mother of Constance. Pew-opener at Ploverleigh church, she is briefly betrothed to Sir Marmaduke Pointdextre, under the influence of the love-philtre, but eventually united with the Notary. *I'm no saucy minx and giddy – Hussies such as them abound – But a clean and tidy widdy Well be-known for miles around!* (*Sorcerer*)

PATIENCE: A dairy maid, loved by Reginald Bunthorne but heart-free until she meets again her childhood sweetheart, Archibald Grosvenor. *Although I may not love you – for you are perfection – there is nothing to prevent your loving me. I am plain, homely, unattractive.* (*Patience*)

PEEP-BO and PITTI-SING: Wards of Ko-Ko and sisters of Yum-Yum.

YUM-YUM: *From three little maids take one away*

PEEP-BO: *Two little maids remain, and they –*

PITTI-SING: *Won't have to wait very long, they say –*

THE THREE: *Three little maids from school!*   (*Mikado*)

PHANTIS: A Judge of the Utopian Supreme Court; one of the two Wise Men appointed to denounce the King on his first lapse from propriety. Unsuccessful suitor of Princess Zara. *I feel sure that she does not regard me with absolute indifference, for she could never look at me without having to go to bed with a sick headache.* (*Utopia*)

PHYLLA: A Utopian maiden. (*Utopia*)

PHYLLIS: An Arcadian shepherdess and Ward in Chancery. Sweetheart of Strephon, she is also wooed by the Lord Chancellor, Earls Mountararat and Tolloller, and their fellow Lords. *Why did five-and-twenty Liberal Peers come down to shoot over*

*your grass-plot last autumn? It couldn't have been the sparrows.
Why did five-and-twenty Conservative Peers come down to fish
your pond? Don't tell me it was the gold-fish! No, no – delays are
dangerous, and if we are to marry, the sooner the better.* (Strephon,
Iolanthe)

PIRATE KING: A renegade nobleman, leading a pirate band of
fellow orphaned nobles. *Many a king on a first-class throne, If he
wants to call his crown his own, Must manage somehow to get
through More dirty work than ever I do.* (*Pirates*)

PISH-TUSH: A noble lord of Titipu. (*Mikado*)

PITTI-SING: See PEEP-BO and PITTI-SING. (*Mikado*)

PLAZA-TORO, DUCHESS OF: Wife of the Duke and mother of
Casilda. *I said to myself, ' That man is a Duke, and I will love
him.' Several of my relations bet me I couldn't, but I did – desper-
ately!* (*Gondoliers*)

PLAZA-TORO, DUKE OF: Count Matadoro, Baron Picadoro, Castilian hidalgo of ninety-five quarterings. Father of Casilda and
director of The Duke of Plaza-Toro, Limited. *That celebrated,
cultivated, underrated nobleman, the Duke of Plaza-Toro!* (*Gondoliers*)

POINT, JACK: Strolling jester, temporarily employed by Sir
Richard Cholmondeley. In love with his fellow artiste, Elsie
Maynard. *See, I am a salaried wit; and is there aught in nature
more ridiculous? A poor, dull, heart-broken man, who must needs
be merry, or he will be whipped; who must rejoice lest he starve;
who must jest you, jibe you, quip you, crank you, wrack you, riddle
you, from hour to hour, from day to day, from year to year, lest he
dwindle, perish, starve, pine, and die!* (*Yeomen*)

POINTDEXTRE, ALEXIS: Son and heir of Sir Marmaduke Pointdextre, betrothed to Aline Sangazure. An officer in the Grenadier Guards, and campaigner for classless marriages.

ALEXIS: *Oh, that the world would break down the artificial barriers
of rank, wealth, education, age, beauty, habits, taste, and temper,
and recognize the glorious principle, that in marriage alone is to be
found the panacea for every ill!*

ALINE: *Continue to preach that sweet doctrine, and you will succeed, oh, evangel of true happiness!* (Sorcerer)

POINTDEXTRE, SIR MARMADUKE: An elderly baronet, in love since youth with Lady Sangazure, whom he eventually marries. Father of Alexis. *Where is the family, other than my own, in which there is no flaw?* (Sorcerer)

POOH-BAH: Lord High Everything Else of Titipu, by virtue of having assumed all the chief offices of State. *I can trace my ancestry back to a protoplasmal primordial atomic globule. Consequently, my family pride is something inconceivable. I can't help it. I was born sneering.* (Mikado)

PORTER, THE RT. HON. SIR JOSEPH, K.C.B. First Lord of the Admiralty, in love with Josephine Corcoran. *Sir Joseph's attentions nauseate me. I know that he is a truly great and good man, for he told me so himself, but to me he seems tedious, fretful, and dictatorial. Yet his must be a mind of no common order, or he would not dare to teach my dear father to dance a hornpipe on the cabin table.* (Pinafore)

PREPOSTEROS: One of the Thespians. *It is enough that I am downtrodden in my profession. I will not submit to imposition out of it. It is enough that as your heavy villain I get the worst of it every night in a combat of six. I will not submit to insult in the day time.* (Thespis)

PRETTEIA: A young Thespian who assumes the role of Venus on Olympus. (Thespis)

PSYCHE, LADY: Florian's sister and Professor of Humanities in the woman's university. She marries Cyril. *Are you indeed that Lady Psyche, who At children's parties drove the conjuror wild, Explaining all his tricks before he did them?* (Cyril, Ida)

QUEEN OF THE FAIRIES: Mentor of Iolanthe, political sponsor of Strephon, and self-invited bride of Private Willis. *It seems that she's a fairy From Andersen's library, And I took her for The proprietor Of a Ladies' Seminary!* (Lord Chancellor, Iolanthe)

RACKSTRAW, RALPH: Able Seaman: foremast-hand aboard H.M.S. *Pinafore*. Foster-son of Mrs Cripps and suitor of

Josephine Corcoran. *There's not a smarter topman in the Navy, your honour, though I say it who shouldn't.* (*Pinafore*)

RUDOLPH, GRAND DUKE OF PFENNIG HALBPFENNIG: Betrothed to the Baroness von Krakenfeldt, but married instead to his childhood's betrothed, the Princess of Monte Carlo. *I never join in merriment – I don't see any joke or jape any – I never tolerate familiarity in shape any – This, joined with an extravagant respect for tuppence-ha'penny, A keynote to my character sufficiently supplies.* (*Grand Duke*)

RUTH: Nurserymaid to Frederic in his infancy, she joined the pirate band with him and hoped to become his wife. *A nurserymaid is not afraid of what you people call work, So I made up my mind to go as a kind of piratical maid-of-all-work.* (*Pirates*)

RUTH: Professional bridesmaid of Rederring, Cornwall. *This is, perhaps, the only village in the world that possesses an endowed corps of professional bridesmaids who are bound to be on duty every day from ten to four.* (*Ruddigore*)

SACHARISSA: A graduate of the woman's university, and its 'lady surgeon'. *Cut off real live legs and arms? . . . I wouldn't do it for a thousand pounds!* (*Ida*)

SALATA: A Utopian maiden. (*Utopia*)

SAMUEL: The Pirate King's lieutenant. *We don't seem to make piracy pay. I'm sure I don't know why, but we don't.* (*Pirates*)

SANGAZURE, ALINE. Daughter of Lady Sangazure, betrothed to Alexis Pointdextre. *Aline is rich, and she comes of a sufficiently old family, for she is the seven thousand and thirty-seventh in direct descent from Helen of Troy.* (*Sorcerer*)

SANGAZURE, LADY ANNABELLA: Widowed mother of Aline. In love from her youth with Sir Marmaduke Pointdextre. *Alas! ah me! and well-a-day! I sigh for love, and well I may, For I am very old and grey.* (*Sorcerer*)

SAPHIR, LADY: One of the twenty love-sick maidens. She marries Colonel Calverley, despite earlier misgivings: *You are not Empyrean. You are not Della Cruscan. You are not even Early English. Oh, be Early English ere it is too late!* (*Patience*)

SCAPHIO: A Judge of the Utopian Supreme Court; one of the

two Wise Men appointed to denounce the King on his first
lapse from propriety. Unsuccessful suitor of Princess Zara, the
first woman he has succeeded in loving. *I have an ideal – a
semi-transparent Being – filled with an inorganic pink jelly – and I
have never yet seen the woman who approaches within measurable
distance of it. All are opaque – opaque – opaque!* (Utopia)

SCYNTHIUS: See ARAC (*Ida*)

SERGEANT OF POLICE: Leader of the force apprehensively pur-
suing the pirates. *When constabulary duty's to be done – To be
done, The policeman's lot is not a happy one.* (Pirates)

SHADBOLT, WILFRED: Head Jailer and Assistant Tormentor in
the Tower of London. 'Betrothed' to Phoebe Meryll. Philo-
sopher and wit *manqué. Aye, I have a pretty wit – a light, airy,
joysome wit, spiced with anecdotes of prison cells and the torture
chamber. Oh, a very delicate wit! I have tried it on many a prisoner,
and there have been some who smiled. Now it is not easy to make a
prisoner smile.* (Yeomen)

SILLIMON: The Thespians' stage-manager. *I ought to be strict with
them and make them do their duty, but I can't. Bless their little
hearts, when I see the pretty little craft come sailing up to me with a
wheedling smile on their pretty little figure-heads, I can't turn
my back on 'em. I'm all bow, though I'm sure I try to be stern!*
(Thespis)

SOLICITOR: Reginald Bunthorne's legal adviser. He marries Lady
Ella. *Heart-broken at my Patience's barbarity, By the advice of my
solicitor, In aid – in aid of a deserving charity, I've put myself up to
be raffled for!* (Patience)

SOPHY, LADY: English governess of the Princesses of Utopia,
subsequently married to their father, King Paramount. *I made
a vow, one early spring, That only to some spotless King, Who
proof of blameless life could bring I'd be united. For I had read, not
long before, Of blameless Kings in fairy lore, And thought the
race still flourished here – Well – I was a maid of fifteen year!*
(Utopia)

SPARKEION: Young Thespian whose marriage to Nicemis is the
cause of the company's outing to Mount Olympus. He is

allocated the role of Phoebus Apollo when the gods leave. *Phoebus am I, with golden ray, The god of day, the god of day, When shadowy night has held her sway, I make the goddess fly.* (*Thespis*)

STANLEY, MAJOR-GENERAL: Father of Mabel, Kate, Isabel and an unspecified number of other daughters. *My military knowledge, though I'm plucky and adventury, Has only been brought down to the beginning of the century: But still in matters vegetable, animal, and mineral, I am the very model of a modern Major-General.* (*Pirates*)

STANLEY, EDITH: One of Major-General Stanley's daughters; sister of Mabel, Isabel and Kate and many others. *Alas! there's not one maiden here Whose homely face and bad complexion Have caused all hope to disappear Of ever winning man's affection!* (*Pirates*)

STANLEY, ISABEL: One of Major-General Stanley's daughters; sister of Mabel, Edith, Kate and many others.

STANLEY, KATE: One of Major-General Stanley's daughters; sister of Mabel, Isabel, and Edith and many others.

STANLEY, MABEL: One of Major-General Stanley's daughters. She falls in love with Frederic. *Oh, family descent, How great thy charm, thy sway how excellent!* (*Pirates*)

STREPHON: An Arcadian shepherd, son of Iolanthe and the Lord Chancellor and sweetheart of Phyllis; elected Liberal-Unionist Member of Parliament. He is a fairy down to the waist, mortal below. *I can make myself invisible down to the waist, but that's of no use when my legs remain exposed to view! My brain is a fairy brain, but from the waist downwards I'm a gibbering idiot. My upper half is immortal, but my lower half grows older every day, and some day or other must die of old age. What's to become of my upper half when I've buried my lower half I really don't know!* (*Iolanthe*)

STUPIDAS: One of the Thespians. (*Thespis*)

TANNHÄUSER, DR: Notary of Speisesaal and legal adviser to the conspiracy to dethrone the Grand Duke. *It is always amusing to the legal mind to see a parcel of laymen bothering themselves*

*about a matter which to a trained lawyer presents no difficulty
whatever. (Grand Duke)*

TARARA: Public Exploder of Utopia, required, if commanded,
to blow up the King and succeed to the throne. *As I'm constitutionally nervous, I must accustom myself by degrees to the
startling nature of my duties. (Utopia)*

TESSA: Venetian contadina, sister of Gianetta and married to
Giuseppe Palmieri. *She is what is called a silly, Still she answers
pretty well.* (Giuseppe, *Gondoliers*)

THESPIS: Manager of the Thessalian Theatres. He stands in for
Jupiter when the gods leave Olympus. *As a man I am naturally
of an easy disposition. As a manager, I am compelled to hold myself
aloof, that my influence may not be deteriorated. As a man, I am
inclined to fraternize with the pauper – as a manager I am compelled
to walk about like this: Don't know yah! Don't know yah! Don't
know yah! (Thespis)*

TIMIDON: The Thespian who assumes the role of Mars on
Olympus. *You told us on taking office to remember two things, to
try experiments and to take it easy. I found I couldn't take it easy
while there are any battles to attend to, so I tried the experiment and
abolished battles. And then I took it easy. The Peace Society ought
to be very much obliged to me. (Thespis)*

TIPSEION: Bibulous Thespian, turned teetotaller, who is allocated
the role of Bacchus on Olympus. *In every respect in which my
duty as the god of wine can be discharged consistently with my duty
as a total abstainer, I will discharge it. But when the functions clash,
everything must give way to the pledge. (Thespis)*

TOLLOLLER, THOMAS, EARL: Leader of the House of Lords.
Friend since boyhood of the Earl of Mountararat and his rival
for the hand of Phyllis. *Of birth and position I've plenty; I've
grammar and spelling for two, And blood and behaviour for twenty.
(Iolanthe)*

TRUSTY, DAME HANNAH: Rose Maybud's adoptive aunt and
former fiancée of Sir Roderic Murgatroyd. *I am pledged . . . to
an eternal maidenhood! Many years ago I was betrothed to a god-
like youth who woo'd me under an assumed name. But on the very*

day upon which our wedding was to have been celebrated, I discovered that he was no other than Sir Roderic Murgatroyd. (*Ruddigore*)

TUCKER, TOM: Midshipmite aboard H.M.S. *Pinafore*.

USHER: Court official. *Gentle, simple-minded Usher.* (Judge, *Trial*)

VITTORIA: A Venetian contadina. (*Gondoliers*)

WARREN: See COLFAX, RICHARD. (*Yeomen*)

WELLS, JOHN WELLINGTON: Proprietor of J. W. Wells & Co.,
Family Sorcerers, 70 St Mary Axe, City of London, purveyor
of the love-philtre. *My name is John Wellington Wells, I'm a
dealer in magic and spells, In blessings and curses And ever-filled
purses, In prophecies, witches, and knells.* (*Sorcerer*)

WILLIS, PRIVATE, of B Company, 1st Grenadier Guards: Sentry
outside Westminster Hall. He marries the Fairy Queen.

QUEEN: *You're a very fine fellow, sir.*

WILLIS: *I am generally admired.*

QUEEN: *I can quite understand it. Now here is a man whose physical
attributes are simply godlike. This man has a most extraordinary
effect upon me. If I yielded to a natural impulse, I should fall down
and worship that man. But I mortify this inclination; I wrestle with
it, and it lies beneath my feet! That is how I treat my regard for that
man!*   (*Iolanthe*)

YEOMEN, FIRST and SECOND: *Tower Warders, Under orders, Gallant pikemen, valiant sworders! Brave in bearing, Foemen scaring,
In their bygone days of daring!* (*Yeomen*)

YUM-YUM: Ward of Ko-Ko and sister of Pitti-Sing and Peep-Bo.
She is betrothed to her guardian, but loves and marries Nanki-
Poo. *Yes, I am indeed beautiful! Sometimes I sit and wonder, in my
artless Japanese way, why it is that I am so much more attractive
than anybody else in the whole world.* (*Mikado*)

ZARA, PRINCESS: Eldest daughter of King Paramount of Utopia
and sister of the Princesses Nekaya and Kalyba. Secretly betrothed to Captain Fitzbattleaxe. *His Majesty's eldest daughter,
Princess Zara, who left our shores five years since to go to England
. . . has taken a high degree at Girton, and is on her way home again,
having achieved a complete mastery over all the elements that have*

tended to raise that glorious country to her present pre-eminent position among civilized nations. (Calynx, *Utopia*)

ZORAH: One of the professional bridesmaids of Rederring, taken as wife by Richard Dauntless. *With Zorah for my missis, There'll be bread and cheese and kisses, Which is just the sort of ration I enjye!* (*Ruddigore*)

The Works and Quotations

THESPIS 1871
or
The Gods Grown Old

UNLESS some searcher succeeds where many others have failed, we shall never see *Thespis* performed in its original form. No copy of the score is known to exist and only two numbers have survived – 'Climbing over rocky mountain', re-used in *The Pirates of Penzance*, and 'Little maid of Arcadee', which enjoyed a brief life of its own as a drawing-room ballad. The few amateur productions of *Thespis* that have been mounted in the years since the Gilbert and Sullivan copyrights expired have made use of music selected from the other works.

On the strength of the text, as judged by today's standards, *Thespis* is no loss: the story is sketchy, the jokes laboured, the quips feeble. Yet, it must have had something for its own time. Presented by John Hollingshead at his Gaiety Theatre, London, on 26 December, 1871 it was inadequately rehearsed and ill performed; yet it was praised by a number of leading critics, who must have perceived in it a glimmer of light trying to penetrate the prevailing murk of coarse melodrama and vulgar ditty which audiences expected in the name of popular entertainment. Perhaps Sullivan's music was sufficiently lively to lift the play to a level we cannot imagine from the text alone. A run of 63 performances was not much; but, at a time before 'Gilbert and Sullivan' meant something to everyone, and in the face of a good deal of bewilderment amongst audiences which must have included a large percentage of men who, in any age, would scarcely respond to such works as theirs, even at their greatest, it was not a bad start. The piece would perhaps have run longer, had the Christmas season, for which it had been conceived, not reached its end. But essentially, it was something for which the English theatre was not yet ready, and it was a fortunate circumstance that the new partners went their separate ways for another four years after it rather than hasten into another immature collaboration.

. . . .

If the text were not so patently feeble, one might be tempted to ascribe the failure of *Thespis* to a revengeful act of the gods it guys. The setting is Mount Olympus, abode of the gods of Greek mythology – though in this piece they prove to be a mixture of Greeks and Romans. What they have in common is decrepitude. Jaded with their occupations, sunk in lethargy, they have allowed their temple to crumble and their influence upon earth and its inhabitants to wane. Mercury, their young messenger, has been turned into a general factotum, running constant errands for his torpid superiors and carrying out their functions for them: 'I do everything and I'm nothing. I've made thunder for Jupiter, odes for Apollo, battles for Mars, and love for Venus. I've married couples for Hymen, and six weeks afterwards, I've divorced them for Cupid – and in return I get all the kicks while they pocket the halfpence.'

His complaints at least stir the senior gods into discussing what might be done to regain their former respect, but they are interrupted by Mars with the news that mortals 'in hundreds, aye in thousands, too!' are at this moment approaching the summit of Olympus. 'A government survey,' Diana suggests. 'Perhaps the Alpine club at their diversion,' is Apollo's idea. 'They seem to be more like a "Cook's Excursion",' observes Mercury, who is more experienced in earthly habits. Defensive thunderbolts and blinding moon-rays being out of the question at such short range, the gods can only retire into the ruined temple to await eventualities.

The 'hundreds and thousands' of interlopers turn out to be a small party of actors and actresses from the Thessalian theatres, on an outing to celebrate the day-long wedding ceremony of two of their number, Sparkeion and Nicemis. Things are not going entirely smoothly for the couple, though. Sparkeion, the youth, is impatient for kisses. Nicemis wishes him to desist until they are thoroughly married. He threatens to pay attentions to Daphne, another member of the company, to whom he had once been engaged. Nicemis retorts that she will encourage their manager, Thespis, to renew his attentions to her: 'I'd just as soon be a manager's wife as a fifth-rate actor's!'

Catching up with them too late to hear this exchange, the rest of the company prepare to enjoy their picnic. Each had undertaken to bring an ingredient towards a meal of lobster salad and claret-cup: so they have – with the exception of the lobster or the claret. General bickering breaks out. Sparkeion begins to make up to Daphne, so Nicemis approaches Thespis, who stands on his managerial dignity and explains that he cannot allow his authority over the company to be undermined by flirting with the half-wife of one of them.

This is all too much for the watching gods. Jupiter, Mars and Apollo shamble out from their hiding place and introduce themselves. All kneel to them except Thespis, who contemptuously tells Jupiter that he doesn't measure up to the way he is usually represented on stage as a 'fine commanding party in the prime of life'. Jupiter ruefully asks his advice. Thespis suggests that the gods take an incognito trip to Earth, mix with the people there for a while and gauge the general opinion of them; then they will know what to do to restore their reputation. While they are away the Thespians will look after Olympus: 'I've a very good company, used to take long parts on the shortest notice. Invest us with your powers and we'll fill your places till you return.' The offer is accepted at once, with the proviso from the gods that Mercury remains on Olympus as consultant should difficulties arise.

Here's a pretty tale for future Iliads and Odyssies,
Mortals are about to personate the gods and goddesses.
Now to set the world in order, we will work in unity.
Jupiter's perplexity is Thespis's opportunity.

The Thespians are allocated their individual roles – Thespis as Jupiter, Sparkeion as Phoebus Apollo, Nicemis as Diana, Timidon as Mars, Daphne as Calliope, and so forth. They discuss their parts excitedly as the weary old gods form a straggling procession and march away.

The passage of a year brings great changes to Olympus. The once-ruined temple has been magnificently restored by the company's scene-painter. Cheerful 'gods and goddesses' lounge about, eating, drinking and smoking. There is an atmosphere of ambrosian luxury; but the effect is not quite complete. Conjugal conflict is still evident. Pretteia, who is filling the role of the absent Venus, has discovered that the goddess is married to either Mars or Vulcan, the former of whom is now represented by Presumptios, Pretteia's actual father, and the latter by her grandfather. Daphne, as Calliope, has found out that Apollo was married to Calliope amongst others, but Nicemis, when it comes to matrimony, instead of sustaining the role of Diana, insists that Apollo continues to be the mortal Sparkeion, her husband.

Still, Thespis is feeling self-satisfied with the results of his year's rule. 'Why, there hasn't been a hitch of any kind since we came up here. Lor! The airs you gods and goddesses give yourselves are perfectly sickening. Why it's mere child's play!' Mercury has other views. One of his duties is to collect all the petitions of people on Earth to the gods and present them once a year. That year is now up.

THESPIS: Oh, then I suppose there are *some* complaints?
MERCURY: Yes, there are *some*.
THESPIS: Oh. Perhaps there are a good many?
MERCURY: There are a good many.
THESPIS: Oh. Perhaps there are a thundering lot?

MERCURY: There are a thundering lot.

THESPIS: Oh!

Jupiter, Apollo and Mars, cloaked and masked, arrive from Earth, dismayed and angry at what they have learned there and demanding Thespis's explanation for the deeper disrepute into which the gods have fallen. He waves their charges of laxity airily aside. The annual court of Olympus is about to sit, at which, he tells them, any few complaints that may have come in will soon be disposed of. The three gods retain their disguise and are introduced to the assembled Olympians by Thespis as influential members of the Athenian Press, come to see fair play.

Mercury carries in tremendous bundles of documents, all petitions from Earth. The first read out is a complaint that for the past six months every day in Athens has been a foggy November Friday, and the people are tired of it. Cymon, the Thespian substitute for Father Time, explains that he had been trying an experiment to abolish Saturdays, with the result that the week has become stuck at Friday; December cannot begin until November is out, which can't happen without a Saturday; and it has been continually wet because Thespis had turned on the rain and forgotten to turn it off again.

Timidon, as Mars, is called to answer a complaint that there have been no battles on Earth during his reign. His answer is that universal peace needed less supervision, so he had instituted it in the interests of taking things easily. The third complaint comes from the associated wine merchants of Mytilene: the year's entire crop of grapes has yielded ginger beer, instead of wine. Tipseion, the stand-in for Bacchus, justifies this on the grounds that Thespis had ordered him to give up his over-indulgence just before he became a god, and now his duty as a total abstainer will not let him allow anything stronger than ginger beer to be grown.

This is too much for the listening gods. They unmask and face the assembly, who all kneel and beg to be allowed to remain on Olympus, where life suits them very well. The other gods return in time to hear Jupiter's dread decree:

D

Away to earth, contemptible comedians,
    And hear our curse, before we set you free;
You shall all be eminent tragedians,
    Whom no one ever goes to see!

Quotations

MERCURY: Oh, I'm the celestial drudge,
    From morning to night I must stop at it,
On errands all day I must trudge,
    And I stick to my work till I drop at it!
In summer I get up at one
    (As a good-natured donkey I'm ranked for it),
Then I go and I light up the Sun,
    And Phoebus Apollo gets thanked for it!
    Well, well, it's the way of the world,
        And will be through all its futurity;
    Though noodles are baroned and earled,
        There's nothing for clever obscurity!

. . . .

JUPITER: The sacrifices and votive offerings have fallen off terribly of late. Why, I can remember the time when people offered us human sacrifices – no mistake about it – human sacrifices! think of that!

DIANA: Ah! Those good old days!

JUPITER: Then it fell off to oxen, pigs and sheep.

APOLLO: Well, there are worse things than oxen, pigs and sheep.

JUPITER: So I've found to my cost. My dear sir – between ourselves, it's dropped off from one thing to another until it has positively dwindled down to preserved Australian beef! What do you think of that?

APOLLO: I don't like it at all.

. . . .

NICEMIS: On mountain top the air is keen,
    And most exhilarating,
And we say things we do not mean
    In moments less elating.
    So please to wait,

> For thoughts that crop,
> *En tête-à-tête,*
> On mountain top,
> May not exactly tally
> With those that you
> May entertain,
> Returning to
> The sober plain
> Of yon relaxing valley.

. . . .

CHORUS: Climbing over rocky mountain,
Skipping rivulet and fountain,
Passing where the willows quiver,
By the ever rolling river,
Swollen with the summer rain.
Threading long and leafy mazes,
Dotted with unnumbered daisies,
Scaling rough and rugged passes,
Climb the hardy lads and lasses,
Till the mountain-top they gain.

. .

THESPIS: I once knew a chap who discharged a function
On the North South East West Diddlesex junction,
He was conspicuous exceeding,
For his affable ways and his easy breeding.
Although a Chairman of Directors,
He was hand in glove with the ticket inspectors,
He tipped the guards with bran-new fivers,
And sang little songs to the engine-drivers.
'Twas told to me with great compunction,
By one who had discharged with unction,
A Chairman of Directors function,
On the North South East West Diddlesex junction.
Fol diddle, lol diddle, lol lol lay . . .

. . . He followed out his whim with vigour,
The shares went down to a nominal figure,
These are the sad results proceeding

From his affable ways and his easy breeding!
The line, with its rails and guards and peelers,
Was sold for a song to marine-store dealers,
The shareholders are all in the work'us,
And he sells pipe-lights in the Regent Circus.
      'Twas told to me etc.

. . . .

SILLIMON: You are playing a part till the real gods return. That's all!
Whether you are supposed to be married to your father – or your
grandfather, what does it matter? This passion for realism is the curse
of the stage!

. . . .

THESPIS: Now that nations can't fight, no two of 'em are on speaking
terms. The dread of fighting was the only thing that kept them civil
to each other. Let battles be restored and peace reign supreme.

ENGLISH comic opera owes more than may be realized to Jacques Offenbach. If his operetta *La Périchole* had been a longer work, Gilbert and Sullivan might not have resumed their seemingly abortive collaboration, and Richard D'Oyly Carte might not have arisen as the timely force that urged them on to immortal fame.

In 1875, at the Royalty Theatre, Soho, *La Périchole* was playing to disappointing audiences, in spite of the work's inherent gaiety and charm. It was too short: a fill-in was needed to offer the audience an evening's money's-worth. Chancing to meet Carte, Gilbert offered him *Trial by Jury*, which he had made into a short entertainment from a ballad of his originally published in *Fun*. He had notions of its being set to music by Carl Rosa. Carte suggested Sullivan instead. Brusque with expectation that he would be rebuffed, Gilbert called on Sullivan and read it to him. The composer was delighted and wrote the effervescent score in a matter of days. The entire work was completed and the production mounted at the Royalty within three weeks, opening on 25 March, 1875. It played second to the Offenbach piece, and might well have been expected to suffer by comparison; but within a few more weeks *La Périchole* had vanished from the bill and Lecocq's *La Fille de Madame Angot* had been substituted, though only as secondary attraction. Audiences were now packing the Royalty to see *Trial by Jury*. The English musical stage revolution had occurred.

The first New York performance was on 15 November 1875.

. . . .

All is bustle in the Court of Justice as members of the jury, spectators and court officials take their seats, and barristers and attorneys shuffle their papers.

> Hark, the hour of ten is sounding:
> Hearts with anxious fears are bounding,
> Hall of Justice crowds surrounding,
>   Breathing hope and fear –
> For today in this arena,
> Summoned by a stern subpoena,
> Edwin, sued by Angelina,
>   Shortly will appear.

Decorum descends as the Court Usher, clad in sober black and brandishing his white rod of office, admonishes the jury to set aside all prejudice, for

> With stern judicial frame of mind
> From bias free of every kind,
>   This trial must be tried.

This advice is, however, lost upon himself, for he reminds them particularly, when listening to the Plaintiff's case, to

> Observe the features of her face –
> The broken-hearted bride.
> Condole with her distress of mind ...

As for the ruffianly Defendant:

> What he may say you needn't mind –
> From bias free of every kind,
>   This trial must be tried!

The 'ruffian' Edwin himself now appears. A pleasant-looking enough young man, and undaunted by the jury's threats, he beckons them to gather round and hear his story of lovesickness turned to boredom, until one morning he had become another's love-sick boy. The all-male jury know how it must have been: they, too, have had their youthful fling. But all that sort of thing is now past: they are respectable chaps, and Edwin need not look to them for sympathy. The virtuous jurymen return to their box, and the Usher calls for silence for the Judge.

Unlike most of his kind, His Lordship is in no hurry to get on with the case. He prefers to spend a little time telling the jury and spectators the rather dubious story of his advancement at the Bar through a tactical engagement to an influential attorney's elderly, ugly daughter. The saga ends with the throwing-over of this *passée* lady, and the Judge addresses himself to the matter in hand, the case of *Angelina* v. *Edwin*. Angelina's entry is almost sensational. The jury are clearly overwhelmed by her beauty; and the Judge, who has been ogling one of the bridesmaids, hastily retrieves the note he has just sent her and gives it to the Usher for Angelina instead. Counsel for the Plaintiff brings a halt to this dalliance by painting a moving picture of his trusting client deceived by a callous traitor. The weeping Angelina is led into the witness-box. She almost faints, and reels, sobbing, on to the chest of the foreman of the jury, whereupon the Judge offers her a seat beside him, on the bench. She accepts it with alacrity and sobs on upon his willing breast. By now the jury are shaking their fists at the Defendant and threatening substantial damages; but when he can make himself heard he draws their attention to the laws of nature, with its constantly changing winds and weathers, the succession of the months, and the phases of the moon:

> Consider the moral, I pray,
> > Nor bring a young fellow to sorrow,
> > Who loves this young lady today,
> > And loves that young lady tomorrow.

Angelina's bridesmaids, who occupy the public seats and have been getting on famously with Edwin throughout the proceedings, rush forward in a body and kneel before the jury, supplicating them to take heed. Edwin's point has clearly impressed the jury, and he is emboldened to offer a solution to the entire matter: if it will make her happy, he will marry Angelina today and his other lady-friend tomorrow. The Judge remarks that this seems to be a reasonable proposition, but Counsel for the Plaintiff submits that to marry two wives at one time is 'Burglaree'. Thus, Edwin's position is that if he refuses to marry Angelina he will be committing Breach of Promise; if he marries her and her successor, he will be guilty of Burglaree. Angelina protests her love for him and exhorts the jury to remember what devotion she is losing when they reckon up her damages. Edwin, repelling her furiously, makes himself out to be a drunkard and bully, and therefore worth very little in terms of cash. This gives the Judge an idea.

> The question, gentlemen – is one of liquor;
>   You ask for guidance – this is my reply:
> He says, when tipsy, he would thrash and kick her,
>   Let's make him tipsy, gentlemen, and try!

All except Edwin object to this. The Judge, now more heedful of the time than he had been when the case began, throws his books and papers in the air and declares that, in order to bring the business to an end, he will marry Angelina himself. At last everyone is suited, and the trial is at an end.

> Though homeward as you trudge,
> You declare my law is fudge,
> Yet of beauty I'm a judge
> ALL
> And a good Judge too!

. . . .

Quotations

CHORUS OF JURYMEN:
> Oh, I was like that when a lad!
>   A shocking young scamp of a rover,
> I behaved like a regular cad;
>   But that sort of thing is all over.
> I'm now a respectable chap
>   And shine with a virtue resplendent,
> And, therefore, I haven't a scrap
>   Of sympathy with the defendant!

. . . .

JUDGE: When I, good friends, was called to the bar,
    I'd an appetite fresh and hearty,
But I was, as many young barristers are,
    An impecunious party.
I'd a swallow-tail coat of a beautiful blue –
    A brief which I bought of a booby –
A couple of shirts and a collar or two,
    And a ring that looked like a ruby!

In Westminster Hall I danced a dance,
    Like a semi-despondent fury;
For I thought I should never hit on a chance
    Of addressing a British Jury –
But I soon got tired of third-class journeys,
    And dinners of bread and water;
So I fell in love with a rich attorney's
    Elderly, ugly daughter.

The rich attorney, he jumped with joy,
    And replied to my fond professions:
'You shall reap the reward of your pluck, my boy,
    At the Bailey and Middlesex Sessions.
You'll soon get used to her looks,' said he,
    'And a very nice girl you'll find her!
She may very well pass for forty-three
    In the dusk, with a light behind her!'

The rich attorney was good as his word;
    The briefs came trooping gaily,
And every day my voice was heard
    At the Sessions or Ancient Bailey.
All thieves who could my fees afford
    Relied on my orations,
And many a burglar I've restored
    To his friends and his relations.

At length I became as rich as the Gurneys –
    An incubus then I thought her,
So I threw over that rich attorney's
    Elderly, ugly daughter.
The rich attorney my character high

Tried vainly to disparage –
And now, if you please, I'm ready to try
This Breach of Promise of Marriage!

. . . .

COUNSEL FOR PLAINTIFF:

May it please you, my lud!
Gentlemen of the jury!

With a sense of deep emotion,
I approach this painful case;
For I never had a notion
That a man could be so base,
Or deceive a girl confiding,
Vows, *etcetera*, deriding.

See my interesting client,
Victim of a heartless wile!
See the traitor all defiant
Wear a supercilious smile!
Sweetly smiled my client on him,
Coyly woo'd and gently won him.

Swiftly fled each honeyed hour
Spent with this unmanly male!
Camberwell became a bower,
Peckham an Arcadian Vale,
Breathing concentrated otto! –
An existence *à la* Watteau.

Picture, then, my client naming,
And insisting on the day:
Picture him excuses framing –
Going from her far away;
Doubly criminal to do so,
For the maid had bought her *trousseau*!

. . . .

DEFENDANT: You cannot eat breakfast all day,
Nor is it the act of a sinner,
When breakfast is taken away.

To turn your attention to dinner;
And it's not in the range of belief,
  That you could hold him as a glutton,
Who, when he is tired of beef,
  Determines to tackle the mutton.
    But this I am willing to say,
      If it will appease her sorrow,
    I'll marry this lady to-day,
      And I'll marry the other to-morrow!

· · · ·

COUNSEL FOR PLAINTIFF:
  In the reign of James the Second,
  It was generally reckoned
  As a rather serious crime
  To marry two wives at one time.

· · · ·

PLAINTIFF: I love him – I love him – with fervour unceasing
      I worship and madly adore;
  My blind adoration is always increasing,
    My loss I shall ever deplore.
  Oh, see what a blessing, what love and caressing
    I've lost, and remember it, pray,
  When you I'm addressing, are busy assessing
    The damages Edwin must pay!

DEFENDANT: I smoke like a furnace – I'm always in liquor,
      A ruffian – a bully – a sot;
  I'm sure I should thrash her, perhaps I should kick her,
    I am such a very bad lot!
  I'm not prepossessing, as you may be guessing,
    She couldn't endure me a day;
  Recall my professing, when you are assessing
    The damages Edwin must pay!

· · · ·

JUDGE: All the legal furies seize you!
No proposal seems to please you,
I can't sit up here all day,
I must shortly get away.
Barristers, and you, attorneys,
Set out on your homeward journeys;
Gentle, simple-minded Usher,
Get you, if you like, to Russ*her*;
Put your briefs upon the shelf,
I will marry her myself!

THE first full-length work by Gilbert and Sullivan was commissioned by D'Oyly Carte for his new Comedy Opéra Company at the Opéra-Comique theatre, which, despite its French name, he intended should become the national base for home-grown comic opera. The story derives from a Christmas 1876 contribution by Gilbert to the periodical, the *Graphic*. *The Sorcerer* was first performed on 17 November, 1877 ran for 178 performances, and proved – as much to the collaborators and Carte as to the Press and public – that so dubious a notion as English comic opera could stand up in confident rivalry to the well-established, sophisticated French *opéra bouffe*. Perfectly sure of himself in the face of no little opposition from Carte's fellow directors, Gilbert set his own style of acting, engaged his own types of performer, and created the convention which has lasted with consistent success ever since.

Even so, *The Sorcerer* was by no means a runaway success in this first season. It was not until its revival, seven years later – by which time *H.M.S. Pinafore, The Pirates of Penzance, Patience* and *Iolanthe* had made the Gilbert and Sullivan works a theatregoers' cult – that *The Sorcerer* really caught on. In 1940 when the D'Oyly Carte Opera Company's costumes and scenery were destroyed in an air raid, and *The Sorcerer* was not revived in England until 1971. The first New York production was on 21 February, 1879.

.   .   .   .

It is somewhere about the middle of the nineteenth century. The village of Ploverleigh – in the West of England, to judge from the villagers' accents, when they remember to use them – is *en fête* for the betrothal of Alexis, son of Sir Marmaduke Pointdextre, to Aline, daughter of Arabella, Lady Sangazure. Only one sad face is to be seen: Constance Partlet, daughter of Mrs

Partlet, the widowed pew-opener, is sighing for her own betrothal whose only substance is in her imagination. The object of her love is Dr Daly, the vicar, who is mourning his lost opportunities of love, obtusely unaware of the adoration that exists before his unperceiving eyes:

> Time was when Love and I were well acquainted.
> Time was when we walked ever hand in hand.
> A saintly youth, with worldly thought untainted,
> None better-loved than I in all the land!
> Time was, when maidens of the noblest station,
> Forsaking even military men,
> Would gaze upon me, rapt in adoration –
> Ah me, I was a fair young curate then!

Despite their happiness at the forthcoming union of their aristocratic families, Sir Marmaduke and Lady Sangazure cannot suppress a few sighs. They have been in love with one another for thirty years, but social delicacy and mutual respect have kept them from declaring themselves. Their courteous greetings and formal conversation cloak seething passion as they watch their children sign the marriage contract before the aged notary. For their part, Alexis and Aline have no doubt about the desirability of being in love. As he puts it:

True happiness comes of true love, and true love should be independent of external influence. It should live upon itself and by itself – in itself love should live for love alone!

Alexis is a man of action, as well as of tautology. He has read a newspaper advertisement by the firm of J. W. Wells & Co., old-established Family Sorcerers of St Mary Axe, London, for a love philtre which is claimed to be infallible. He proposes to buy a quantity, distribute it through the village, and thus ensure that every adult in the place shall learn the secret of pure and lasting happiness. The principal of the firm, Mr John Wellington Wells, is at this very moment indulging himself in the refreshment tent. He is sent for, and assures Alexis that whoever imbibes the philtre will become unconscious immediately, to fall in love on waking twelve hours later with the first person upon whom he or she claps eyes. For morality's sake, already-married persons are immune. Alexis instructs him to pour a quantity into the teapot from which the villagers are about to be served. Mr Wells obeys, uttering an incantation to assistant sprites and demons to inspire his dreadful deed.

> Now shrivelled hags, with poison bags,
>   Discharge your loathsome loads!
> Spit flame and fire, unholy choir!
>   Belch forth your venom, toads!
> Ye demons fell, with yelp and yell,
>   Shed curses far afield –
> Ye fiends of night, your filthy blight
>   In noisome plenty yield!

It is a dramatic and noisy operation, but the villagers are unaware of it when they arrive. Their minds are on the feast. Unwittingly, they crowd round for the distribution of teacups, while Dr Daly, the deftest hand in the neighbourhood at brewing tea, officiates with the pot. All drink, except Alexis, Aline and Mr Wells. By the time the betrothed couple have sung a paean to true love – 'rich harvest of gladness, peace-bearing tillage', and more in that vein – the revellers are staggering about, rubbing their eyes, and struggling in vain to retain their faculties. But John Wellington Wells's claims for his philtre have not been exaggerated. Within minutes, the majority of the population of Ploverleigh is prostrate and snoring blissfully.

Quite how the three conspirators conduct themselves for the next twelve hours is nowhere stated. No doubt the lovers continue their idealistic justification of what they have perpetrated, while Mr Wells makes free with the substantial remains of the interrupted banquet, avoiding only the teapot. By midnight, however, they are gathered together, by the light of the moon and Mr Wells's lantern. The prone populace begin to stir. At Mr Wells's suggestion, the three retire 'While Love, the House-maid, lights her kitchen fire'. The villagers arise, gape at one another, discover that they are in love, exchange potentially rash

vows, and celebrate with a rustic dance. Now certain complica-
tions start to emerge. Constance's first encounter after wakening
has not been with her already-beloved vicar, but with the aged
notary. Sir Marmaduke has been impelled to propose to, and
has been accepted by, Mrs Partlet. One look from Lady Sangazure at Mr Wells is enough to tell him the truth: 'Oh, horrible! –
she's going to adore me!' He tries to fend her off:

MR WELLS: Hate me! I drop my H's – have through life!
LADY SANGAZURE: Love me! I'll drop them too!
MR WELLS: Hate me! I always eat peas with a knife!
LADY SANGAZURE: Love me! I'll eat like you!

When this sort of thing produces no effect, he tells her he is
engaged to a Pacific island maiden. Anguished, Lady Sangazure
leaves, threatening to bury what must be a life-long woe in her
family vault. Only Dr Daly remains unfulfilled by the philtre's
effects. He is under its influence, surely enough, but every maiden
he has looked at has already been snapped up by some other love-
sick villager. He sighs, 'I never remarked it before, but the young
maidens of this village are very comely. So likewise are the
middle-aged. Also the elderly. All are comely – and all are
engaged!' He seeks solace in playing his flageolet, unaware that
fate is about to play a tune upon him. Anxious to ensure that
their love shall be everlasting, Alexis has been pressing Aline to
drink the philtre. She has refused on the grounds that, if he
cannot trust her love to endure without artificial aids, he has no
righ to claim it. Accused in return of wishing to reserve her future
freedom, she has given in and sipped the philtre. Perhaps because
she has drunk directly from the bottle, and not of the diluted
mixture in the teapot, she does not fall asleep for the statutory
twelve hours, but turns round and sees Dr Daly, with whom she
falls instantly in love. He returns her avowals, while Alexis rages
impotently, powerless against the magic's effect on them.

Alexis appeals to Mr Wells for advice. He is told that there is
only one means by which the spell may be removed: either he or
Wells himself must sacrifice his life to Ahrimanes – presumably a

relative of Ahriman, the Zoroastrian spirit of evil and deceit. Wells would be glad to oblige, only it would not be fair to his Company, whose stocktaking is due next week. Alexis offers himself up, but Aline stays him. Dr Daly has decently offered to leave the country, and there will be no one left for her to adore if Alexis departs in sacrifice. Mr Wells suggests they put the decision to popular vote. Led by Sir Marmaduke, the populace decree that, as the one who has caused all the trouble in the first place, Mr Wells must go. He bows to popular opinion. The ground opens and John Wellington Wells sinks into flickering red flames and out of sight. The love spell is cancelled instantaneously and all rejoin their former partners. Sir Marmaduke, whose commissariat appears ever-ready, bids the villagers to his mansion for yet another feast, and they dance off, singing of eggs, ham, strawberry jam, rollicking buns and gay Sally Lunns.

Quotations

DR DALY: Had I a headache? sighed the maids assembled;
　　　　Had I a cold? welled forth the silent tear;
　　　　Did I look pale? then half a parish trembled;
　　　　And when I coughed all thought the end was near!
　　　　I had no care – no jealous doubts hung o'er me –
　　　　For I was loved beyond all other men.
　　　　Fled gilded dukes and belted earls before me –
　　　　Ah me, I was a pale young curate then!

· · · ·

ALEXIS: The cause progresses but slowly. Still I have made some converts to the principle, that men and women should be coupled in matrimony without distinction of rank. I have lectured on the subject at Mechanics' Institutes, and the mechanics were unanimous in favour of my views. I have preached in workhouses, beershops, and Lunatic Asylums, and I have been received with enthusiasm. I have addressed navvies on the advantages that would accrue to them if they married wealthy ladies of rank, and not a navvy dissented!

E

ALINE: Noble fellows! And yet there are those who hold that the uneducated classes are not open to argument! And what do the countesses say?

ALEXIS: Why, at present, it can't be denied, the aristocracy hold aloof.

ALINE: Ah, the working man is the true intelligence after all!

ALEXIS: He is a noble creature when he is quite sober.

. . . .

ALEXIS: Good day – I believe you are a Sorcerer.

MR WELLS: Yes, sir, we practise Necromancy in all its branches. We've a choice assortment of wishing-caps, divining-rods, amulets, charms, and counter-charms. We can cast you a nativity at a low figure, and we have a horoscope at three-and-six that we can guarantee. Our Abudah chests, each containing a patent Hag who comes out and prophesies disasters, with spring complete, are strongly recommended. Our Aladdin lamps are very chaste, and our Prophetic Tablets, foretelling everything – from a change of Ministry down to a rise in Unified – are much inquired for. Our penny Curse – one of the cheapest things in the trade – is considered infallible.We have some very superior Blessings, too, but they're very little asked for. We've only sold one since Christmas – to a gentleman who bought it to send to his mother-in-law – but it turned out that he was afflicted in the head, and it's been returned on our hands. But our sale of penny Curses, especially on Saturday nights is tremendous.We can't turn 'em out fast enough.

> Oh! my name is John Wellington Wells,
> I'm a dealer in magic and spells,
>   In blessings and curses
>   And ever-filled purses,
> In prophecies, witches, and knells.
>
> If you want a proud foe to 'make tracks' –
> If you'd melt a rich uncle in wax –
>   You've but to look in
>   On our resident Djinn,
> Number seventy. Simmery Axe!
>
> We've a first-class assortment of magic;
>   And for raising a posthumous shade
> With effects that are comic or tragic,
>   There's no cheaper house in the trade.

Love-philtre – we've quantities of it;
    And for knowledge if any one burns,
We keep an extremely small prophet, a prophet
    Who brings us unbounded returns:

For he can propheys
With a wink of his eye
Peep with security
Into futurity,
Sum up your history,
Clear up a mystery,
Humour proclivity
For a nativity – for a nativity!
Mirrors so magical,
Tetrapods tragical,
Bogies spectacular,
Answers oracular,
Facts astronomical,
Solemn or comical,
And, if you want it, he
Makes a reduction on taking a quantity!

    Oh!
If any one anything lacks,
He'll find it all ready in stacks,
    If he'll only look in
    On the resident Djinn,
Number seventy, Simmery Axe!

. . . .

ALEXIS: I am anxious from purely philanthropical motives to distribute
    this philtre, secretly, among the inhabitants of this village. I shall of
    course require a quantity. How do you sell it?...
MR WELLS: In buying a quantity, sir, we should strongly advise your
    taking it in the wood, and drawing it off as you happen to want it.
    We have it in four-and-a-half and nine gallon casks – also in pipes and
    hogsheads for laying down, and we deduct 10 per cent for prompt
    cash.
ALEXIS: I should mention that I am a Member of the Army and Navy
    Stores.

MR WELLS: In that case we deduct 25 per cent.

. . . .

CHORUS: Now to the banquet we press;
    Now for the eggs and the ham;
Now for the mustard and cress,
    Now for the strawberry jam!
Now for the tea of our host,
    Now for the rollicking bun,
Now for the muffin and toast,
    Now for the gay Sally Lunn!

. . . .

ALINE: How joyful they all seem in their new-found happiness! The whole village has paired off in the happiest manner. And yet not a match has been made that the hollow world would not consider ill-advised!

ALEXIS: But we are wiser – far wiser – than the world. Observe the good that will become of these ill-assorted unions. The miserly wife will check the reckless expenditure of her too frivolous consort, the wealthy husband will shower innumerable bonnets on his penniless bride, and the young and lively spouse will cheer the declining days of her aged partner with comic songs unceasing!

ALINE: What a delightful prospect for him!

. . . .

ALEXIS: My dear father . . . it can hardly be necessary to assure you that any wife of yours is a mother of mine.

. . . .

ALINE: Zorah is very good, and very clean, and honest, and quite, quite sober in her habits: and that is worth far more than beauty, dear Sir Marmaduke.

DR DALY: Yes; beauty will fade and perish, but personal cleanliness is practically undying, for it can be renewed whenever it discovers symptoms of decay.

. . . .

MR WELLS: Hate me! I drop my H's – have through life!
LADY SANGAZURE: Love me! I'll drop them too!

MR WELLS: Hate me! I always eat peas with a knife!

LADY SANGAZURE: Love me! I'll eat like you!

MR WELLS: Hate me! I spend the day at Rosherville!

LADY SANGAZURE: Love me! that joy I'll share!

MR WELLS: Hate me! I often roll down One Tree Hill!

LADY SANGAZURE: Love me! I'll join you there!

LADY SANGAZURE: Love me! my prejudices I will drop!

MR WELLS: Hate me! that's not enough!

LADY SANGAZURE: Love me! I'll come and help you in the shop!

MR WELLS: Hate me! the life is rough!

LADY SANGAZURE: Love me! my grammar I will all forswear!

MR WELLS: Hate me! abjure my lot!

LADY SANGAZURE: Love me! I'll stick sunflowers in my hair!

MR WELLS: Hate me! they'll suit you not!

or

The Lass that Loved a Sailor

H.M.S. *Pinafore*, the craft which was to bring home so much treasure for Gilbert and Sullivan and their backers, several times came close to foundering. For all the apparent spontaneity of its music and wit, the work was not composed easily: Gilbert had to struggle with the text, and Sullivan laboured at the music through bouts of excruciating physical pain from the kidney complaint which harassed him throughout adult life. It opened satisfactorily enough at the Opéra-Comique on 25 May, 1878 but within a few days was playing to decreasing houses. Several weeks of heatwave were partially to blame, together with a disapproving word-of-mouth in certain quarters about the work's poor taste in making fun of England's most hallowed institution, the Royal Navy. It was not until Sullivan included a nightly pot-pourri from its music in a series of promenade concerts at the Opera House, Covent Garden, that H.M.S. *Pinafore* became a craze and played to packed houses. It was further threatened the following year when Carte's fellow directors broke with him and mounted a rival production of the work, first at the Aquarium Theatre and then at the Olympic, which involved an alarming fight during an Opéra-Comique performance as men from the breakaway company tried to remove the scenery and properties, and Carte's employees battled to stop them.

For all this and the drawn-out litigation which ensued, *Pinafore* achieved 617 performances in this first run, by far the record then for any musical work originated in England. These included 46 performances by a cast entirely composed of children in *The Children's Pinafore*, which opened at the Opéra-Comique on 16 December, 1879. *Pinafore* took the United States by storm, beginning the enduringly warm American appreciation of the Gilbert and Sullivan works. As a measure against the many

unauthorized versions playing in America, the partners took out
a company of their own late in 1879. They were received like
national heroes, and their 'official' *Pinafore*, produced by Gilbert,
conducted by Sullivan, and using leading artists from England,
at the Fifth Avenue Theatre, New York, was hailed as a revelation. But pirated, and often mangled, versions continued to be
presented in many parts of the country, and there existed no
legal means of suppressing them. The first New York production
of all had been on 15 January, 1879.

. . . .

The scene is the quarter-deck of the man-of-war, H.M.S. *Pinafore*, lying at anchor at Portsmouth. Sea and sky are blue, and
the tars are in high good humour.

> We sail the ocean blue,
> And our saucy ship's a beauty;
> We're sober men and true,
> And attentive to our duty.

Their spirits are enhanced by the arrival aboard of a familiar
(if mis-named) friend, Little Buttercup, a large and rosy bumboat
woman, bearing her basket of seamen's comforts, including snuff,
tobacco, treacle, toffee, chops, chickens, polonies and peppermint
drops. Only one discordant element mars the scene – Dick Deadeye, a one-eyed seaman of repellent aspect, triangular posture and
cynical utterance. But even Deadeye cannot depress the spirits of
his messmates, who treat him with amiable dislike so long as he
refrains from trying their tempers too far.

One other member of the ship's company is taking no part in
the gay proceedings. Ralph Rackstraw, 'the smartest lad in all
the fleet', has his mind upon nightingales, moonlight, melancholy mountain echoes, and the like. He is in love, and, alas,
with a lass above his station: his captain's daughter, Josephine
Corcoran. Ralph's shipmates agree with him that he is aiming a
trifle above himself, but upon Deadeye's chipping in with the
observation that 'captains' daughters don't marry foremast

hands', they are turned to sympathy for Ralph. These musings are interrupted by the appearance of their popular commander, Captain Corcoran. But even this resourceful and well-bred officer, who never (well, hardly ever) needs to resort to bad language or abuse to maintain their respect, nourishes a secret sorrow. He confides to Little Buttercup that his daughter Josephine is sought in marriage by the First Lord of the Admiralty, Sir Joseph Porter, but 'does not seem to tackle kindly to it'. Buttercup is readily sympathetic towards His Lordship. She knows something of the pain of unreturned love, she confesses with emotion, and Captain Corcoran's admiring glance follows her as she goes.

Josephine is sorrowful, too. Her father prises her secret gently from her: her heart is given to a member of his own crew, but as the proud daughter of a captain, R.N., she has determined to carry her love secretly with her to the tomb, rather than reveal it to its object. Further discussion is interrupted by the approaching sound of singing and the boom of saluting nine-pounders. Pressing a photograph of Sir Joseph Porter into Josephine's hands, Captain Corcoran urges her to go and study it in her cabin, in the hope that it will bring her to a more reasonable frame of mind. The crew assemble to welcome the approaching party, which is a large and almost entirely female one. The ladies are Sir Joseph Porter's sisters, cousins and aunts who accompany him wherever he goes. The sailors' pleasure at greeting this bevy of beauty is matched by the ladies' delight to be visiting them, for

> Sailors sprightly
> Always rightly
> Welcome ladies so politely.

A marine's drum rolls and Sir Joseph Porter, K.C.B., strides on to the quarter-deck, resplendent in white breeches, gold-faced tunic, cocked hat and eye-glass. Although his pride is second to none, he does not hesitate to tell the assembly the story of his go-getting rise to success and fame. He inspects and admires

Pinafore's crew, especially commending his unbeknown rival in love, Ralph Rackstraw. Having lectured their captain sharply upon the importance of politeness in handling seamen, he bears the humiliated officer away to his cabin for a word 'on a tender and sentimental subject', leaving the crew with the reflection that 'a British sailor is any man's equal, excepting mine'. This gives new encouragement to Ralph, who determines to keep his love for Josephine a secret no longer, to the approval of everyone except Dick Deadeye. When he next encounters her, Ralph blurts out his simple passion:

In me there meet a combination of antithetical elements which are at eternal war with one another. Driven hither by objective influences – thither by subjective emotions – wafted one moment into blazing day, by mocking hope – plunged the next into the Cimmerian darkness of tangible despair, I am but a living ganglion of irreconcilable antagonisms.

Although this artless eloquence goes straight to Josephine's heart, she remains the captain's daughter. She spurns him, and Ralph summons his messmates to hear his farewell words before he kills himself. But as he claps the pistol to his head, Josephine hurries back to admit her love for him. General rejoicing prevails, together with whispered plans to smuggle the couple ashore to be married that very night.

That night, the moon is up, and Captain Corcoran brings his mandolin on to the quarter-deck to accompany his melancholy song. Everything had been so comfortable until recently. A commander beloved by all his crew, a slander-free life – and now, his crew acting strangely, his daughter partial to a tar, and Sir Joseph Porter threatening him with a court martial because of it: everything is at sixes and sevens. Little Buttercup, who has lingered aboard long past the time when she should have returned ashore, offers the captain her sympathy and gives him a plain hint of her feelings for him. He tells her that he fears they can never be more than friends. Buttercup reminds him that she has gipsy blood in her veins and sings a mystical song to the effect that

'Things are seldom what they seem'. Though bemused by her allusions, the captain manages to make it a duet.

In an effort to further Sir Joseph Porter's suit, Captain Corcoran suggests to him that since it is probably Josephine's awe for his great rank that prevents her from returning his affection, he should assure her that it is a standing rule at the Admiralty that love levels all ranks. Sir Joseph does so, little realizing that Josephine's concern is not with the disparity between herself and one of higher rank, but with one beneath her. The trio of happy relief in which Josephine, her father and Sir Joseph express their delight in this solution is thus sung to some cross-purpose, and Captain Corcoran's joy is short-lived. No sooner have Josephine and Sir Joseph gone their separate ways than Dick Deadeye shambles up to reveal the plans he has overheard for that night's secret elopement. The captain has just time to envelop himself in a boat cloak and crouch beside *Pinafore*'s wheel before a tip-toeing procession of sailors, led by Josephine and Rackstraw, makes its way towards the ship's side. Sudden sounds halt them in their tracks, but Deadeye reassures them that it is only the cat. The 'cat' it is – a cat-o'-nine-tails, brandished by their captain as he confronts them and demands an explanation. Rackstraw gives him one:

> I humble, poor, and lowly born,
> The meanest in the port division –
> The butt of epauletted scorn –
> The mark of quarter-deck derision –
> Have dared to raise my wormy eyes
> Above the dust to which you mould me
> In manhood's glorious pride to rise,
> I am an Englishman – behold me!

Even so patriotic a sentiment cannot assuage the infuriated captain.

> In uttering a reprobation
>   To any British tar,
> I try to speak with moderation,
>   But you have gone too far.

> I'm very sorry to disparage
> A humble foremast lad,
> But to seek your captain's child in marriage,
> Why, damme, it's too bad!

A shocked hush falls. Sir Joseph's female relatives had arrived just in time to hear the captain relieve himself of this oath, and Sir Joseph appears on the poopdeck as he repeats it. Corcoran's hasty attempts to justify his bad language are brushed aside by the First Lord. He orders the captain below. Sir Joseph is prepared, however, to hear the story of what has happened from other lips. He turns to Ralph Rackstraw, who smugly tells him that 'love burns as brightly in the fo'c'sle as it does on the quarter-deck, and Josephine is the fairest bud that ever blossomed upon the tree of a poor fellow's wildest hopes'. Sir Joseph, appalled, orders him to be taken below, too, and put in chains.

Seeing Ralph led away is too much for Little Buttercup. She proceeds to confess a long-concealed blunder. In her youth, she had practised baby-farming. Two of her simultaneous charges had been an infant of lowly birth and another of the 'upper crust'. The crime which she has had for so long borne upon her conscience had been to mix the two up, a matter of some relevance to the present situation, in that

> The well-born babe was Ralph –
> Your captain was the other! ! !

This changes everything. Corcoran and Ralph are summoned back on deck, and appear in one another's uniforms. Josephine no more a captain's daughter, is of no further interest to Sir Joseph, who resigns her to Captain Rackstraw; Able Seaman Corcoran is no longer restrained by disparity of position from offering himself to Little Buttercup; while Sir Joseph, after a quick look round his attendant females, reluctantly accepts his Cousin Hebe's offer to soothe and comfort his declining days.

Quotations

BUTTERCUP: For I'm called Little Buttercup – dear Little Buttercup,
    Though I could never tell why,
    But still I'm called Buttercup – poor Little Buttercup,
    Sweet Little Buttercup I;

    I've snuff and tobaccy, and excellent jacky,
    I've scissors and watches, and knives;
    I've ribbons and laces to set off the faces
    Of pretty young sweethearts and wives.

    I've treacle and toffee, I've tea and I've coffee.
    Soft tommy and succulent chops;
    I've chickens and conies, and pretty polonies,
    And excellent peppermint drops.

    Then buy of your Buttercup – dear little Buttercup,
    Sailors should never be shy;
    So, buy of your Buttercup – poor Little Buttercup;
    Come, of your Buttercup buy!

. . .

BOATSWAIN: Don't take no heed of *him*; that's only poor Dick Deadeye.

DICK: I say – it's a beast of a name, ain't it – Dick Deadeye?

BUTTERCUP: It's not a nice name.

DICK: I'm ugly too, ain't I?

BUTTERCUP: You are certainly plain.

DICK: And I'm three-cornered too, ain't I?

BUTTERCUP: You are rather triangular.

DICK: Ha! ha! That's it. I'm ugly, and they hate me for it; for you all hate me, don't you?

ALL: We do!

DICK: There!

BOATSWAIN: Well, Dick, we wouldn't go for to hurt any fellow creetur's feelings, but you can't expect a chap with such a name as Dick Deadeye to be a popular character – now can you?

DICK: No.

. . . .

RALPH: It's a strange anomaly, that the daughter of a man who hails from the quarter-deck may not love another who lays out on the fore-yard arm. For a man is but a man, whether he hoists his flag at the main-truck or his slacks on the main-deck.

. . . .

CAPTAIN: I am the Captain of the *Pinafore*;
ALL: And a right good captain, too!
CAPTAIN: You're very, very good,
        And be it understood,
    I command a right good crew.
ALL: We're very, very good,
        And be it understood,
    He commands a right good crew.
CAPTAIN: Though related to a peer,
    I can hand, reef, and steer,
        And ship a selvagee;
    I am never known to quail
    At the fury of a gale,
        And I'm never, never sick at sea!
ALL: What, never?
CAPTAIN: No, never!
ALL: What, *never*?
CAPTAIN: Well – hardly ever!

. . . .

SIR JOSEPH: I am the monarch of the sea,
        The ruler of the Queen's Navee,
    Whose praise Great Britain loudly chants.
COUSIN HEBE: And we are his sisters, and his cousins, and his aunts!
RELATIVES: And we are his sisters, and his cousins, and his aunts! His sisters, and his cousins, and his aunts!
SIR JOSEPH: When at anchor here I ride,
        My bosom swells with pride,
    And I snap my fingers at a foeman's taunts:
COUSIN HEBE: And so do his sisters, and his cousins, and his aunts!
ALL: And so do his sisters, and his cousins, and his aunts! His sisters, and his cousins, and his aunts!

SIR JOSEPH: But when the breezes blow,
         I generally go below,
         And seek the seclusion that a cabin grants!
COUSIN HEBE: And so do his sisters, and his cousins, and his aunts!
ALL: And so do his sisters, and his cousins, and his aunts!
         His sisters and his cousins,
          Whom he reckons up by dozens,
           And his aunts!

. . . .

SIR JOSEPH: When I was a lad I served a term
        As office boy to an Attorney's firm.
        I cleaned the windows and I swept the floor,
        And I polished up the handle of the big front door.
         I polished up that handle so carefullee
          That now I am the Ruler of the Queen's Navee!
           CHORUS: – He polished, etc.

        As office boy I made such a mark
        That they gave me the post of a junior clerk.
        I served the writs with a smile so bland,
        And I copied all the letters in a big round hand –
         I copied all the letters in a hand so free,
          That now I am the Ruler of the Queen's Navee!
           CHORUS: – He copied, etc.

        In serving writs I made such a name
        That an articled clerk I soon became;
        I wore clean collars and a brand-new suit
        For the pass examination at the Institute.
         And that pass examination did so well for me,
          That now I am the Ruler of the Queen's Navee!
           CHORUS: – And that pass examination, etc.

        Of legal knowledge I acquired such a grip
        That they took me into the partnership.
        And that junior partnership, I ween,
        Was the only ship that I ever had seen.
         But that kind of ship so suited me,
          That now I am the Ruler of the Queen's Navee!
           CHORUS: – But that kind, etc.

I grew so rich that I was sent
By a pocket borough into Parliament.
I always voted at my party's call,
And I never thought of thinking for myself at all.
    I thought so little, they rewarded me
    By making me the Ruler of the Queen's Navee!
        CHORUS: – He thought so little, etc.

Now, landsmen all, whoever you may be,
If you want to rise to the top of the tree,
If your soul isn't fettered to an office stool,
Be careful to be guided by this golden rule –
    Stick close to your desks and never go to sea,
    And you all may be Rulers of the Queen's Navee!
        CHORUS: – Stick close, etc.

. . . .

RALPH, BOATSWAIN, BOATSWAIN'S MATE:
    A British tar is a soaring soul,
        As free as a mountain bird,
    His energetic fist should be ready to resist
        A dictatorial word.
    His nose should pant and his lip should curl,
    His cheeks should flame and his brow should furl,
    His bosom should heave and his heart should glow,
    And his fist be ever ready for a knock-down blow.
        CHORUS: – His nose should pant, etc.
    His eyes should flash with an inborn fire,
        His brow with scorn be wrung;
    He never should bow down to a domineering frown,
        Or the tang of a tyrant tongue.
    His foot should stamp and his throat should growl,
    His hair should twirl and his face should scowl;
    His eyes should flash and his breast protrude,
    And this should be his customary attitude.
        CHORUS: – His foot should stamp, etc.

. . . .

BUTTERCUP: Things are seldom what they seem,
            Skim milk masquerades as cream;
            Highlows pass as patent leathers;
            Jackdaws strut in peacock's feathers.

CAPTAIN: Very true,
            So they do.

BUTTERCUP: Black sheep dwell in every fold;
            All that glitters is not gold;
            Storks turn out to be but logs;
            Bulls are but inflated frogs.

CAPTAIN: So they be,
            Frequentlee.

BUTTERCUP: Drops the wind and stops the mill;
            Turbot is ambitious brill;
            Gild the farthing if you will,
            Yet it is a farthing still . . .

CAPTAIN: Though I'm anything but clever,
            I could talk like that for ever;
            Once a cat was killed by care;
            Only brave deserve the fair.

BUTTERCUP: Very true,
            So they do.

CAPTAIN: Wink is often good as nod;
            Spoils the child who spares the rod;
            Thirsty lambs run foxy dangers;
            Dogs are found in many mangers.

BUTTERCUP: Frequentlee,
            I agree.

CAPTAIN: Paw of cat the chestnut snatches;
            Worn-out garments show new patches;
            Only count the chick that hatches;
            Men are grown-up catchy catchies.

BUTTERCUP: Yes, I know,
            That is so.

                              .   .   .   .

CAPTAIN: Never mind the why and wherefore,
            Love can level ranks, and therefore,

Though his lordship's station's mighty,
Though stupendous be his brain,
Though your tastes are mean and flighty
And your fortune poor and plain,

CAPTAIN AND SIR JOSEPH:
Ring the merry bells on board-ship,
Rend the air with warbling wild,
For the union of $\binom{\text{his}}{\text{my}}$ lordship
With a humble captain's child!

CAPTAIN: For a humble captain's daughter –
JOSEPHINE: For a gallant captain's daughter –
SIR JOSEPH: And a lord who rules the water –
JOSEPHINE: And a tar who ploughs the water!
ALL: Let the air with joy be laden,
Rend with songs the air above,
For the union of a maiden
With the man who owns her love!

. . . .

CAPTAIN: Sir Joseph, I cannot express to you my delight at the happy result of your eloquence. Your argument was unanswerable.

SIR JOSEPH: Captain Corcoran, it is one of the happiest characteristics of this glorious country that official utterances are invariably regarded as unanswerable.

. . . .

BOATSWAIN: He is an Englishman!
For he himself has said it,
And it's greatly to his credit,
That he is an Englishman!
ALL: That he is an Englishman!
BOATSWAIN: For he might have been a Roosian,
A French, or Turk, or Proosian,
Or perhaps Itali-an!
ALL: Or perhaps Itali-an!
BOATSWAIN: But in spite of all temptations
To belong to other nations,
He remains an Englishman!

F

or

The Slave of Duty

THIS work is aptly named, in view of the interesting arrangements made by Gilbert and Sullivan to combat its piracy in
America. Its first English run lasted exactly one matinee; and
not in London, but at the Royal Bijou Theatre, Paignton, in
Devonshire, on 30 December, 1879. The cast wore costumes
improvised from the ones they were wearing in H.M.S. *Pinafore*.
The scripts they carried on stage were incomplete textually and
even more so musically, for both composer and author were on
the other side of the Atlantic, working against time on the
version which was to open at the Fifth Avenue Theatre, New
York, on the evening following the British premiere.

This strange juxtaposition was an attempt to establish simultaneous copyright in the two countries. It did not deter the
plunderers, but the presence of the idolized Gilbert and Sullivan
in America helped send the work off to tremendous success there
and enabled them to set up first-class productions at several other
centres and so show up the tawdry standards of most unauthorized versions.

The first major presentation in England was at the Opéra-
Comique on 3 April, 1880. The work is shorter than most. It was
coupled on this first occasion with a 'New and Original Vaude-
ville', *In the Sulks*, with music by Alfred Cellier and book by
Frank Desprez, but today generally shares the bill with *Cox and
Box*, adapted by F. C. Burnand from J. Maddison Morton's farce
Box and Cox, with music by Arthur Sullivan (first publicly pro-
duced 11 May, 1867). In order to meet the American deadline,
Pirates was completed in great haste by a sick and exhausted
Sullivan who wrote the Overture only a matter of hours before
the curtain rose.

. . . .

At one of the many rocky parts of the Cornish sea-coast, a band of pirates is making merry. The bumpers which pass between them contain, not grog or rum, but sherry, an idiosyncratic tipple for pirates at first sight, though the reason for so aristocratic a preference will emerge. They are celebrating the release from his indentures of Frederic, who is about to become 21 years of age. He alone is unhappy. The apprenticeship just completed should never have begun in the first place, as his child-hood's nurse, Ruth, who serves the band as 'a kind of piratical maid-of-all-work', explains. Instructed by Frederic's father to apprentice him to a pilot:

> Mistaking my instructions, which within my brain did gyrate,
> I took and bound this promising boy apprentice to a *pirate*.
> A sad mistake it was to make and doom him to a vile lot.
> I bound him to a pirate – you – instead of to a pilot.

Having faithfully fulfilled his obligations, Frederic is torn between loyalty to his comrades and duty to society. 'Individually,' he assures them, 'I love you all with affection unspeakable, but, collectively, I look upon you with a disgust that amounts to absolute detestation. Oh! pity me, my beloved friends, for such is my sense of duty that, once out of my indentures, I shall feel myself bound to devote myself heart and soul to your extermination.'

The pirates are sympathetic, recognizing, anyway, that they can offer him little incentive to remain with them. They do not thrive at their trade. To a man, they are tender-hearted orphans, congenitally incapable of molesting any fellow orphan. Word of this has got about, and, to judge from the protestations of the crews of the last three ships they have taken, Great Britain's mercantile navy is recruited solely from orphan asylums: the ships have been released, and piracy is not paying.

During his servitude, Frederic has been constantly at sea from the age of 8 and has never seen any woman's face except Ruth's. Her pleas that she is beautiful and as fine a candidate for a wife as he will find do not altogether convince him: and, even though assured by the pirate lieutenant that 'there are the remains of a fine woman about Ruth', he prefers to judge her by comparison. His chance is at hand. To Ruth's dismay, a bevy of young beauties is approaching at this very moment, preparing to take off their shoes and stockings for a paddle. Frederic leaps forward and warns them that they are amidst pirates; then he begs them to help redeem him from his wild profession by carrying him away in marriage. None seems willing, until the entry of Mabel, whose unselfish heart is touched by the plight of the 'poor wandering one'. The other girls tactfully withdraw to talk about the weather and leave the two alone; but within minutes they are all surrounded by the returning pirate band, who gleefully spell out their fate:

> Here's a first-rate opportunity
> To get married with impunity,
> And indulge in the felicity
> Of unbounded domesticity.
> You shall quickly be parsonified,
> Conjugally matrimonified,
> By a doctor of divinity,
> Who resides in this vicinity.

The pirates' delight is soon ended in a way that is by now too familiar to them. The girls disclose that they are the daughters of Major-General Stanley, who, making a timely appearance, pleads

> Oh, men of dark and dismal fate,
> Forgo your cruel employ,
> Have pity on my lonely state,
> I am an orphan boy!

It is too much, as usual, for the pirates: they allow the girls and their father to go. Ruth comes to kneel before Frederic and begs him not to leave her. He upbraids her for her deceit, and pushes her away.

The General has saved his daughters from the pirates' clutches, but at much cost to his conscience. Night after night he sits, surrounded by the girls, in the ruined chapel he had acquired when he bought his estate, and broods upon the dishonour his lie has brought upon the purchased ancestors in the tombs about him. He is contemplating seeking out the Pirate King to confess all, but Frederic dissuades him. He has assembled a force of policemen, led by a sergeant, to march against his former comrades. The police are in a highly nervous state, which they can only alleviate by slapping their chests and singing ' Tarantara! Tarantara!' They are persuaded to leave at length, and the General and his daughters go too, leaving Frederic amongst the ruins. He is not alone for long: the Pirate King and Ruth slip on to the scene and place a pistol each to his ears. Their true weapon, though, is a chronological paradox, which, they say, had occurred to one of the band after Frederic had left it.

Some person in authority, I don't know who, very likely the Astronomer Royal,
Has decided that, although for such a beastly month as February,
  twenty-eight days as a rule are plenty,
One year in every four his days shall be reckoned as nine-and-twenty.
Through some singular coincidence – I shouldn't be surprised if it were
  owing to the agency of an ill-natured fairy –
You are the victim of this clumsy arrangement, having been born in
  leap-year, on the twenty-ninth of February,
And so, by a simple arithmetical process, you'll easily discover,
That though you've lived twenty-one years, yet, if we go by birthdays,
  you're only five and a little bit over!

The implication is that, having signed indentures for apprenticeship until his twenty-first birthday, which will not now occur until the year 1940, Frederic is still a member of the pirate band. He struggles to determine his duty, and loyalty comes out top. He tells the Pirate King that Major-General Stanley is no orphan, and never has been one. The King declares that Tremorden Castle, the General's home, shall be attacked that night and the deceiver slain.

The King and Ruth go, and Mabel returns, to be told by Frederic that he will not be free to claim her until he comes of age – in 1940. Not surprisingly, she pleads with him not to leave

her 'to pine alone and desolate' in the meantime; but he insists
on living up to the sub-title of the opera and goes off to rejoin
the pirates. As Mabel is pulling herself together with the assurance
that he will return for her in fifty-one years' time, the police
return, evidently relieved at having failed to find the pirates.
Mabel dispatches them again, and they march off, reflecting that,
'When constabulary duty's to be done, the policeman's lot is not
a happy one.'

The police have not gone far when they hear the pirates
approaching with stealthy cacophony. The police prudently hide,
and the pirates do likewise as they see the Major-General approaching. He is allowed time to sing something about breezes,
trees, rovers and lovers, and to be joined by his peignoir-clad
daughters, before the pirates pounce and seize him. They in turn
are attacked by the police. Alas for law and order, it is the pirates
who prevail, standing with drawn swords over the prostrate
constabulary. Sensing that the Sergeant is about to assert
that his force is entirely composed of orphans, the Pirate King
warns him off. But the Sergeant has an even stronger card to
play.

> On your allegiance we've a stronger claim –
> We charge you yield, in Queen Victoria's name!

It is the pirates' turn to kneel submissively. The General orders
them to be marched away in custody, but Ruth intervenes.

RUTH: One moment! let me tell you who they are.
          They are no members of the common throng;
          They are all noblemen who have gone wrong!

GENERAL: No Englishman unmoved that statement hears,
          Because, with all our faults, we love our House of Peers.
          I pray you, pardon me, ex-Pirate King,
          Peers will be peers, and youth will have its fling.
          Resume your ranks and legislative duties,
          And take my daughters, all of whom are beauties.

Quotations

PIRATE KING: Oh, better far to live and die
Under the brave black flag I fly,
Than play a sanctimonious part,
With a pirate head and a pirate heart.
Away to the cheating world go you,
Where pirates all are well-to-do;
But I'll be true to the song I sing,
And live and die a Pirate King.

. . . .

MABEL: Poor wandering one!
Though thou hast surely strayed,
Take heart of grace,
Thy steps retrace,
Poor wandering one!
Poor wandering one!
If such poor love as mine
Can help thee find
True peace of mind –
Why, take it, it is thine!
Take heart, fair days will shine;
Take any heart – take mine!

. . . .

GIRLS: Yes, yes, let's talk about the weather

How beautifully blue the sky,
The glass is rising very high,
Continue fine I hope it may,
And yet it rained but yesterday.
To-morrow it may pour again
(I hear the country wants some rain),
Yet people say, I know not why,
That we shall have a warm July.

. . . .

MAJOR-GENERAL: I am the very model of a modern Major-General,
I've information vegetable, animal, and mineral,
I know the kings of England, and I quote the fights historical,
From Marathon to Waterloo, in order categorical;

I'm very well acquainted too with matters mathematical,
I understand equations, both the simple and quadratical,
About binomial theorem I'm teeming with a lot o' news –
With many cheerful facts about the square of the hypotenuse . . .

. . . .

PIRATE KING: Although our dark career
Sometimes involves the crime of stealing,
We rather think that we're
Not altogether void of feeling.
Although we live by strife,
We're always sorry to begin it,
For what, we ask, is life
Without a touch of Poetry in it?

ALL: Hail, Poetry, thou heaven-born maid!
Thou gildest e'en the pirate's trade:
Hail, flowing fount of sentiment!
All hail, Divine Emollient!

. . . .

SERGEANT: When the foeman bares his steel,
Tarantara! tarantara!
We uncomfortable feel,
Tarantara!
And we find the wisest thing,
Tarantara! tarantara!
Is to slap our chests and sing
Tarantara!
For when threatened with emeutes,
Tarantara! tarantara!

And your heart is in your boots,
Tarantara!
There is nothing brings it round,
Like the trumpet's martial sound,
Like the trumpet's martial sound.

. . . .

SERGEANT: When a felon's not engaged in his employment –
POLICE: His employment,
SERGEANT: Or maturing his felonious little plans –
POLICE: Little plans,
SERGEANT: His capacity for innocent enjoyment –
POLICE: 'Cent enjoyment
SERGEANT: Is just as great as any honest man's –
POLICE: Honest man's.
SERGEANT: Our feelings we with difficulty smother –
POLICE: 'Culty smother
SERGEANT: When constabulary duty's to be done –
POLICE: To be done.
SERGEANT: Ah, take one consideration with another –
POLICE: With another,
SERGEANT: A policeman's lot is not a happy one.
POLICE: When constabulary duty's to be done –
To be done,
The policeman's lot is not a happy one.
SERGEANT: When the enterprising burglar's not a-burgling –
POLICE: Not a-burgling,
SERGEANT: When the cut-throat isn't occupied in crime –
POLICE: 'Pied in crime,
SERGEANT: He loves to hear the little brook a-gurgling –
POLICE: Brook a-gurgling,
SERGEANT: And listen to the merry village chime –
POLICE: Village chime.
SERGEANT: When the coster's finished jumping on his mother –
POLICE: On his mother,
SERGEANT: He loves to lie a-basking in the sun –
POLICE: In the sun.
SERGEANT: Ah, take one consideration with another –
POLICE: With another,

SERGEANT: The policeman's lot is not a happy one.
POLICE: When constabulary duty's to be done –
                To be done,
      The policeman's lot is not a happy one –
                Happy one.

. . . .

PIRATES: Come, friends, who plough the sea,
      Truce to navigation,
      Take another station;
    Let's vary piracee
    With a little burglaree!

or

Bunthorne's Bride

BEHIND the fun of Gilbert's lines stands the quite serious business of satire. Generally his targets are common human attitudes – hypocrisy, pomposity, class distinction, and so forth; but with *Patience* he descended from the general to the particular and burlesqued the aesthetic movement of the time, typified by Oscar Wilde, Walter Pater, J. M. Whistler, and their self-professed disciples. At the same time, by contrasting his precious *poseurs* with the bluff, earthy officers of the 35th Heavy Dragoons, Gilbert contrived to satirize the unimaginative military mind as well; and, for good measure, used the love-sick maidens who hang upon the rival poets' words and vacillate between them and the Dragoons to typify that portion of the gullible, easily-led public who will scamper after every new craze.

Patience was first presented on 23 April, 1881 at the Opéra-Comique, the last of the Gilbert and Sullivan works to be originated in that increasingly inadequate theatre. It ran for 176 performances at the Opéra Comique and 402 at the Savoy. Despite Gilbert's misgivings, it did well in America, where the first presentation opened on 22 September in that same year. The fashion for aestheticism was not nearly so established there as in England at that time; but the piece succeeded well enough on its own merits and was rather more than fortuitously helped by a lecture series by Oscar Wilde – long-haired, knee-breeched and lily-clutching – which carried the craze across the Atlantic just in time. Richard D'Oyly Carte, as it happened, was Wilde's lecture agent.

• • • •

Twenty love-sick maidens we,
Love-sick all against our will.

> Twenty years hence we shall be
> Twenty love-sick maidens still.

The cause of this *malaise* amongst the aesthetically draped young ladies who languish beside the moat of Castle Bunthorne is that establishment's owner, Reginald Bunthorne, who combines castle keeping with poesy and expounding the virtues of all that is preciously medieval. The maidens are rivals for his love, yet united in their rivalry; but, as the least ethereal of them, the rugged Lady Jane, reveals, they are probably all wasting their time.

JANE: Fools and blind! The man loves – wildly loves!
ANGELA: But whom? None of us!
JANE: No, none of us. His weird fancy has lighted, for the nonce, on Patience, the village milkmaid!
SAPHIR: On Patience? Oh, it cannot be!
JANE: Bah! But yesterday I caught him in her dairy, eating fresh butter with a tablespoon. To-day he is not well!

The maddening feature, to them, is that the innocent Patience has never loved anyone – except a great-aunt – and does not know what to do so can imply, except that it appears to make those who suffer from it extremely miserable. She brings a message which she hopes will cheer the maidens up a little: the 35th Dragoon Guards have halted in the village and are on their way to this very spot.

ANGELA: The 35th Dragoon Guards!
SAPHIR: They are fleshly men, of full habit!
ELLA: We care nothing for Dragoon Guards!
PATIENCE: But, bless me, you were all engaged to them a year ago!
SAPHIR: A year ago!
ANGELA: My poor child, you don't understand these things. A year ago they were very well in our eyes, but since then our tastes have been etherealized, our perceptions exalted. Come, it is time to lift up our voices in morning carol to Reginald.

They hurry off into the castle and the Dragoons march on, full of an assurance which is unexpectedly pricked when the ladies return and do not notice them. Their eyes are only for Reginald Bunthorne, who is absorbed in poetic composition – or, rather, appears to be; for it is clear (if not to the enraptured maidens and enraged soldiers) that he is only too aware of his surroundings.

> Though my book I seem to scan
>> In a rapt ecstatic way,
> Like a literary man
>> Who despises female clay,
> I hear plainly all they say,
> Twenty love-sick maidens they!

The Dragoons claim the maidens' attention long enough to register their protests, but are told that they are simply not aesthetic enough.

SAPHIR: You are not Empyrean. You are not Della Cruscan. You are not even Early English. Oh, be Early English ere it is too late!

JANE (*looking at their uniforms*): Red and Yellow! Primary colours! Oh, South Kensington!

DUKE: We didn't design our uniforms, but we don't see how they could be improved.

JANE: No, you wouldn't. Still, there *is* a cobwebby grey velvet, with a tender bloom like cold gravy, which, made Florentine fourteenth-century, trimmed with Venetian leather and Spanish altar lace, and surmounted with something Japanese – it matters not what – would at least be Early English!

This insult to the British uniform – a uniform, in Colonel Calverley's words, 'that has been as successful in the courts of Venus as on the field of Mars' – makes the Dragoons stump angrily away. With the maidens gone, too, Bunthorne is able to confess to himself that he is an aesthetic sham who happens to know a good movement on which to cash in when he sees one. When Patience returns alone he opens his heart to her, but she fearfully replies that she cannot under any circumstances love him. He leaves desolate, wailing as he goes his unpublished poem 'Heart Foam':

> Oh, to be wafted away
>   From this black Aceldama of sorrow,
> Where the dust of an earthy to-day
>   Is the earth of a dusty to-morrow!

The Lady Angela, finding Patience in tears, inquires the reason. The simple maid confesses her inability to feel so universal an emotion as love. Angela begs her to try, assuring her that love is an essentially unselfish thing. The argument strikes home. Seeing it to be wicked of herself to reject anything that is unselfish, Patience determines that she will set about falling in love at once; indeed, will not go to bed until she is head over ears in love with somebody. Fortunately for her domestic arrangements, there approaches one Archibald Grosvenor, poet of the school of simplicity, self-styled trustee of beauty for the enjoyment and delectation of his fellow creatures. When they were both babes of a few years old, he and Patience had played together and felt a little touch from Cupid. Now, taller, stouter, and so beautiful that he is loved madly at first sight by every woman he encounters, he has come to claim the one whom he has loved 'with a Florentine fourteenth-century frenzy' for fifteen years. Love, it seems, has at last been revealed to Patience; but, in the midst of their rapture, a thought occurs to her.

GROSVENOR? What's the matter?

PATIENCE: Why, you are perfection! A source of endless ecstasy to all who know you!

GROSVENOR: I know I am. Well?

PATIENCE: Then, bless my heart, there can be nothing unselfish in loving *you*!

GROSVENOR: Merciful powers! I never thought of that!

PATIENCE: To monopolize those features on which all women love to linger! It would be unpardonable!

GROSVENOR: Why, so it would! Oh, fatal perfection, again you interpose between me and my happiness!

PATIENCE: Oh, if you were but a thought less beautiful than you are!

GROSVENOR: Would that I were; but candour compels me to admit that
I am not!
PATIENCE: Our duty is clear; we must part, and for ever!

A further thought strikes her: even if she may not love him
because of his beauty, there is nothing to prevent his loving her
for her plainness, homeliness and unattractiveness. They settle
for this compromise, and sadly go their separate ways.

Bunthorne, rose-crowned and garlanded, but looking none
the less extremely miserable, returns, led by the maidens like a
pet dog on a lead of roses. The Dragoons arrive, astonished to
see him thus. He explains that, heart-broken by Patience's rejection, he has taken his solicitor's advice, which is to put himself
up for auction in aid of a deserving charity. Lieutenant the Duke
of Dunstable seizes the chance to make a renewed plea on his
fellow officers' behalf, and moves the maidens almost to the
point of yielding; but Bunthorne intervenes with some brisk
sales-talk:

> Such a judge of blue-and-white and other kinds of pottery –
> From early Oriental down to modern terra-cotta-ry –
> Put in half a guinea – you may draw him in a lottery –
>   Such an opportunity may not occur again.

The maidens surge forward to buy tickets, then blindfold
themselves, ready for the draw. Just as Lady Jane is groping for
the first ticket from the bag, Patience returns, kneels to Bunthorne
and begs his pardon. She explains that, since it would be an
unselfish act to love him against her will, she is prepared to do so.
He accepts readily. The other maidens turn once more to the
relieved officers, and all appears to be settled to everyone's satisfaction until Archibald Grosvenor wanders on to the scene,
deeply immersed in a book. One look at him is enough to draw
the maidens away from the soldiers, to kneel around Grosvenor
and declare their love for him.

Playing a 'cello in a woody glade, Lady Jane laments the passing of her charms, but consoles herself that with the rest of
the maidens occupied with Grosvenor, she has only to wait for

Bunthorne to tire of Patience and turn to her – though he had better not take too long about it. She carries her instrument off, as the maidens carry theirs – more archaic in type – on. Grosvenor appears to be trying to read, despite their flutings and pipings, but he is secretly sighing for Patience. They beg him to read one of his poems, and he reluctantly assents. His style emerges somewhat in contrast to his rival poet's.

> Teasing Tom was a very bad boy,
> A great big squirt was his favourite toy;
> He put live shrimps in his father's boots,
> And sewed up the sleeves of his Sunday suits;
> He punched his little sisters' heads,
> And cayenne-peppered their four-post beds,
> He plastered their hair with cobbler's wax,
> And dropped hot halfpennies down their backs.
>   The consequence was he was lost totally,
>   And married a girl in the *corps de bally*!

His hearers are ready to swoon with admiration, but he sings them the fable of the magnet who, although he attracted most other metals, loved only a silver churn. Sadly, they take the hint, and depart.

Grosvenor's silver churn – Patience – approaches him, to his delight, but it is only for assurance that he still loves her. She has no intention of failing in her duty to love Bunthorne, even though he treats her badly. Bunthorne and Lady Jane see her talking to Grosvenor and upbraid her. Sick of being deprived of general adulation by his rival, Bunthorne plots to shame him out of the district and goes off discussing the details with Lady Jane. Their place is taken by the three senior Dragoons – Colonel Calverley, Major Murgatroyd and Lieutenant the Duke of Dunstable. A transformation has taken place in them. As a desperate attempt to regain the maidens' affection, they have adopted the angular attitudes of the Brotherhood. The poses they strike as they see the Ladies Angela and Saphir approach are not very expert, but they appear to have their effect.

ANGELA: Oh, Saphir – see – see! The immortal fire has descended on them, and they are of the Inner Brotherhood – perceptively intense and consummately utter.

SAPHIR: How Botticellian! How Fra Angelican! Oh, Art, we thank thee for this boon!

COLONEL: I'm afraid we're not quite right.

ANGELA: Not supremely, perhaps, but oh, so all-but! Oh, Saphir, are they not quite too all-but?

SAPHIR: They are indeed jolly utter!

MAJOR: I wonder what the Inner Brotherhood usually recommend for cramp.

As the Colonel explains, 'We are doing this at some personal inconvenience with a view of expressing the extremity of our devotion to you.' Such tenacity of purpose touches the ladies, and the question only remains who pairs off with whom. The Duke votes himself odd man out, and they all dance off happily together.

Grosvenor and Bunthorne come face to face, and Bunthorne threatens to put a curse on his rival if he will not cut his hair, make himself as commonplace-looking as possible and adopt an altogether matter-of-fact conversational mode. Grosvenor readily agrees. He is sick of adulation and Bunthorne is welcome to have it back. Grosvenor goes and Bunthorne indulges in a triumphant dance, to the astonishment of Patience, who has never seen him less than surly. He tells her that having completed his ill-natured act towards his rival he is a changed man: 'I have reformed. I have modelled myself upon Mr Grosvenor. Henceforth I am mildly cheerful. My conversation will blend amusement with instruction. I shall still be aesthetic; but my aestheticism will be of the most pastoral kind.'

It dawns upon Patience that, in this event, she is no longer able to love him unselfishly, and so is free. He is just protesting that he would rather resume his old ways, and keep her, when Grosvenor reappears, hair cut and ordinarily dressed. He is followed by the Dragoons and by the maidens, who, now that their idol has shed aestheticism, have done the same and returned to being ordinarily cheerful young women. Patience falls into Grosvenor's arms; the Duke of Dunstable selects Lady Jane for his bride; and everyone else pairs off, leaving only Reginald Bunthorne – despite the opera's sub-title – brideless.

Quotations

ANGELA: Ah, Patience, if you have never loved, you have never known true happiness!

PATIENCE: But the truly happy always seem to have so much on their minds. The truly happy never seem quite well.

JANE: There is a transcendentality of delirium – an acute accentuation of supremest ecstasy – which the earthy might easily mistake for indigestion. But it is *not* indigestion – it is aesthetic transfiguration!

. . . .

COLONEL: If you want a receipt for that popular mystery,
     Known to the world as a Heavy Dragoon,
    Take all the remarkable people in history,
     Rattle them off to a popular tune.
    The pluck of Lord Nelson on board of the *Victory* –
    Genius of Bismarck devising a plan –
    The humour of Fielding (which sounds contradictory) –
     Coolness of Paget about to trepan –
    The science of Jullien, the eminent musico –
     Wit of Macaulay, who wrote of Queen Anne –
    The pathos of Paddy, as rendered by Boucicault –
     Style of the Bishop of Sodor and Man –
    The dash of a D'Orsay, divested of quackery –
    Narrative powers of Dickens and Thackeray –
    Victor Emmanuel – peak-hunting Peveril –
    Thomas Aquinas, and Doctor Sacheverell –
     Tupper and Tennyson – Daniel Defoe –
     Anthony Trollope and Mr Guizot!
      Take of these elements all that is fusible,
      Melt 'em all down in a pipkin or crucible,
      Set 'em to simmer and take off the scum,
      And a Heavy Dragoon is the residium!

CHORUS: Yes! Yes! Yes! Yes!
    A Heavy Dragoon is the residium!

COLONEL: If you want a receipt for this soldier-like paragon,
    Get at the wealth of the Czar (if you can) –
    The family pride of a Spaniard from Arragon –
    Force of Mephisto pronouncing a ban –
    A smack of Lord Waterford, reckless and rollicky –
    Swagger of Roderick, heading his clan –
    The keen penetration of Paddington Pollaky –
    Grace of an Odalisque on a divan –
    The genius strategic of Caesar or Hannibal –
    Skill of Sir Garnet in thrashing a cannibal –
    Flavour of Hamlet – the Stranger, a touch of him –
    Little of Manfred (but not very much of him) –
    Beadle of Burlington – Richardson's show –
    Mr. Micawber and Madame Tussaud!
      Take of these elements all that is fusible, etc.

. . . .

BUNTHORNE: It is a wild, weird, fleshly thing; yet very tender, very yearning, very precious. It is called, 'Oh, Hollow! Hollow! Hollow!'
PATIENCE: Is it a hunting song?
BUNTHORNE: A hunting song? No, it is *not* a hunting song. It is the wail of the poet's heart on discovering that everything is commonplace. To understand it, cling passionately to one another and think of faint lilies.

        '*Oh, Hollow! Hollow! Hollow!*'

    What time the poet hath hymned
    The writhing maid, lithe-limbed,
      Quivering on amaranthine asphodel,
    How can he paint her woes,
    Knowing, as well he knows,
      That all can be set right with calomel?

    When from the poet's plinth
    The amorous colocynth
      Yearns for the aloe, faint with rapturous thrills,

How can he hymn their throes
Knowing, as well he knows,
   That they are only uncompounded pills?
Is it, and can it be,
Nature hath this decree,
   Nothing poetic in the world shall dwell?
Or that in all her works
Something poetic lurks,
   Even in colocynth and calomel?
     I cannot tell.

      . . . .

COLONEL: When I first put this uniform on,
     I said, as I looked in the glass,
      'It's one to a million
      That any civilian
     My figure and form will surpass.
      Gold lace has a charm for the fair,
      And I've plenty of that, and to spare,
       While a lover's professions,
       When uttered in Hessians,
      Are eloquent everywhere!'
        A fact that I counted upon,
        When I first put this uniform on!

      . . . .

BUNTHORNE: Am I alone,
     And unobserved? I am!
   Then let me own
     I'm an aesthetic sham!
   This air severe
     Is but a mere
           Veneer!
   This cynic smile
     Is but a wile
           Of guile!
   This costume chaste
     Is but good taste
           Misplaced!
    Let me confess!
A languid love for lilies does *not* blight me!

Lank limbs and haggard cheeks do *not* delight me!
 I do *not* care for dirty greens
  By any means.
  I do *not* long for all one sees
   That's Japanese.
  I am *not* fond of uttering platitudes
   In stained-glass attitudes.
  In short, my mediaevalism's affectation,
  Born of a morbid love of admiration!

If you're anxious for to shine in the high aesthetic
 line as a man of culture rare,
You must get up all the germs of the transcendental
 terms, and plant them everywhere.
You must lie upon the daisies and discourse in novel
 phrases of your complicated state of mind,
The meaning doesn't matter if it's only idle chatter
 of a transcendental kind.
    And every one will say,
    As you walk your mystic way,
'If this young man expresses himself in terms too
 deep for *me*,
Why, what a very singularly deep young man this
 deep young man must be!' ...

    • • • •

JANE: Silvered is the raven hair,
  Spreading is the parting straight,
 Mottled the complexion fair,
  Halting is the youthful gait,
 Hollow is the laughter free,
  Spectacled the limpid eye –
 Little will be left of me
  In the coming by and by!

 Fading is the taper waist,
  Shapeless grows the shapely limb,
 And although severely laced,
  Spreading is the figure trim!
 Stouter than I used to be,
  Still more corpulent grow I –

There will be too much of me
In the coming by and by!

. . . .

GROSVENOR: A magnet hung in a hardware shop,
And all around was a loving crop
Of scissors and needles, nails and knives,
Offering love for all their lives;
But for iron the magnet felt no whim,
Though he charmed iron, it charmed not him;
From needles and nails and knives he'd turn,
For he'd set his love on a Silver Churn!

ALL: A Silver Churn?

GROSVENOR: A Silver Churn!
His most aesthetic
Very magnetic
Fancy took this turn –
'If I can wheedle
A knife or a needle,
Why not a Silver Churn?'

CHORUS: His most aesthetic, etc.

GROSVENOR: And Iron and Steel expressed surprise,
The needles opened their well-drilled eyes,
The penknives felt 'shut up', no doubt,
The scissors declared themselves 'cut out',
The kettles they boiled with rage, 'tis said,
While every nail went off its head,
And hither and thither began to roam,
Till a hammer came up – and drove them home.

ALL: It drove them home?

GROSVENOR: It drove them home!
While this magnetic,
Peripatetic
Lover he lived to learn,
By no endeavour
Can magnet ever
Attract a Silver Churn!

. . . .

DUKE, COLONEL, AND MAJOR:

> It's clear that mediaeval art alone retains its zest,
> To charm and please its devotees we've done our
>   little best.
> We're not quite sure if all we do has the Early English
>   ring;
> But, as far as we can judge, it's something like this
>   sort of thing:
>> You hold yourself like this
>> You hold yourself like that
> By hook and crook you try to look both angular and
>   flat
>> We venture to expect
>> That what we recollect,
> Though but a part of true High Art, will have its due
>   effect.

. . . .

BUNTHORNE: When I go out of door,
> Of damozels a score
>> (All sighing and burning,
>> And clinging and yearning)
> Will follow me as before.
> I shall, with cultured taste,
> Distinguish gems from paste,
>> And 'Hi diddle diddle'
>> Will rank as an idyll,
> If I pronounce it chaste!

BUNTHORNE AND GROSVENOR:

> A most intense young man,
> A soulful-eyed young man,
> An ultra-poetical, super-aesthetical,
> Out-of-the-way young man!

GROSVENOR: Conceive me, if you can,
> An every-day young man:
>> A commonplace type,
>> With a stick and a pipe,
> And a half-bred black-and-tan;

Who thinks suburban 'hops'
More fun than 'Monday Pops',
Who's fond of his dinner,
And doesn't get thinner
On bottled beer and chops.

BUNTHORNE AND GROSVENOR:
A common place young man,
A matter-of-fact young man,
A steady and stolid-y, jolly Bank-holiday
Every-day young man!

BUNTHORNE: A Japanese young man,
A blue-and-white young man,
Francesca di Rimini, miminy, piminy,
Je-ne-sais-quoi young man!

GROSVENOR: A Chancery Lane young man,
A Somerset House young man,
A very delectable, highly respectable,
Threepenny-bus young man!

BUNTHORNE: A pallid and thin young man,
A haggard and lank young man,
A greenery-yallery, Grosvenor Gallery,
Foot-in-the-grave young man!

GROSVENOR: A Sewell & Cross young man,
A Howell & James young man,
A pushing young particle – 'What's the next article?' –
Waterloo House young man!

IOLANTHE 1882

or

The Peer and the Peri

By 1882, with their partnership in its seventh year, Gilbert and Sullivan had satirized between them the Law, the Clergy, the Navy, the Police, the Army, and the aesthetic movement – and much more by association. Parliament's inevitable turn came with *Iolanthe*, which also took another considerable tilt at the Law. One of Gilbert's *Bab Ballads*, 'The Fairy Curate', about a curate who is half-fairy, half-mortal, and has a mother chronologically younger than himself, was the starting-point for his inspiration, but the element of political satire rose from his working-out of the story.

Iolanthe was the first new work to be presented at the Savoy Theatre, which Richard D'Oyly Carte had had built on the site of the medieval Savoy Manor between the Strand and the Thames Embankment – and, incidentally, had made the first theatre to be entirely electrically lighted. *Patience* had transferred to this large and comfortable house on 10 October, 1881: *Iolanthe* opened there on 25 November, 1882. Perhaps because Gilbert's fun-poking on this occasion edged nearer to delicate susceptibilities, the new work came in for some criticism and one song had to be dropped for this reason. Generally, though, there was a rapturous and profitable reception for a charming, urbanely witty work with some of Sullivan's most sparkling music. A company from London gave a simultaneous New York premiere in yet another attempt to cut the ground away from beneath potential pirates' feet.

．．．．

Gaily though they trip, blithely though they sing, the fairies of Arcady are conscious that their purposeless but pleasant revels have not been what they were since the banishment of Iolanthe,

the composer of their songs, arranger of their dances, and general inspiration of their activities. Some twenty-five years previously, Iolanthe had committed the supreme offence against fairy laws of marrying a mortal. Only because of the all-surpassing love felt for her by the Queen of the Fairies had the statutory sentence of death been commuted to one of life imprisonment, with a choice of all the pleasant places of the earth in which to serve it. Disconcertingly, Iolanthe had settled for the bottom of a stream. For a quarter of a century she has been working out her sentence in these watery surroundings, standing on her head.

Now at last in the face of her subjects' persuasions the Queen is prepared to relent. Iolanthe is summoned from her exile, and her Queen is as overjoyed as any of the others to see her return. After the first transports of delight, however, she must satisfy her curiosity as to Iolanthe's eccentric choice of place of exile. Iolanthe replies that she had wanted to be near the son of her illicit marriage, Strephon, who had been born shortly after her banishment. Strephon, who is now 24, is an Arcadian shepherd with the singular quality of being half a fairy. Appropriately enough at this moment, he appears, dancing, singing and accompanying himself upon the flageolet. If he is surprised to find his mother no longer at the bottom of the stream, but on dry land and right way up, he gives no sign of it; for Strephon's thoughts are wholly occupied with Phyllis, a beautiful Ward in Chancery with whom he is in love. Things are not running smoothly for him. He has not dared reveal his fairyhood, for fear of alarming his intended; and, as an apparent mere mortal shepherd, he has gained no favour in the Lord Chancellor's eyes as a suitor worthy of one of his wards. Careless of the legal consequences, however, Strephon is determined to wait no longer: he will marry his Phyllis this very day. Admiring his mettle, the Queen of the Fairies prescribes an intellectual sphere of action in which to occupy his agile fairy brain.

QUEEN: . . . I've a borough or two at my disposal. Would you like to go into Parliament?

IOLANTHE: A fairy Member! That would be delightful!

STREPHON: I'm afraid I should do no good there – you see, down to the waist, I'm a Tory of the most determined description, but my legs are a couple of confounded Radicals, and, on a division, they'd be sure to take me into the wrong lobby. You see, they're two to one, which is a strong working majority.

QUEEN: Don't let that distress you; you shall be returned as a Liberal-Conservative, and your legs shall be our peculiar care.

With a parting admonition to Strephon to call upon them at any time of stress, the fairies trip away, only in the nick of time if Strephon is to keep his secret from his loved one, for Phyllis is now approaching. She is not convinced that married life and eternal happiness are synonymous; she is concerned about the penal servitude Strephon might incur for marrying a Ward in Chancery, and is, besides, not unaware that the Lord Chancellor himself and half the British peerage seem to be interestedly aware of her attractions. But Strephon will not hear of waiting for her to come of age.

STREPHON: Two years. Have you ever looked in the glass?
PHYLLIS: No, never.
STREPHON: Here, look at that (*showing her a pocket mirror*), and tell me if you think it rational to expect me to wait two years?
PHYLLIS (*looking at herself*): No. You're quite right – it's asking too much. One must be reasonable.

They swear a never-ending love and wander off arm in arm, just in time to miss the entry of a richly-robed body of peers, who, besides exalted rank, have at least one thing in common – love for Phyllis. The Lord Chancellor, who follows them in wig and black-and-gold gown, hastens to disabuse them of any notion that they are the only ones attracted by her. His own regard for her is such that his constitution is being rapidly undermined: 'Three months ago I was a stout man, I need say no more'. . . .

The feelings of a Lord Chancellor who is in love with a Ward of Court are not to be envied. What is his position? Can he give his own consent to his own marriage with his own Ward? Can he marry his own Ward without his own consent? And if he marries his own Ward without his own consent, can he commit himself for contempt of his own Court? And if he commits himself for contempt of his own Court, can he appear by counsel before himself, to move for arrest of his own judgment? Ah, my Lords, it is indeed painful to have to sit upon a woolsack which is stuffed with such thorns as these!

Lord Mountararat, the deputy-leader of the House of Lords, brings Phyllis from her cottage. All sing her praises – ecstatically if rather patronizingly – but Phyllis haughtily rejects them all, confessing that her heart is already given. Strephon appears, to declare himself her betrothed. The peers, gathering up their wounded pride along with their robes, make as dignified a departure as the circumstances will allow. The Lord Chancellor remains to demand Strephon's explanation of his defiance of the Court of Chancery.

STREPHON: When chorused Nature bids me take my love, shall I reply, 'Nay, but a certain Chancellor forbids it'? Sir, you are England's Lord High Chancellor, but are you Chancellor of birds and trees, King of the winds and Prince of thunderclouds?

LORD CHANCELLOR: No. It's a nice point. I don't know that I ever met it before. But my difficulty is that at present there's no evidence before the Court that chorused Nature has interested herself in the matter.

STREPHON: No evidence! You have my word for it. I tell you that she bade me take my love.

LORD CHANCELLOR: Ah! but, my good sir, you mustn't tell us what she told you – it's not evidence. Now an affidavit from a thunderstorm, or a few words on oath from a heavy shower, would meet with all the attention they deserve.

He departs, leaving a much less resolute Strephon. Iolanthe comes to her son and by way of comfort reminds him that he can at least defy the Lord Chancellor with his fairy half; but, as Strephon gloomily points out, what would be the use of his body being free if his legs were working out seven years' penal servitude. Iolanthe promises to go to her Queen and ask for special consideration for the case. While mother and son are talking closely and affectionately, the peers tiptoe up with Phyllis and try to overhear them. They are only partially successful. As a fairy, Iolanthe has never aged beyond a certain desirable point in her teens, which, in appearance, rather complements Strephon's 24, and the eavesdroppers misconstrue their innocent words. Phyllis cannot contain herself and renounces her love for Strephon. His protest that 'this lady's my mother!' reduces the peers to derisory laughter. Phyllis sends him on his way, and, turning to Lord Mountararat, and his colleague and Leader of the House Lord Tolloller, declares herself ready to accept either of them. Strephon calls upon the Queen of the Fairies to help him. Attended by her fairies – every one of them a sister to Iolanthe and aunt to Strephon – she appears at once, but fails to impress the noble lords. The Lord Chancellor tells her to be off and the peers support him. The furious Queen decides to teach them all a lesson: Strephon shall enter Parliament at once, and with all the influence of fairy backing.

QUEEN: Every bill and every measure
      That may gratify his pleasure,
      Though your fury it arouses,
      Shall be passed by both your Houses!
      You shall sit, if he sees reason,
      Through the grouse and salmon season;
      He shall end the cherished rights
      You enjoy on Friday nights:
      He shall prick that annual blister,
      Marriage with deceased wife's sister:
      Titles shall ennoble, then,
      All the Common Councilmen:
      Peers shall teem in Christendom,
        And a Duke's exalted station
      Be attainable by Com-
        Petitive Examination!

In Palace Yard, Westminster, with the lighted windows of the Houses of Parliament against a night sky, Private Willis, of B Company, 1st Grenadier Guards, is ruminating in his sentry-box when suddenly the Yard is full of fairies celebrating Strephon's success as a Parliamentarian. The peers stamp in, voicing quite different sentiments about him.

LORD MOUNTARARAT: ... This ridiculous protégé of yours is playing the deuce with everything! To-night is the second reading of his Bill to throw the Peerage open to Competitive Examination!

LORD TOLLOLLER: And he'll carry it, too!

LORD MOUNTARARAT: Carry it? Of course he will! He's a Parliamentary Pickford – he carries everything!

The fairies begin to discern a certain charm about their lordships, but the Queen of the Fairies appears and rebukes them for even contemplating marriage with mortals. When they have gone, Phyllis enters Palace Yard half in tears, but cannot think why. Of one thing she is certain: she is *not* pining for Strephon. Lords Mountararat and Tolloller follow her and conduct a difficult wrangle as to which of them is best fitted to bring her lasting happiness. They consider a duel, but such is their friendship that neither can contemplate losing it and so leaving the survivor to inevitable remorse. The result is that when Phyllis persuades them that she is not worth spoiling their friendship for, they agree, and go off happily without her.

Another miserable denizen of Westminster is the Lord Chancellor. Mountararat and Tolloller are much distressed to discover him slumped on a seat, exhausted by insomnia and unrequited love. They encourage him to pluck up the courage to make one more approach to himself in his official capacity, respectfully and with a proper show of deference, to see if his arguments cannot at last prevail. Much heartened, he determines to do so.

Strephon, who has found Parliamentary triumph to be no substitute for Phyllis's love, encounters her in Palace Yard and, with no further reason for concealing it, confesses that he is half a fairy. She assures him that she would rather marry half a mortal she loves than half a dozen she doesn't. The anomaly of his mother's apparent youth is satisfactorily cleared up and Phyllis is happy to accept that any young lady she may happen to find Strephon kissing in future is certain to be an elderly relative.

Iolanthe enters, and they tell her that their engagement is on again. Strephon begs his mother to use her fairy eloquence to persuade the Lord Chancellor to let them marry. Agitated, she tells him her secret: the Lord Chancellor is her mortal husband who believes her dead, and she is bound by fairy law, under penalty of death, never to undeceive him. Iolanthe veils herself swiftly and the lovers tiptoe away as the Lord Chancellor re-appears. Now he is jubilant.

Victory! Victory! Success has crowned my efforts, and I may consider myself engaged to Phyllis! At first I wouldn't hear of it – it was out of the question. But I took heart. I pointed out to myself that I was no stranger to myself; that, in point of fact, I had been personally acquainted with myself for some years. This had its effect. I admitted that I had watched my personal advancement with considerable interest, and I handsomely added that I yielded to no one in admiration for my private and pro-fessional virtues. This was a great point gained. I then endeavoured to work upon my feelings. Conceive my joy when I distinctly perceived a tear glistening in my own eye! Eventually, after a severe struggle with myself, I reluctantly – most reluctantly – consented.

Iolanthe kneels at his feet and pleads Strephon's suit. The Lord Chancellor sternly rejects it, telling her that Phyllis is to be his own bride. Iolanthe reveals that she is his wife. He recognizes her and sobs with joy. Fairy wails are heard approaching and the Queen enters to pronounce Iolanthe's doom. But even as the Queen is raising her spear the peers emerge from the shadows and one of the fairies steps forward to confess that she and her sisters have all become fairy duchesses, marchionesses, countesses, viscountesses and baronesses. This throws the Queen into a dilemma. She cannot slaughter the entire company, and yet fairy law is quite clear upon the subject. But the Lord Chancellor, as an old Equity draftsman, is equal to the situation. The law merely needs amending by one word, to read that every fairy shall die who *doesn't* marry a mortal. The Queen's eye lights at once upon Private Willis.

QUEEN: To save my life, it is necessary that I marry at once. How should you like to be a fairy guardsman?

WILLIS: Well, ma'am, I don't think much of the British soldier who wouldn't ill-convenience himself to save a female in distress.

A pair of wings, emblazoned with the Grenadier Guards' crest, spring from his shoulders. The Queen turns to the peers and invites them to become fairies, too. They accept; wings sprout, and off they all fly to Fairyland.

Quotations

IOLANTHE: Then the Lord Chancellor has at last given his consent to your marriage with his beautiful ward, Phyllis?

STREPHON: Not he, indeed. To all my tearful prayers he answers me, 'A shepherd lad is no fit helpmate for a Ward of Chancery.' I stood in court, and there I sang him songs of Arcadee, with flageolet accompaniment – in vain. At first he seemed amused, so did the Bar; but quickly wearying of my song and pipe, bade me get out. A servile usher then, in crumpled bands and rusty bombazine, led me, still singing, into Chancery Lane! I'll go no more, I'll marry her to-day, and brave the upshot, be it what it may!

. . . .

CHORUS: Loudly let the trumpet bray!
                    Tantantara!
            Proudly bang the sounding brasses!
                    Tantantara! Tzing! Boom!
As upon its lordly way
    This unique procession passes,
                    Tantantara! Tzing! Boom!
Bow, bow, ye lower middle classes!
Bow, bow, ye tradesmen, bow, ye masses!
Blow the trumpets, bang the brasses!
                    Tantantara! Tzing! Boom!
We are peers of highest station,
Paragons of legislation,
Pillars of the British nation!
                    Tantantara! Tzing! Boom! . . .

. . . .

LORD CHANCELLOR: The Law is the true embodiment
Of everything that's excellent.
It has no kind of fault or flaw,
And I, my Lords, embody the Law.
The constitutional guardian I
Of pretty young Wards in Chancery,
All very agreeable girls – and none
Are over the age of twenty-one.
A pleasant occupation for
A rather susceptible Chancellor!

ALL: A pleasant, etc.

LORD CHANCELLOR: But though the compliment implied
Inflates me with legitimate pride,
It nevertheless can't be denied
That it has its incovenient side.
For I'm not so old, and not so plain,
And I'm quite prepared to marry again,
But there'd be the deuce to pay in the Lords
If I fell in love with one of my Wards!
Which rather tries my temper, for
I'm *such* a susceptible Chancellor!

ALL: Which rather, etc.

LORD CHANCELLOR: And every one who'd marry a Ward
Must come to me for my accord,
And in my court I sit all day,
Giving agreeable girls away,
With one for him – and one for he –
And one for you – and one for ye –
And one for thou – and one for thee –
But never, oh, never a one for me!
Which is exasperating for
A highly susceptible Chancellor!

· · · ·

LORD TOLLOLLER: Spurn not the nobly born
With love affected,
Nor treat with virtuous scorn
The well-connected ...

H

Spare us the bitter pain
   Of stern denials,
Nor with low-born disdain
   Augment our trials.
Hearts just as pure and fair
May beat in Belgrave Square
As in the lowly air
   Of Seven Dials!
Blue blood! blue blood!
   Of what avail art thou
   To serve us now?
Though dating from the Flood
   Blue blood!

· · · ·

LORD CHANCELLOR: When I went to the Bar as a very young man,
   (Said I to myself – said I),
I'll work on a new and original plan
   (Said I to myself – said I),
I'll never assume that a rogue or a thief
Is a gentleman worthy implicit belief,
Because his attorney has sent me a brief
   (Said I to myself – said I).

Ere I go into court I will read my brief through
   (Said I to myself – said I),
And I'll never take work I'm unable to do
   (Said I to myself – said I),
My learned profession I'll never disgrace
By taking a fee with a grin on my face,
When I haven't been there to attend to the case
   (Said I to myself – said I!).

I'll never throw dust in a juryman's eyes
   (Said I to myself – said I),
Or hoodwink a judge who is not over-wise
   (Said I to myself – said I),
Or assume that the witnesses summoned in force
In Exchequer, Queen's Bench, Common Pleas,
   or Divorce,

> Have perjured themselves as a matter of course
>> (Said I to myself – said I!).
> In other professions in which men engage
>> (Said I to myself – said I),
> The Army, the Navy, the Church, and the Stage
>> (Said I to myself – said I),
> Professional licence, if carried too far,
> Your chance of promotion will certainly mar –
> And I fancy the rule might apply to the Bar
>> (Said I to myself – said I!)

. . . .

STREPHON (*to* IOLANTHE):
> When darkly looms the day,
> And all is dull and grey,
> To chase the gloom away,
>> On thee I'll call!

PHYLLIS (*to* LORD MOUNTARARAT):
> What was that?

LORD MOUNTARARAT (*to* PHYLLIS):
> I think I heard him say,
> That on a rainy day,
> To while the time away,
>> On her he'd call!

CHORUS: We think we heard him say, etc.

IOLANTHE (*to* STREPHON):
> When tempests wreck thy bark,
> And all is drear and dark,
> If thou shouldst need an Ark,
>> I'll give thee one!

PHYLLIS (*to* LORD TOLLOLLER):
> What was that?

LORD TOLLOLLER (*to* PHYLLIS):
> I heard the minx remark,
> She'd meet him after dark,
> Inside St. James's Park,
>> And give him one!

. . . .

PRIVATE WILLS: When all night long a chap remains
                      On sentry-go, to chase monotony
             He exercises of his brains,
                 That is, assuming that he's got any.
             Though never nurtured in the lap
             Of luxury, yet I admonish you,
             I am an intellectual chap,
                 And think of things that would astonish you.
                 I often think it's comical –
                     Fal, lal, la, la! Fal, lal, la!
                 How Nature always does contrive –
                     Fal, lal, la, la, la!
                     That every boy and every gal
                         That's born into the world alive
                     Is either a little Liberal
                         Or else a little Conservative!
                         Fal, lal, la, la! Fal, lal, la, la!
                     Is either a little Liberal
                         Or else a little Conservative!
             When in that House M.P.s divide,
                 If they've a brain and cerebellum, too,
             They've got to leave that brain outside,
                 And vote just as their leaders tell 'em to.
             But then the prospect of a lot
             Of dull M.P.s in close proximity,
             All thinking for themselves, is what
                 No man can face with equanimity.
                 Then let's rejoice with loud Fal la – Fal, lal, la, la!
                     Fal, lal, la!
                 That Nature always does contrive –
                     Fal, lal, la, la, la!
                 That every boy and every gal
                     That's born into the world alive
                 Is either a little Liberal
                     Or else a little Conservative!
                     Fal, lal, la, la! Fal, lal, la, la!
                 Is either a little Liberal
                     Or else a little Conservative!

                         .   .   .   .

LORD MOUNTARARAT: . . . It so happens that if there is an institution in Great Britain which is not susceptible of any improvement at all, it is the House of Peers!

> When Britain really ruled the waves –
>   (In good Queen Bess's time)
> The House of Peers made no pretence
> To intellectual eminence,
>   Or scholarship sublime;
> Yet Britain won her proudest bays
> In good Queen Bess's glorious days:

CHORUS: Yes, Britain won, etc.

LORD MOUNTARARAT: When Wellington thrashed Bonaparte,
>   As every child can tell,
>   The House of Peers, throughout the war,
>   Did nothing in particular,
>   And did it very well:
>   Yet Britain set the world ablaze
>   In good King George's glorious days

CHORUS: Yes, Britain set, etc.

LORD MOUNTARARAT: And while the House of Peers withholds
>   Its legislative hand,
>   And noble statesmen do not itch
>   To interfere with matters which
>   They do not understand
>   As bright will shine Great Britain's rays
>   As in King George's glorious days!

CHORUS: As bright will shine, etc.

· · · ·

QUEEN OF THE FAIRIES: On fire that glows
>   With heat intense
>   I turn the hose
>   Of common sense,
>   And out it goes
>   At small expense!
>   We must maintain
>   Our fairy law;
>   That is the main
>   On which to draw –

In that we gain
A Captain Shaw!
Oh, Captain Shaw!
Type of true love kept under!
Could thy Brigade
With cold cascade
Quench my great love, I wonder!

.   .   .   .

LORD CHANCELLOR:

When you're lying awake with a dismal headache,
    and repose is taboo'd by anxiety,
I conceive you may use any language you choose to indulge in,
    without impropriety;
For your brain is on fire – the bedclothes conspire of usual
    slumber to plunder you:
First your counterpane goes, and uncovers your toes, and your
    sheet slips demurely from under you;
Then the blanketing tickles – you feel like mixed pickles – so
    terribly sharp is the pricking,
And you're hot, and you're cross, and you tumble and toss till
    there's nothing 'twixt you and the ticking.
Then the bedclothes all creep to the ground in a heap, and you
    pick 'em all up in a tangle;
Next your pillow resigns and politely declines to remain at its
    usual angle!
Well, you get some repose in the form of a doze, with hot
    eye-balls and head ever aching.
But your slumbering teems with such horrible dreams that
    you'd very much better be waking;
For you dream you are crossing the Channel, and tossing about
    in a steamer from Harwich –
Which is something between a large bathing machine and a very
    small second-class carriage –
And you're giving a treat (penny ice and cold meat) to a party
    of friends and relations –
They're a ravenous horde – and they all came on board at Sloane
    Square and South Kensington Stations.

And bound on that journey you find your attorney (who started
  that morning from Devon);
He's a bit undersized, and you don't feel surprised when he
  tells you he's only eleven.
Well, you're driving like mad with this singular lad (by the by,
  the ship's now a four-wheeler),
And you're playing round games, and he calls you bad names
  when you tell him that 'ties pay the dealer';
But this you can't stand, so you throw up your hand, and you
  find you're as cold as an icicle,
In your shirt and your socks (the black silk with gold clocks),
  crossing Salisbury Plain on a bicycle;
And he and the crew are on bicycles too – which they've
  somehow or other invested in –
And he's telling the tars all the particulars of a company he's
  interested in –
It's a scheme of devices, to get at low prices all goods from
  cough mixtures to cables
(Which tickled the sailors), by treating retailers as though they
  were all vegetables –
You get a good spadesman to plant a small tradesman (first
  take off his boots with a boot-tree)
And his legs will take root, and his fingers will shoot, and they'll
  blossom and bud like a fruit-tree –
From the greengrocer tree you get grapes and green pea,
  cauliflower, pineapple, and cranberries,
While the pastrycook plant cherry brandy will grant, apple
  puffs, and three-corners, and Banburys –
The shares are a penny, and ever so many are taken by
  Rothschild and Baring,
And just as a few are allotted to you, you awake with a
  shudder despairing –
You're a regular wreck, with a crick in your neck, and no wonder
  you snore, for your head's on the floor, and you've needles and
  pins, from your soles to your shins, and your flesh is a-creep,
  for your left leg's asleep, and you've cramp in your toes, and a
  fly on your nose, and some fluff in your lung, and a feverish
  tongue, and a thirst that's intense, and a general sense that you
  haven't been sleeping in clover;

But the darkness has passed, and it's daylight at last, and the
night has been long – ditto ditto my song – and thank
goodness they're both of them over!

· · · ·

LORD CHANCELLOR:　I'll take heart
　　　　　　　　　　And make a start –
　　　　　　　　　　Though I fear the prospect's shady –
　　　　　　　　　　Much I'd spend
　　　　　　　　　　To gain my end –
　　　　　　　　　　Faint heart never won fair lady!
ALL:　　　　　　　　Faint heart never won fair lady!
　　　　　　　　　　Nothing venture, nothing win –
　　　　　　　　　　Blood is thick, but water's thin –
　　　　　　　　　　In for a penny, in for a pound –
　　　　　　　　　　It's love that makes the world go round!

or

Castle Adamant

A FEW weeks after the first night of *Princess Ida* at the Savoy on
5 January, 1884 Sir Arthur Sullivan, as he had now become,
informed D'Oyly Carte that he would write no more works in
which, as he saw it, the music lived subordinate to the words,
and serious situations were being misused as vehicles for humour.
He was ill and depressed and had collapsed immediately after
conducting the first performance of the new piece, whose rela-
tively poor returns during its nine-months' run might have
appeared to justify his disillusionment. Despite the fact that it was
destined to be followed next year by what would be the most
popular Gilbert and Sullivan work of all, *The Mikado*, the imme-
diate aftermath of *Princess Ida* marked the beginning of the end
of the partnership.

The work itself has been one of the least performed of all,
partly because of its staging demands, partly because it is more
enjoyed by aficionados for Gilbert and Sullivan than by audiences
at large; yet it is full of fine things, satirizing the New Woman's
demand for emancipation, in a story, in blank verse, based on
Tennyson's *The Princess*. As for Sullivan's music, when he wrote
to Carte bemoaning that 'My tunes are in danger of becoming
mere repetitions of my former pieces, my concerted movements
are getting to possess a strong family likeness', they were the ill-
judged words of fatigue, ill-health and a growing resentment of
what he saw as Gilbert's dominance.

First New York production was on 11 February, 1884.

. . . .

In a pavilion attached to King Hildebrand's palace, soldiers and
courtiers are scanning the distance through opera-glasses and
telescopes. They are watching for the arrival of King Gama, a

neighbouring monarch whose daughter had been betrothed twenty years before to Hildebrand's son, Prince Hilarion. He is due to bring her this day to keep his troth; but when, at length, a small party of people bearing Gama's arms heaves into view, there is no princess visible amongst them. Hildebrand vows that any backsliding by Gama will mean war, while Hilarion quietly wonders what it will be like to meet a bride whom he has not encountered since she was one year old and he was two.

The visiting party has crossed the river and entered the palace. Gama's three hulking sons, Arac, Guron and Scynthius, enter first, followed by their royal father, who proceeds to live up to his misanthropic reputation.

GAMA: So this is Castle Hildebrand? Well, well!
            Dame Rumour whispered that the place was grand;
            She told me that your taste was exquisite,
            Superb, unparalleled!
HILDEBRAND (*gratified*): Oh, really, King!
GAMA: But she's a liar! How old you've grown!
            Is this Hilarion? Why, you've changed too –
            You were a singularly handsome child!

But all his repertoire of insults cannot save him from having eventually to admit that he cannot produce Princess Ida. She has retired to Castle Adamant, one of his many country houses, to conduct a woman's university where a hundred girls live only for learning and eschew the society of men.

FLORIAN: Are there no males whatever in those walls?
GAMA: None, gentlemen, excepting letter mails –
            And they are driven (as males often are
            In other large communities) by women.
            Why, bless my heart, she's so particular
            She'll scarcely suffer Dr Watts's hymns –
            And all the animals she owns are 'hers'!
            The ladies rise at cockcrow every morn –
CYRIL: Ah, then they have male poultry?
GAMA: Not at all,
            The crowing's done by an accomplished hen!

Hildebrand is not to be diverted. He gives orders for an ulti-
matum to be delivered to Castle Adamant: either Ida comes out
to fulfil the marriage bargain, or Gama and his sons will be
hanged. They are marched away to a dungeon, while Hilarion
and his two courtier friends, Cyril and Florian, eagerly prepare
to leave for the woman's university, confident that their masculine charms will be enough to overcome Ida's resistance without resort to threats.

In Castle Adamant the ladies are earnestly discussing their
curriculum of classical studies, remarking in passing on the
coarseness of Man. Their Professor of Abstract Science, Lady
Blanche, reads out the punishment list for the latest series of
digressions, and Ida herself delivers an elephantine sermon about
woman's supremacy over man and the need for a Women's
Liberation movement. Lady Blanche listens cynically: she sees
herself as rightful Principal of the college, and vows that her
time shall come.

What has come, meanwhile, is Hildebrand's trio of emissaries,
tumbling over the wall as soon as Blanche has departed, rubbing
themselves where broken glass, stinging nettles and other defences
have done their job. They are cheerfully confident, nevertheless,
and the sight of some discarded academic robes suggests immediately that they disguise themselves as three noble lady under-
graduates seeking admission to the university. No sooner have
they done so than Ida appears, interrogates them, and is satisfied.

The Princess goes her way unsuspecting; but there can be no
deceiving the next maiden to encounter the three young men,
for she is the Lady Psyche, Professor of Humanities and sister to
Florian. Certain that she will recognize him and his companions,
her childhood's playfellows, they decide to confide in her. As
they do, they are overheard by Melissa, Lady Blanche's daughter,
who has never seen a man and is as much attracted by Florian as
he is by her. Both she and Psyche are moved to admit that there
may be some flaw in Ida's views on males, after all, and the
five of them celebrate the revelation in a gay song. They dance
away, but Melissa is detained by her mother's arrival.

BLANCHE: Those are the three new students?
MELISSA: Yes they are.
         They're charming girls.
BLANCHE: Particularly so.
         So graceful, and so very womanly!
         So skilled in all a girl's accomplishments!
MELISSA: Yes – very skilled.
BLANCHE: They sing so nicely too!
MELISSA: They *do* sing nicely!
BLANCHE: Humph! It's very odd.
         Two are tenors, one is a baritone!

So the secret is dangerously out; but Melissa knows her
mother's jealousy of Ida, and persuades her that by assisting
Hilarion's bid to claim the Princess as his bride she will clear the
way to her own advancement.

Melissa loses no time in telling Florian that they are discovered
and urges him to fly at once, taking her with him. He is only too
willing, but the sound of the luncheon bell detains him, for
'Cursed with an appetite keen I am', and there is a nice piece of
cold roast lamb approaching. Unfortunately, the 'Daughters of
the Plough' who carry in the luncheon also bear strong waters,
and before long Cyril is becoming tipsy and indiscreet. His
companions are unable to prevent him singing an old kissing-
song in praise of female charms. Hilarion hits him. It sobers
Cyril instantly, but the Princess has already seen through the
deception. In her agitation she runs on to the bridge over the
stream, loses her balance and falls in. Hilarion dives after her and
saves her. The situation would seem to be saved, too, by this,
but Ida's principles are stronger than her sense of gratitude.

PRINCESS: The man whose sacrilegious eyes
          Invade our strict seclusion, dies.
          Arrest these coarse intruding spies!

Though the ladies plead for them, too, the three are bound and
led away. Melissa hurries in with the news that an armed band
is at the castle gate, demanding admittance in King Hildebrand's

name. The Princess issues orders to deny them entry, but it is too late: the gate is battered down and the soldiers swarm in, leading Gama's three sons in chains. Hildebrand himself confronts the Princess, threatening to level the place and execute his three hostages if she will not become Hilarion's bride. She accuses him of bluffing; he retorts that she may have until the following afternoon to make up her mind.

The Princess commands defiance, but her maidens' hearts are not in the task: they are too afraid of getting hurt. Princess Ida recognizes that the ideals she has laboured to instil into them have failed to take root, and is only too glad to accept an offer from Hilarion, Florian and Cyril to fight on her side. Her father, King Gama, enters, pale and distraught, with a message from Hildebrand. That monarch is loth to fight with women, so suggests that Gama's three sons should engage in combat with Hilarion and his two friends, and that the outcome should settle the issue. Solely out of pity for her father, she agrees. Arac, Guron and Scynthius remove their cumbersome armour and the six men cross swords. Encouraged from the battlements by the soldiers and maidens, they fight until Gama's sons lie wounded on the ground. Ida has no alternative but to resign and let the triumphant Blanche replace her as Principal.

PRINCESS: So ends my cherished scheme! Oh, I had hoped
    To band all women with my maiden throng,
    And make them all abjure tyrannic Man!

HILDEBRAND: A noble aim!

PRINCESS: You ridicule it now;
    But if I carried out this glorious scheme,
    At my exalted name Posterity
    Would bow in gratitude!

HILDEBRAND: But pray reflect –
    If you enlist all women in your cause,
    And make them all abjure tyrannic Man,
    The obvious question then arises, 'How
    Is this Posterity to be provided?'

PRINCESS: I never thought of that! My Lady Blanche,
    How do you solve the riddle?

BLANCHE: Don't ask me –
                Abstract Philosophy won't answer it.

Cyril claims Psyche's hand, and Florian Melissa's. Ida turns to Hilarion and confesses that her views had been mistaken. In Tennyson's own words, she tells him

> 'We will walk the world
> Yoked in all exercise of noble end!
> And so through those dark gates across the wild
> That no man knows! Indeed, I love thee – Come!'

Quotations

HILARION: Ida was a twelvemonth old,
        Twenty years ago!
    I was twice her age, I'm told,
        Twenty years ago!
    Husband twice as old as wife
    Argues ill for married life,
    Baleful prophecies were rife,
        Twenty years ago!

    Still, I was a tiny prince
        Twenty years ago.
    She has gained upon me, since
        Twenty years ago.
    Though she's twenty-one, it's true,
    I am barely twenty-two –
    False and foolish prophets you,
        Twenty years ago!

· · · ·

ARAC: We are warriors three,
            Sons of Gama, Rex.
        Like most sons are we,
            Masculine in sex.

ALL THREE: Yes, yes, yes,
            Masculine in sex.

ARAC: Politics we bar,
    They are not our bent;
On the whole we are
    Not intelligent.

ALL THREE: No, no, no,
    Not intelligent.

ARAC: But with doughty heart,
    And with trusty blade
We can play our part –
    Fighting is our trade.

ALL THREE: Yes, yes, yes,
    Fighting is our trade.

. . . .

GAMA: If you give me your attention, I will tell you what I am:
    I'm a genuine philanthropist – all other kinds are sham.
    Each little fault of temper and each social defect
    In my erring fellow-creatures I endeavour to correct.
    To all their little weaknesses I open people's eyes;
    And little plans to snub the self-sufficient I devise;
    I love my fellow-creatures – I do all the good I can –
    Yet everybody says I'm such a disagreeable man!
        And I can't think why!

To compliment inflated I've a withering reply;
And vanity I always do my best to mortify;
A charitable action I can skilfully dissect;
And interested motives I'm delighted to detect;
I know everybody's income and what everybody earns;
And I carefully compare it with the income-tax returns;
But to benefit humanity however much I plan,
Yet everybody says I'm such a disagreeable man!
        And I can't think why!

I'm sure I'm no ascetic; I'm as pleasant as can be;
You'll always find me ready with a crushing repartee,
I've an irritating chuckle, I've a celebrated sneer,
I've an entertaining snigger, I've a fascinating leer.

To everybody's prejudice I know a thing or two;
I can tell a woman's age in half a minute – and I do.
But although I try to make myself as pleasant as I can,
Yet everybody says I am a disagreeable man!
    And I can't think why!

      • • • •

HILARION: Expressive glances
    Shall be our lances,
      And pops of Sillery
      Our light artillery.
    We'll storm their bowers
    With scented showers
    Of fairest flowers
      That we can buy!

      • • • •

ARAC, GURON AND SCYNTHIUS:
    For a month to dwell
    In a dungeon cell;
      Growing thin and wizen
      In a solitary prison,
    Is a poor look-out
    For a soldier stout,
      Who is longing for the rattle
      Of a complicated battle –
    For the rum-tum-tum
    Of the military drum,
      And the guns that go boom! boom!

      • • • •

MELISSA: Pray, what authors should she read
    Who in Classics would succeed?
PSYCHE: If you'd climb the Helicon,
    You should read Anacreon,
    Ovid's *Metamorphoses*,
    Likewise Aristophanes,
    And the works of Juvenal:
    These are worth attention, all;

But if you will be advised,
You will get them Bowdlerized!

CHORUS: Ah! we will get them Bowdlerized!

SACHARISSA: Pray you, tell us, if you can,
What's the thing that's known as Man?

PSYCHE: Man will swear and Man will storm –
Man is not at all good form –
Man is of no kind of use –
Man's a donkey – Man's a goose –
Man is coarse and Man is plain –
Man is more or less insane –
Man's a ribald – Man's a rake,
Man is Nature's sole mistake!

CHORUS: We'll a memorandum make –
Man is Nature's sole mistake!

. . . .

BLANCHE: Attention, ladies, while I read to you
The Princess Ida's list of punishments.
The first is Sacharissa. She's expelled!

ALL: Expelled!

BLANCHE: Expelled, because although she knew
No man of any kind may pass our walls,
She dared to bring a set of chessmen here!

SACHARISSA: I meant no harm! they're only men of wood!

BLANCHE: They're men with whom you give each other mate,
And that's enough! The next is Chloe.

CHLOE: Ah!

BLANCHE: Chloe will lose three terms, for yesterday,
When looking through her drawing-book, I found
A sketch of a perambulator!

ALL: (*horrified*) Oh!

BLANCHE: *Double* perambulator, shameless girl!

. . . .

FLORIAN: A Woman's college! maddest folly going!
What can girls learn within its walls worth knowing?
I'll lay a crown (the Princess shall decide it)
I'll teach them twice as much in half-an-hour outside it.

I

HILARION: Hush, scoffer; ere you sound your puny thunder,
List to their aims, and bow your head in wonder!
They intend to send a wire
        To the moon – to the moon;
And they'll set the Thames on fire
        Very soon – very soon;
Then they learn to make silk purses
        With their rigs – with their rigs,
From the ears of Lady Circe's
        Piggy-wigs – piggy-wigs.
And weasels at their slumbers
        They trepan – they trepan;
To get sunbeams from cucumbers,
        They've a plan – they've a plan.
They've a firmly rooted notion
They can cross the Polar Ocean,
And they'll find Perpetual Motion,
        If they can – if they can.

                    .   .   .   .

PRINCESS: The world is but a broken toy,
        It's pleasure hollow – false its joy,
        Unreal its loveliest hue,
                Alas!
        Its pains alone are true,
                Alas!
        Its pains alone are true.

                    .   .   .   .

LADY PSYCHE: A Lady fair, of lineage high,
        Was loved by an Ape, in the days gone by.
        The Maid was radiant as the sun,
        The Ape was a most unsightly one –
                So it would not do –
                His scheme fell through
        For the Maid, when his love took formal shape,
                Expressed such terror
                At his monstrous error,
        That he stammered an apology and made his 'scape,

The picture of a disconcerted Ape.

With a view to rise in the social scale,
He shaved his bristles, and he docked his tail,
He grew moustachios, and he took his tub,
And he paid a guinea to a toilet club –
    But it would not do,
    The scheme fell through –
For the Maid was Beauty's fairest Queen,
    With golden tresses,
    Like a real princess's,
While the Ape, despite his razor keen,
Was the apiest Ape that ever was seen!

He bought white ties, and he bought dress suits,
He crammed his feet into bright tight boots –
And to start in life on a brand-new plan,
He christened himself Darwinian Man!
    But it would not do,
    The scheme fell through –
For the Maiden fair, whom the monkey craved,
    Was a radiant Being,
    With a brain far-seeing –
While Darwinian Man, though well-behaved,
At best is only a monkey shaved!

. . . .

CYRIL: Would you know the kind of maid
        Sets my heart aflame-a?
    Eyes must be downcast and staid,
        Cheeks must flush for shame-a!
        She may neither dance nor sing,
        But, demure in everything,
        Hang her head in modest way,
        With pouting lips that seem to say,
    'Oh, kiss me, kiss me, kiss me, kiss me,
        Though I die of shame-a!'
    Please you, that's the kind of maid
        Sets my heart aflame-a!

. . . .

GAMA: Whene'er I spoke
       Sarcastic joke
          Replete with malice spiteful,
       This people mild
       Politely smiled,
          And voted me delightful!
       Now when a wight
       Sits up all night
          Ill-natured jokes devising,
       And all his wiles
       Are met with smiles,
          It's hard, there's no disguising!

    Oh, don't the days seem lank and long
      When all goes right and nothing goes wrong,
      And isn't your life extremely flat
      With nothing whatever to grumble at!
          When German bands
          From music stands
      Played Wagner imperfectly –
          I bade them go –
          They didn't say no,
      But off they went directly!
          The organ boys
          They stopped their noise
      With readiness surprising,
          And grinning herds
          Of hurdy-gurds
      Retired apologizing!

          I offered gold
          In sums untold
      To all who'd contradict me –
          I said I'd pay
          A pound a day
      To anyone who kicked me –
          I bribed with toys
          Great vulgar boys
      To utter something spiteful,

> But bless you, no!
> They *would* be so
> Confoundedly politeful!
>
> In short, these aggravating lads,
> They tickle my tastes, they feed my fads,
> They give me this and they give me that,
> And I've nothing whatever to grumble at!

. . . .

ARAC: This helmet, I suppose,
> Was meant to ward off blows,
> It's very hot,
> And weighs a lot,
> As many a guardsman knows,
> As many a guardsman knows.
> So off that helmet goes.

ALL: Yes, yes, yes,
> So off that helmet goes!

ARAC: This tight-fitting cuirass
> Is but a useless mass,
> It's made of steel,
> And weighs a deal,
> This tight-fitting cuirass
> Is but a useless mass.
> A man is but an ass
> Who fights in a cuirass,
> So off goes that cuirass.

ALL: Yes, yes, yes,
> So off goes that cuirass!

ARAC: These brassets, truth to tell,
> May look uncommon well,
> But in a fight
> They're much too tight,
> They're like a lobster shell!
> They're like a lobster shell!

ALL: Yes, yes, yes,
          They're like a lobster shell!

ARAC: These things I treat the same
              (I quite forget their name)
                 They turn one's legs
                 To cribbage pegs –
              Their aid I thus disclaim,
              Their aid I thus disclaim.
              Though I forget their name!
              Though I forget their name
              Their aid I thus disclaim.

ALL: Yes, yes, yes,

               Their aid $\left. \begin{array}{c} \text{we} \\ \text{they} \end{array} \right\}$ thus disclaim!

THE MIKADO

or

The Town of Titipu

THE present author was lucky enough to be in Tokyo in 1948 and thus able to see the production of *The Mikado*, with an American-Japanese cast, that had been sponsored by the U.S.-dominated occupation forces as part of the scheme to 'democratize' that nation. The production was not bad and the experiment was considered a success: an ancestor of the reigning Son of Heaven had been allowed to be burlesqued in public. The Japanese are nothing if not perceptive, and no doubt they recognized easily enough the difference between genuine insult and gentle ribbing. They probably also saw that although he had set his story in Japan, Gilbert had not been satirizing the Japanese at all, taking deadly aim at a number of very English hypocrisies. The widely talked-about Japanese Exhibition in London in 1884-5 had given him the cue for the new work demanded by Carte to replace the failing *Princess Ida* and he had seen how doubly funny and effective his satire might be made by placing it in a Japanese milieu. To Sullivan, Gilbert's outline of his new idea came as an immense relief. Jaded by the labours of *Ida*, impatient with Gilbert's wish to write something with 'supernatural and improbable elements', yet required by his contract with Carte to compose something soon, he rose to the occasion with music that would sweep the world in its own right. Again, the contrast with the orientalism of the visual spectacle heightens the effect of the music, which is amongst the most 'English' Sullivan ever wrote.

The Mikado opened at the Savoy on 14 March, 1885 and ran for 672 performances, which remained the record for that theatre for a quarter of a century. Extraordinary plans were carried out to smuggle a London company into New York, where, at the Fifth Avenue Theatre, they were able to open on 20 July, 1885.

In so doing they forestalled an unauthorized presentation by a few days and ran on for some 250 performances. Many other countries into which the Gilbert and Sullivan magic had not yet permeated received *The Mikado* rapturously, and it remains easily the most popular of all their works.

. . . .

A group of gentlemen of the city of Titipu, in Japan, are accosted outside the Palace by a shabby fellow carrying a *samisen* – the Japanese equivalent of a guitar – and a bundle of music. He introduces himself as Nanki-Poo, a wandering minstrel with a versatile repertoire of ballads ranging from the most meltingly sentimental to the rumbustiously patriotic, with rousing sea ditties somewhere between. He has come to seek out Yum-Yum, ward of a cheap tailor named Ko-Ko, with whom he had fallen in love at sight while taking round the cap for the Titipu town band a year before. She had, disappointingly, turned out to be engaged to her guardian; but word has recently reached Nanki-Poo that Ko-Ko has fallen foul of a stern new decree prohibiting flirting, under penalty of death, and is to be executed. Thus, Yum-Yum will be freed of her obligation, and he has come to claim her.

The noblemen disabuse him. The Mikado's ruling that all who flirt, leer or wink (unless connubially linked) shall forthwith be beheaded has proved so abhorrent throughout the land that a way round it has been found. Someone has had the ingenious idea of appointing a condemned man Lord High Executioner, on the argument that he will not be able to obey the Mikado by cutting off anyone else's head until he has first obeyed him by cutting off his own, a thing he is scarcely likely to do. Ko-Ko's timely conviction has secured him the first appointment to this office, the highest a citizen can attain; so he is still alive, Yum-Yum remains engaged to him, and Nanki-Poo has had a month's wasted journey.

Nanki-Poo is understandably appalled; as, it appears, had been all the great officers of State, who would have had to serve under the former tailor. They have all resigned, and a haughty aristocrat of infinite lineage, Pooh-Bah, has condescended to replace them single-handed: 'It is consequently my degrading duty to serve this upstart as First Lord of the Treasury, Lord Chief Justice, Commander-in-Chief, Lord High Admiral, Master of the Buckhounds, Groom of the Back Stairs, Archbishop of Titipu, and Lord Mayor, both acting and elect, all rolled into one. And at a salary! A Pooh-Bah paid for his services! I a salaried minion! But I do it! It revolts me, but I do it!'

Nanki-Poo wanders disconsolately away, and Ko-Ko himself appears, handsomely attended as befits his station. He has come to consult Pooh-Bah about the budget for his forthcoming wedding festivities, which are required to continue for a week.

POOH-BAH: Speaking as your Private Secretary, I should say that, as the city will have to pay for it, don't stint yourself, do it well.

KO-KO: Exactly – as the city will have to pay for it. That is your advice.

POOH-BAH: As Private Secretary. Of course you will understand that, as Chancellor of the Exchequer, I am bound to see that due economy is observed.

KO-KO: Oh! But you said just now 'Don't stint yourself, do it well!'

POOH-BAH: As Private Secretary.

KO-KO: And now you say that the economy must be observed.

POOH-BAH: As Chancellor of the Exchequer.

KO-KO: I see. Come over here, where the Chancellor can't hear us. Now, as my Solicitor, how do you advise me to deal with this difficulty?

POOH-BAH: Oh, as your Solicitor, I should have no hesitation in saying 'Chance it —'.

KO-KO: Thank you. I will.

POOH-BAH: If it were not that, as Lord Chief Justice, I am bound to see that the law isn't violated.

KO-KO: I see. Come over here where the Chief Justice can't hear us. Now, then, as First Lord of the Treasury?

POOH-BAH: Of course, as First Lord of the Treasury, I could propose a special vote that would cover all expenses, if it were not that, as Leader of the Opposition, it would be my duty to resist it, tooth and nail. Or, as Paymaster-General, I could so cook the accounts that, as Lord High Auditor, I should never discover the fraud. But then, as Archbishop of Titipu, it would be my duty to denounce my dishonesty and give myself into my own custody as First Commissioner of Police.

KO-KO: That's extremely awkward.

POOH-BAH: I don't say that all these distinguished people couldn't be squared; but it is right to tell you that they wouldn't be sufficiently degraded in their own estimation unless they were insulted with a very considerable bribe.

KO-KO: The matter shall have my careful consideration.

They leave, in earnest discussion, as the bride Yum-Yum comes upon the scene, shuffling in dainty Japanese fashion together with her sisters Peep-Bo and Pitti-Sing – three little maids from school – followed by a chorus of fellow ex-pupils. Ko-Ko returns to claim a brief embrace from his bride-to-be on account of their wedding, which is to take place that afternoon. But she catches sight of Nanki-Poo and as soon as Ko-Ko has departed confesses to the minstrel that she has no wish to marry her guardian at all. Yet to refuse would be futile. Ko-Ko would never let her marry Nanki-Poo. To wait until she is of age to please herself would be useless, since 'in Japan girls do not arrive at years of discretion until they are fifty'; and, finally, a mere musician is not much of a catch.

NANKI-POO: What if I should prove that, after all, I am no musician?

YUM-YUM: There! I was certain of it, directly I heard you play!

NANKI-POO: What if I should prove that I am no other than the son of his Majesty the Mikado?

He goes on to explain how he comes to be wandering the country as an itinerant second trombonist. He had inadvertently captivated an elderly lady at his father's Court, named Katisha. Under the Mikado's strict moral law this had become a matter of marriage or execution, and, fancying neither, Nanki-Poo had assumed the disguise which he has worn ever since. This revelation, though interesting, is of little use to Yum-Yum and himself as things now stand: she is to become Ko-Ko's bride this very afternoon. After exchanging some forbidden kisses, she and Nanki-Poo leave sadly, in opposite directions.

For his part, Ko-Ko is about to receive an unpleasant surprise. It comes in a letter from the Mikado himself. His Majesty has noticed that there have been no executions in Titipu for a year, and has decreed that unless someone is beheaded within a month the post of Lord High Executioner shall be abolished and the city reduced to the rank of village. Pooh-Bah reminds Ko-Ko that he is already under sentence of death for flirting, so he should cut off his own head without delay. Ko-Ko demurs. Self-decapitation would be suicide, and suicide is a capital offence.

His best idea is to appoint Pooh-Bah Lord High Substitute, an honour which even that Lord High Everything Else feels compelled to decline. Just at that moment, Nanki-Poo returns, carrying a rope, with which, he tells them, he is about to terminate an unendurable existence, because the girl he loves must marry Ko-Ko. The latter suggests that, if Nanki-Poo is determined to die, he might as well do so on the execution block, and provide the Mikado's required victim. He can go to his death in a month's time as the central figure of a grand public ceremonial – 'a procession – bands – dead march – bells tolling – all the girls in tears – Yum-Yum distracted – then, when it's all over, general rejoicings, and a display of fireworks in the evening. *You* won't see them, but they'll be there all the same.' In the meantime, he will live like a fighting-cock at Ko-Ko's expense.

Nanki-Poo counters with the proposal that he be married to Yum-Yum tomorrow and beheaded in a month, threatening to hang himself at once if Ko-Ko refuses. The Lord High Executioner has little alternative. Only begging Nanki-Poo not to prejudice the girl against him during their month of marriage, he consents.

Expressions of gratitude are interrupted by the melodramatic arrival in their midst of an ill-favoured woman who reveals herself to be Katisha, come to reclaim her false lover, Nanki-Poo. They spurn her. When her threats against Yum-Yum fail to quell the merrymaking, she launches into an attempted disclosure of Nanki-Poo's true identity. It is Yum-Yum who is resourceful enough to whip the crowd into enough noise at the right moment to prevent the crucial words being audible. Foiled, Katisha thrusts the crowd aside and retreats, vowing vengeance.

Later, seated in her garden, Yum-Yum is being assisted in her bridal toilet by her maidens. She counts herself the happiest girl in Japan, until Peep-Bo and Pitti-Sing somewhat tactlessly remind her how short-lived her pleasure is to be. Nanki-Poo is at hand to cheer them up.

NANKI-POO: A month? Well, what's a month? Bah! These divisions of time are purely arbitrary. Who says twenty-four hours makes a day?
PITTI-SING: There's a popular impression to that effect.
NANKI-POO: Then we'll efface it. We'll call each second a minute – each minute an hour – each hour a day – and each day a year. At that rate we've about thirty years of married happiness before us!

Even this consolatory device proves vulnerable, though. Ko-Ko brings the disturbing information that a corollary to the law against flirting is that when a married man is beheaded his wife is buried alive. Yum-Yum's ardour cools noticeably, and Nanki-Poo finds himself in a position where, if he insists on her going through with their marriage, he condemns her to a notably stuffy death, and if he releases her she is free to marry Ko-Ko at once. He threatens instant suicide again. The dilemma is unexpectedly solved when news is brought that the Mikado himself is about to enter the city, come to ascertain that his orders have been carried out. Desperate to please, Ko-Ko offers to swear an affidavit that he has executed Nanki-Poo, if only the latter will desist from his renewed threat of suicide and go away at once. He may even marry Yum-Yum and take her with him. As Archbishop of Titipu, Pooh-Bah will perform the ceremony in five minutes; and as Lord High Everything Else, Pooh-Bah will perhaps verify that the execution has taken place.

POO-BAH: Am I to understand that all of us high Officers of State are required to perjure ourselves to ensure your safety?
KO-KO: Why not? You'll be grossly insulted, as usual.
POOH-BAH: Will the insult be cash down, or at a date?
KO-KO: It will be a ready-money transaction.

Pooh-Bah agrees and takes Nanki-Poo and Yum-Yum away. They have barely gone when a magnificent procession arrives, heralding the Mikado and Katisha. When the Mikado is suitably enthroned, Pooh-Bah and Ko-Ko appear before him. The latter presents a certificate of execution and they describe the event in increasingly lurid detail. But Katisha has been reading the certificate, and has seen the victim's name – Nanki-Poo, her false lover and son of the Mikado. She shows His Majesty the paper.

MIKADO: I forget the punishment for compassing the death of the Heir Apparent.

KO-KO, POOH-BAH, PITTI-SING: Punishment.

MIKADO: Yes. Something lingering, with boiling oil in it, I fancy. Something of that sort. I think boiling oil occurs in it, but I'm not sure. I know it's something humorous, but lingering, with either boiling oil or melted lead. Come, come, don't fret – I'm not a bit angry.

KO-KO: If your Majesty will accept our assurance, we had no idea –

MIKADO: Of course –

PITTI-SING: I knew nothing about it.

POOH-BAH: I wasn't there.

MIKADO: That's the pathetic part of it. Unfortunately, the fool of an Act says 'compassing the death of the Heir Apparent'. There's not a word about a mistake.

KO-KO, PITTI-SING, POOH-BAH: No!

MIKADO: Or not knowing –

KO-KO: No!

MIKADO: Or having no notion –

PITTI-SING: No!

MIKADO: Or not being there –

POOH-BAH: No!

MIKADO: There should be, of course –

KO-KO, PITTI-SING, POOH-BAH: Yes!

MIKADO: But there isn't.

KO-KO, PITTI-SING, POOH-BAH: Oh!

MIKADO: That's the slovenly way in which these Acts are always drawn. However, cheer up, it'll be all right. I'll have it altered next session.

Now, let's see about your execution – will after luncheon suit you? Can you wait till then?

KO-KO, PITTI-SING, POOH-BAH: Oh, yes – we can wait till then!

MIKADO: Then we'll make it after luncheon.

POOH-BAH: I don't want any lunch.

MIKADO: I'm really very sorry for you all, but it's an unjust world, and virtue is triumphant only in theatrical performances.

There is only one way out for them – to bring Nanki-Poo back to life. He declines: 'I'm a dead man, and I'm off for my honeymoon.' Mention of Katisha's presence makes him even more determined. If she heard that he was alive and married to Yum-Yum she would insist on his execution, and his widow would be buried alive. He suggests that, instead, Ko-Ko should persuade Katisha to marry *him*. The prospect revolts the latter, but he can see no other alternative to execution. There is still an obstacle – Katisha. Hardly surprisingly, she rejects the abrupt offer of marriage from the man who has just slain the object of her love. It takes a plaintive song about a suicidal little tom-tit to move her; but it does, and she and Ko-Ko hurry off to the Registrar.

As soon as Katisha is securely married, the conspirators urge her forward to beg the Mikado's forgiveness for them all. He refuses. Just in time, Nanki-Poo enters with Yum-Yum. The Mikado sees that his son is alive after all, Katisha sees that she has been tricked, and Ko-Ko hastens to get out his explanation before she takes him to pieces.

KO-KO: It's like this: When your Majesty says, 'Let a thing be done', it's as good as done – practically it *is* done – because your Majesty's will is law. Your Majesty says, 'Kill a gentleman', and a gentleman is told off to be killed. Consequently, that gentleman is as good as dead – practically, he *is* dead – and if he is dead, why not say so?

MIKADO: I see. Nothing could possibly be more satisfactory!

It is a sentiment that has been echoed by millions of admirers of this most brilliant of all the Gilbert and Sullivan works.

Quotations

NOBLES: If you want to know who we are,
    We are gentlemen of Japan:
On many a vase and jar –
    On many a screen and fan,
      We figure in lively paint:
      Our attitude's queer and quaint –
      You're wrong if you think it ain't, oh!

If you think we are worked by strings,
    Like a Japanese marionette,
You don't understand these things:
    It is simply Court etiquette.
      Perhaps you suppose this throng
      Can't keep it up all day long?
      If that's your idea, you're wrong, oh!

       . . . .

NANKI-POO: A wandering minstrel I –
      A thing of shreds and patches
      Of ballads, songs and snatches,
    And dreamy lullaby!

My catalogue is long,
      Through every passion ranging,
      And to your humours changing
    I tune my supple song!
        Are you in sentimental mood?
        I'll sigh with you,
          Oh, sorrow!
        On maiden's coldness do you brood?
        I'll do so, too –
          Oh, sorrow, sorrow!
    I'll charm your willing ears
    With songs of lovers' fears
    While sympathetic tears
      My cheeks bedew –
        Oh, sorrow, sorrow!

But if patriotic sentiment is wanted,
  I've patriotic ballads cut and dried;
For where'er our country's banner may be planted,
  All other local banners are defied!
Our warriors, in serried ranks assembled,
  Never quail – or they conceal it if they do –
And I shouldn't be surprised if nations trembled
  Before the mighty troops of Titipu!

CHORUS: We shouldn't be surprised, etc.

NANKI-POO: And if you call for a song of the sea,
  We'll heave the capstan round,
With a yeo heave ho, for the wind is free,
Her anchor's a-trip and her helm's a-lee,
  Hurrah for the homeward bound!

CHORUS: Yeo-ho – heave-ho –
Hurrah for the homeward bound!

NANKI-POO: To lay aloft in a howling breeze
    May tickle a landsman's taste,
But the happiest hour a sailor sees
    Is when he's down
    At an inland town,
With his Nancy on his knees, yeo-ho!
  And his arm around her waist!

CHORUS: Then man the capstan – off we go,
    As the fiddler swings us round,
With a yeo heave ho,
And a rumbelow,
    Hurrah for the homeward bound!

. . . .

POOH-BAH: Our logical Mikado, seeing no moral difference between the dignified judge who condemns a criminal to die, and the industrious mechanic who carries out the sentence, has rolled the two offices into one, and every judge is now his own executioner.

. . . .

NOBLES: Behold the Lord High Executioner!
   A personage of noble rank and title –
  A dignified and potent officer,
   Whose functions are particularly vital!
    Defer, defer,
  To the Lord High Executioner!

· · · ·

KO-KO: Taken from the county jail
   By a set of curious chances;
  Liberated then on bail,
   On my own recognizances;
  Wafted by a favouring gale
   As one sometimes is in trances
  To a height that few can scale,
   Save by long and weary dances;
  Surely, never had a male
   Under such-like circumstances
  So adventurous a tale,
   Which may rank with most romances.

· · · ·

KO-KO: As some day it may happen that a victim must be
   found,
  I've got a little list – I've got a little list
  Of Society offenders who might well be underground,
   And who never would be missed – who never would
   be missed!

  There's the pestilential nuisances who write for
   autographs –
  All people who have flabby hands and irritating
   laughs –
  All children who are up in dates, and floor you
   with 'em flat –
  All persons who in shaking hands, shake hands with
   you like *that* –
  And all third persons who on spoiling tête-à-têtes
   insist –

K

They'd none of 'em be missed – they'd none of 'em
be missed!

. . . .

THE THREE MAIDS: Three little maids from school are we,
Pert as a school-girl well can be,
Filled to the brim with girlish glee,
Three little maids from school!
YUM-YUM: Everything is a source of fun.
PEEP-BO: Nobody's safe, for we care for none!
PITTI-SING: Life is a joke that's just begun!
THE THREE MAIDS: Three little maids from school!
Three little maids who, all unwary,
Come from a ladies' seminary,
Freed from its genius tutelary –
Three little maids from school!

. . . .

KO-KO, POOH-BAH, PISH-TUSH:
To sit in solemn silence in a dull, dark dock,
In a pestilential prison, with a life-long lock,
Awaiting the sensation of a short, sharp shock,
From a cheap and chippy chopper on a big black block!

. . . .

PITTI-SING: For he's going to marry Yum-Yum –
ALL: Yum-Yum!
PITTI-SING: Your anger pray bury,
For all will be merry,
I think you had better succumb –
ALL: Cumb – cumb!
PITTI-SING: And join our expressions of glee.
On this subject I pray you be dumb –
ALL: Dumb – dumb.
PITTI-SING: You'll find there are many
Who'll wed for a penny –
The word for your guidance is 'Mum' –
ALL: Mum – mum!
PITTI-SING: There's lots of good fish in the sea!

. . . .

YUM-YUM, PITTI-SING, NANKI-POO AND PISH-TUSH:

> Brightly dawns our wedding day;
>> Joyous hour, we give thee greeting!
>> Whither, whither art thou fleeting?
> Fickle moment, prithee stay!
>> What though mortal joys be hollow?
>> Pleasures come, if sorrows follow:
> Though the tocsin sound, ere long,
>> Ding dong! Ding dong!
> Yet until the shadows fall
> Over one and over all,
> Sing a merry madrigal –
> Fal-la – fal-la! etc. (*ending in tears*)

> Let us dry the ready tear,
>> Though the hours are surely creeping
>> Little need for woeful weeping,
> Till the sad sundown is near.
>> All must sip the cup of sorrow –
>> I to-day and thou to-morrow;
> This the close of every song –
>> Ding dong! Ding dong!
> What, though solemn shadows fall,
> Sooner, later, over all?
> Sing a merry madrigal –
> Fal-la – fal-la! etc.

. . . .

YUM-YUM:
> Here's a how-de-do!
> If I marry you,
>> When your time has come to perish,
>> Then the maiden whom you cherish
>> Must be slaughtered, too!
>> Here's a how-de-do!

NANKI-POO:
> Here's a pretty mess!
> In a month, or less,
> I must die without a wedding!
> Let the bitter tears I'm shedding

	Witness my distress,
	Here's a pretty mess!
KO-KO:	Here's a state of things!
	To her life she clings!
Matrimonial devotion	
Doesn't seem to suit her notion –	
	Burial it brings!
	Here's a state of things!

. . . .

CHORUS: Miya sama, miya sama,

On n'm-ma no mayé ni

Pira-Pira suru no wa

Nan gia na

Toko tonyaré tonyaré na?

MIKADO: From every kind of man

Obedience I expect;

I'm the Emperor of Japan –

KATISHA: And I'm his daughter-in-law elect!

He'll marry his son

(He's only got one)

To his daughter-in-law elect!

MIKADO: My morals have been declared

Particularly correct;

KATISHA: But they're nothing at all, compared

With those of his daughter-in-law elect!

Bow – Bow –

To his daughter-in-law elect!

ALL: Bow – Bow –

To his daughter-in-law elect.

. . . .

MIKADO: A more humane Mikado never

Did in Japan exist,

To nobody second,

I'm certainly reckoned

A true philanthropist.

It is my very humane endeavour
  To make, to some extent,
    Each evil liver
    A running river
  Of harmless merriment . . .

. . . The advertising quack who wearies
  With tales of countless cures,
    His teeth, I've enacted,
    Shall all be extracted
  By terrified amateurs.
The music-hall singer attends a series
  Of masses and fugues and 'ops'
    By Bach, interwoven
    With Spohr and Beethoven,
  At classical Monday Pops.

The billiard sharp whom any one catches,
  His doom's extremely hard –
    He's made to dwell –
    In a dungeon cell
  On a spot that's always barred.
And there he plays extravagant matches
  In fitless finger-stalls
    On a cloth untrue,
    With a twisted cue
  And elliptical billiard balls!

CHORUS: My object all sublime
  I shall achieve in time –
To let the punishment fit the crime –
  The punishment fit the crime;
And make each prisoner pent
Unwillingly represent
A source of innocent merriment!
  Of innocent merriment!

· · · ·

KO-KO: The criminal cried, as he dropped him down,
    In a state of wild alarm –
  With a frightful, frantic, fearful frown,
    I bared my big right arm.

I seized him by his little pig-tail,
    And on his knees fell he,
        As he squirmed and struggled,
        And gurgled and guggled,
    I drew my snickersnee!
        Oh, never shall I
        Forget the cry,
    Or the shriek that shrieked he,
        As I gnashed my teeth,
        When from its sheath
    I drew my snickersnee!

PITTI-SING: He shivered and shook as he gave the sign
    For the stroke he didn't deserve;
When all of a sudden his eye met mine,
    And it seemed to brace his nerve;
For he nodded his head and kissed his hand,
    And he whistled an air, did he,
        As the sabre true
        Cut cleanly through
    His cervical vertebrae!
        When a man's afraid,
        A beautiful maid
    Is a cheering sight to see;
        And it's oh, I'm glad
        That moment sad
    Was soothed by sight of me!

POOH-BAH: Now though you'd have said that head was dead
    (For its owner dead was he),
It stood on its neck, with a smile well-bred,
    And bowed three times to me!
It was none of your impudent off-hand nods,
    But as humble as could be;
        For it clearly knew
        The deference due
    To a man of pedigree!
        And it's oh, I vow,
        This deathly bow
    Was a touching sight to see;
        Though trunkless, yet

It couldn't forget
The deference due to me!

. . . .

KATISHA: You hold that I am not beautiful because my face is plain. But
you know nothing; you are still unenlightened. Learn, then, that it is
not in the face alone that beauty is to be sought. My face is unattractive!
POOH-BAH: It is.
KATISHA: But I have a left shoulder-blade that is a miracle of loveliness.
People come miles to see it. My right elbow has a fascination that few
can resist.
POOH-BAH: Allow me!
KATISHA: It is on view Tuesdays and Fridays, on presentation of visiting
card.

. . . .

NANKI-POO: The flowers that bloom in the spring,
          Tra la,
     Breathe promise of merry sunshine –
As we merrily dance and we sing,
          Tra la,
We welcome the hope that they bring,
          Tra la,
Of a summer of roses and wine.
     And that's what we mean when we say
          that a thing
     Is welcome as flowers that bloom in
          the spring.
          Tra la la la la, etc.
ALL: Tra la la la la, etc.
KO-KO: The flowers that bloom in the spring,
          Tra la,
     Have nothing to do with the case.
I've got to take under my wing,
          Tra la,
A most unattractive old thing,
          Tra la,
     With a caricature of a face,
          And that's what I mean when I say, or I sing,

'Oh, bother the flowers that bloom in the spring.
    Tra la la la la, etc.

     . . . .

KO-KO: On a tree by a river a little tom-tit
    Sang 'Willow, titwillow, titwillow!'
And I said to him, 'Dicky-bird, why do you sit
    Singing "Willow, titwillow, titwillow"?'
'Is it weakness of intellect, birdie?' I cried,
'Or a rather tough worm in your little inside?'
With a shake of his poor little head, he replied,
    'Oh, willow, titwillow, titwillow!'

He slapped at his chest, as he sat on that bough,
    Singing, 'Willow, titwillow, titwillow!'
And a cold perspiration bespangled his brow,
    Oh, willow, titwillow, titwillow!

He sobbed and he sighed, and a gurgle he gave,
Then he threw himself into the billowy wave,
And an echo arose from the suicide's grave –
    'Oh, willow, titwillow, titwillow!'
Now I feel just as sure as I'm sure that my name
    Isn't Willow, titwillow, titwillow,
That 'twas blighted affection that made him exclaim,
    'Oh, willow, titwillow, titwillow!'
And if you remain callous and obdurate, I
Shall perish as he did, and you will know why,
Though I probably shall not exclaim as I die,
    'Oh, willow, titwillow, titwillow!'

     . . . .

KO-KO: There is beauty in extreme old age –
     Do you fancy you are elderly enough?
     Information I'm requesting
     On a subject interesting:
    Is a maiden all the better when she's tough?
KATISHA: Throughout this wide dominion
     It's the general opinion
    That she'll last a good deal longer when she's tough.
KO-KO: Are you old enough to marry, do you think?

Won't you wait until you're eighty in the shade?
    There's a fascination frantic
    In a ruin that's romantic;
Do you think you are sufficiently decayed?

KATISHA: To the matter that you mention
    I have given some attention,
And I think I am sufficiently decayed.

BOTH: If that is so,
    Sing derry down derry!
    It's evident, very,
        Our tastes are one!
Away we'll go,
    And merrily marry,
    Nor tardily tarry
        Till day is done!

or

The Witch's Curse

DESCRIBED as 'an entirely original supernatural opera', in two
acts, *Ruddigore* was first produced at the Savoy Theatre on 22
January, 1887. Early the previous year Gilbert had suggested to
Sullivan that they burlesque the still-popular stage melodrama
convention of aristocratic villain, innocent maiden, simple sailor-
man and family ghost – or ghosts. Sullivan's preoccupations were
with his new oratorio *The Golden Legend*, a setting of Long-
fellow's poem, commissioned for the Leeds Festival of October
that year. As a result, the score of *Ruddygore* (as it was originally
to be entitled) remained still unfinished at the end of 1886, and he
did not finish work on it until a week before the actual first night.

The new opera had a mixed reception. It was complicated to
stage and some of the mechanical effects went wrong. Sections
of the gallery cried, 'Take it away – give us back *The Mikado*!'
Gilbert and Sullivan took note and considerably changed Act 2.
They also re-spelt the title. It had been suggested that ladies could
not bring themselves to pronounce the original. An *i* was substituted for the offending *y*. Although the pronunciation remained
unchanged, prudery was satisfied, and *Ruddigore* ran for nearly a
year. First American production was on 21 February, 1887.

. . . .

The setting is the village of Rederring on the Cornish coast.
Outside the cottage of the local beauty, Rose Maybud, the only
endowed corps of professional bridesmaids in the world laments
the lack of calls upon its service.

> Rose, all glowing
>   With virgin blushes, say –
> Is anybody going
> To marry you today?

Rose's adoptive aunt, Dame Hannah, assures them that no such prospect is in view. Desperate for a client, they urge her to take a husband herself, but she replies that she is pledged to eternal maidenhood. The god-like youth whom long ago she had been about to marry had turned out to be Sir Roderic Murgatroyd, one of the Bad Baronets of Ruddigore, inheritor of the curse imposed upon all his line by a witch burnt at the stake by the first baronet, Sir Rupert.

> 'Each lord of Ruddigore
> Despite his best endeavour
> Shall do one crime, or more,
> Once, every day, for ever!'

The bridesmaids depart disconsolately. Rose emerges from her cottage to set out upon some errand of charity, and is admonished by Dame Hannah for dissipating the good nature which would be better bestowed upon a husband than in the distribution of peppermint rock to old Gaffer Gadderby, false teeth to pretty little Ruth Rowbottom, and a pound of snuff to the poor orphan girl on the hill.

Rose replies that the unknown parents who hung her (in a plated dish-cover) from the knocker of the workhouse door left her one precious legacy, a book of etiquette, by whose strict precepts she has judged all suitors. None has measured up to its standards. Her heart might point out one apparently worthy of her; but 'it's manners out of joint to point'. Whispered professions of love are all very well; but whispering is contrary to etiquette. And as for the notion of dropping a hint through Dame Hannah: 'It says you mustn't hint, in print!'

Despite her inhibitions, Rose is willing enough; only the object of her affections is as constrained as herself. Robin Oakapple, a prosperous farmer, can only convey his feelings by telling Rose of the love of an imaginary friend for an unidentified maid.

> If I were the maid I should fan his honest flame . . .

She can only respond in kind:

> If I were the youth I should speak to her today ...

Inevitably, such conversation gets them nowhere. Robin's melancholy is noted by his faithful servant, old Adam Goodheart, who greets his master in forbidden fashion as Sir Ruthven Murgatroyd. He knows Robin's secret. Twenty years ago, rather than inherit the family curse, young Sir Ruthven had fled his ancestral home and established himself in Rederring as Robin Oakapple, leaving title and curse to his younger brother, Despard.

In infancy, Sir Ruthven had been 'put out to nurse' and had acquired a foster-brother, Richard Dauntless, who became his dearest friend. For ten years now the foster-brothers have not met, for Richard Dauntless has been away making a name for himself in the Royal Navy. Now at last he comes home, a brown and brawny son-of-the-sea. Unrequested, he gives a lively account of an action in the revenue sloop *Tom-Tit*, and follows it with a hornpipe.

Robin warns Richard that the secret of his identity must still be kept and confides in him his love for Rose. Richard consults his heart, with which he is on exceptionally communicative terms, and is advised by it to offer to do Robin's courting for him. Robin agrees eagerly. He is aware of his own qualities, but knows himself to be modesty personified – too diffident, modest and shy for romantic advancement.

When Richard sets eyes on Rose he becomes even more enthusiastic about the undertaking. Robin's interests are set aside. Richard's forthright tactics are sanctioned by the book of etiquette ('Keep no one in unnecessary suspense'), and within a few minutes of meeting Dick and Rose are betrothed.

Robin's disappointment makes him declare at last his love for Rose, who, weighing the gentleman farmer's prospects against a lowly mariner's, consults *her* heart and is advised to reverse her decision. She does, telling Richard that should her heart change her mind again, she will let him know. She and Robin go off to prepare for their wedding.

A strange figure appears outside Rose's cottage. It is Mad Margaret, the rejected sweetheart of Sir Despard Murgatroyd. She sings a curious song, revealing the deranged mind of one spurned in love. She is frightened away by the sound of lusty singing, heralding the approach of a chorus of Bucks and Blades, come to exchange the attentions of city ladies of gentle degree for temporary pastoral delights. They are followed by a gaunt, dark-visaged personage, Sir Despard Murgatroyd, Bad Baronet of Ruddigore, who cautions his hearers against an existence of crime and its deleterious effects upon the countenance. The merrymakers shrink from him and leave him to brood alone upon his scheme for atonement.

'I get my crime over the first thing in the morning, and then, ha! ha! for the rest of the day I do good – I do good – I do good! Two days since, I stole a child and built an orphan asylum. Yesterday I robbed a bank and endowed a bishopric. To-day I carry off Rose Maybud, and atone with a cathedral!'

But the cathedral is never to be built, nor the crime committed; for Richard Dauntless's heart has been at him again, and has urged him to reveal to Sir Despard that the rightful Bad Baronet is Sir Ruthven, alias Robin Oakapple. Overjoyed to hear that he is at last free to live a blameless life, Sir Despard delays only long enough for Robin's wedding celebrations to get well under way before making a dramatic entry.

> Hold, bride and bridegroom, ere you wed each other,
> I claim young Robin as my elder brother!

Robin cannot deny it. Unable to accept her betrothed in his new role, Rose offers herself to Sir Despard. He, however, is now free to renew his long-broken vow to Mad Margaret. Only Richard remains available: he needs no persuading. The merrymaking resumes, and as the guests dance Robin's face is already suffusing with uncharacteristic evil.

But wickedness does not come easily to so mild a nature. An ineffectual conference takes place in the picture gallery of

Ruddigore Castle, Robin's new home. From the walls, full-length portraits of the baronets of Ruddigore from the time of James I look down, as Robin makes a brave show of his new status to Adam Goodheart, which the faithful retainer endeavours to match. Neither has his heart in it. Robin cannot think of a crime for the day. Old Adam endeavours to suggest one.

ADAM: Richard Dauntless is here with pretty Rose Maybud, to ask your consent to their marriage. Poison their beer.

ROBIN: No – not that – I know I'm a bad Bart., but I'm not as bad a Bart. as all that.

ADAM: Well, there you are, you see! It's no use my making suggestions if you don't adopt them.

ROBIN: How would it be, do you think, were I to lure him here with cunning wile – bind him with good stout rope to yonder post – and then, by making hideous faces at him, curdle the heart-blood in his arteries, and freeze the very marrow in his bones? How say you, Adam, is not the scheme well planned?

ADAM: It would be simply rude – nothing more.

In any case, Richard has come prepared. He unfurls a small flag and waves it protectively over Rose's head. Robin staggers back: 'Foiled – and by a Union Jack!'

The happy throng dances away, leaving Robin alone with his ancestors' portraits. Turning to them, he pleads for a merciful removal of the curse which has blighted his honest life. As he flings himself down, sudden darkness falls, to lift again to the sound of singing which seems to travel from the distance of years.

> Painted emblems of a race,
>   All accurst in days of yore,
>   Each from his accustomed place
>   Steps into the world once more.

The Bad Baronets of Ruddigore step from their frames and march round the cowering Robin, heaping scorn upon him. From the end of the gallery one more formidable than the rest advances – Sir Roderic, the late Lord of Ruddigore from whom

Robin's title is immediately descended. For all his terror, Robin cannot help pitying the ghastly host, but Sir Roderic hastens to reassure him that they are a jollier crew than he seems to suppose, and supports his contention with a grisly, gleeful song of grave-yard revels. But the spectres mean business. Robin is submitted to an inquisition into his criminal progress, and is found sadly wanting. Making a false income-tax return, forging his own will and disinheriting his own unbegotten son scarcely qualify in the eyes of his accomplished ancestors. Sir Roderic warns him that unless he improves immediately, say, by carrying off a lady, he must expect to perish in inconceivable agonies. When Robin replies that he respects ladies too much, he is given a sample of the torments awaiting him. He consents without more ado. His ancestors, having demanded his pardon for persecuting him, return to their frames.

Robin sends Adam Goodheart off in haste to abduct any village maiden he cares to choose. Robin leaves the picture gallery for some more congenial part of the castle, and just misses the arrival of a man and woman in sober black, who turn out to be a reformed Despard and Mad Margaret, groom and bride of a week. Margaret is still a little mad, and given to outbursts of passionate gratitude towards the man who had once jilted her, until calmed by his masterly use of their cautionary code-word, 'Basingstoke!'

They have come to urge Robin to abandon his horrible calling and become a pure and blameless ratepayer. When Robin is reminded that responsibility for all Despard's crimes of the past ten years has been transferred to him as rightful bearer of the title all along, he resolves to atone with his death.

The departure of the newly-weds coincides with the return of old Adam, dragging with him an abducted maiden. She is Dame Hannah. She berates Robin soundly for his unchivalrous behavi-our and, seizing a sword from the wall, contemptuously tosses him her own small dagger and proceeds to fight. Robin, thoroughly unnerved, calls out to his Uncle Roderic to save him, and that worthy steps majestically out of his frame once

more. Dame Hannah's astonishment at seeing the picture come
to life is equalled by Sir Roderic's at seeing her there:

RODERIC: 'Little Nannikin!'
HANNAH: 'Roddy-doddy!'

The ancestor who had urged Robin to sterner criminal efforts
now reproves him for carrying off the lady to whom he –
Roderic – had once been engaged. Robin is dismissed from their
presence, and the former lovers sing a sad duet of a constant little
flower and the fickle oak in whose shelter she had once wished
only to remain.

Robin bursts back in upon them, followed by Richard, Rose,
Despard, Margaret and all the other inhabitants of Rederring.
He has had an inspiration: since a baronet of Ruddigore who
refuses to commit his daily crime must die; and since to make
such a refusal is tantamount, therefore, to committing suicide;
and since suicide is a crime – then Sir Roderic, who had died after
refusing to continue his life of evil, had no business to die at all.
Thus, the curse should not have been handed on, and Robin
considers himself free from obligations he ought not to have
inherited. This discovery suits everyone. Sir Roderic, declaring
himself 'practically alive' again, is free to marry Dame Hannah;
Despard and Margaret can forget their concern for Robin's wel-
fare and settle down to do good works in Basingstoke; and
Robin can claim his Rose, who is prepared to love him unreservedly at last.

As for Richard Dauntless, deprived of his ill-gained betrothal,
Rederring can provide ready compensation from amongst the
ranks of its pretty bridesmaids.

> If you ask me why I do not pipe my eye,
> Like an honest British sailor, I reply,
> That with Zorah for my missis,
> There'll be bread and cheese and kisses,
> Which is just the sort of ration I enjye!

Quotations

HANNAH: Sir Rupert Murgatroyd
  His leisure and his riches
He ruthlessly employed
  In persecuting witches.
With fear he'd make them quake –
He'd duck them in his lake –
    He'd break their bones
    With sticks and stones,
And burn them at the stake!

Once, on the village green,
  A palsied hag he roasted,
And what took place, I ween,
  Shook his composure boasted;
For, as the torture grim
Seized on each withered limb,
    The writhing dame
    'Mid fire and flame
Yelled forth this curse on him:

'Each lord of Ruddigore,
  Despite his best endeavour,
Shall do one crime, or more,
  Once, every day, for ever!
This doom he can't defy,
However he may try,
    For should he stay
    His hand, that day
In torture he shall die!'

The prophecy came true:
  Each heir who held the title
Had, every day, to do
  Some crime of import vital;
Until, with guilt o'erplied,
'I'll sin no more!' he cried,
    And on the day
    He said that say,
In agony he died!

CHORUS: And thus, with sinning cloyed,
          Has died each Murgatroyd,
              And so shall fall,
              Both one and all,
          Each coming Murgatroyd!

                              . . . .

ROSE: If somebody there chanced to be
          Who loved me in a manner true,
      My heart would point him out to me,
          And I would point him out to you.
      But here it says one of those who point,
          Their manners must be out of joint –
              You may not point –
              You must not point –
          It's manners out of joint, to point!
      Had I the love of such as he,
          Some quiet spot he'd take me to,
      Then he could whisper it to me,
          And I could whisper it to you.
      But whispering, I've somewhere met,
      Is contrary to etiquette:
              Where can it be?
              Now let me see –
                  Yes, yes!
          It's contrary to etiquette!

                              . . . .

RICHARD: I shipped, d'ye see, in a Revenue sloop,
              And, off Cape Finistere,
                  A merchantman we see,
                  A Frenchman, going free,
              So we made for the bold Mounseer,
                      D'ye see?
              We made for the bold Mounseer.
          But she proved to be a Frigate – and she up with her ports,
              And fires with a thirty-two!
                  It come uncommon near,
                  But we answered with a cheer,

Which paralysed the Parley-voo,
D'ye see?
Which paralysed the Parley-voo!

Then our Captain he up and he says, says he,
'That chap we need not fear, –
We can take her, if we like,
She is sartin for to strike,
For she's only a darned Mounseer,
D'ye see?
She's only a darned Mounseer!
But to fight a French fal-lal – it's like hittin' of a gal –
It's a lubberly thing for to do;
For we, with all our faults,
Why, we're sturdy British salts,
While she's only a poor Parley-voo,
D'ye see?
While she's only a poor Parley-voo!'

So we up with our helm, and we scuds before the breeze
As we gives a compassionating cheer;
Froggee answers with a shout
As he sees us go about,
Which was grateful of the poor Mounseer,
D'ye see?
Which was grateful of the poor Mounseer!
And I'll wager in their joy they kissed each other's cheek
(Which is what them furriners do),
And they blessed their lucky stars
We were hardy British tars
Who had pity on a poor Parley-voo,
D'ye see?
Who had pity on a poor Parley-voo!

. . . .

RICHARD: Let your heart be your compass, with a clear conscience for your binnacle light, and you'll sail ten knots on a bowline, clear of shoals, rocks, and quicksands! Well, now, what does my heart say in this here difficult situation? Why, it says, 'Dick,' it says – (it calls me Dick acos it's known me from a babby) – 'Dick,' it says, '*you* ain't

shy – *you* ain't modest – speak you up for him as is!' Robin my lad ·
just you lay me alongside, and when she's becalmed under my lee,
I'll spin her a yarn that shall sarve to fish you two together for life!

. . . .

ROBIN: My boy, you may take it from me,
That of all the afflictions accurst
With which a man's saddled
And hampered and addled,
A diffident nature's the worst.

Though clever as clever can be –
A Crichton of early romance –
You must stir it and stump it,
And blow your own trumpet,
Or, trust me, you haven't a chance!

Now take, for example, *my* case:
I've a bright intellectual brain –
In all London city
There's no one so witty –
I've thought so again and again.
I've a highly intelligent face –
My features cannot be denied –
But whatever I try, sir,
I fail in – and why, sir?
I'm modesty personified!

As a poet, I'm tender and quaint –
I've passion and fervour and grace –
From Ovid and Horace
To Swinburne and Morris,
They all of them take a back place.
Then I sing and I play and I paint:
Though none are accomplished as I,
To say so were treason:
You ask me the reason?
I'm diffident, modest, and shy!

If you wish in the world to advance,
Your merits you're bound to enhance,

You must stir it and stump it,
And blow your own trumpet,
Or, trust me, you haven't a chance!

. . . .

MAD MARGARET: Cheerily carols the lark
Over the cot.
Merrily whistles the clerk
Scratching a blot.
But the lark
And the clerk,
I remark,
Comfort me not!

Over the ripening peach
Buzzes the bee.
Splash on the billowy beach
Tumbles the sea.
But the peach
And the beach
They are each
Nothing to me!

And why!
Who am I?
Daft Madge! Crazy Meg!
Mad Margaret! Poor Peg!
He! he! he! he! he! (*chuckling*)

Mad, I?
Yes, very!
But why?
Mystery!
Don't call!

No crime –
'Tis only
That I'm
Love – lonely!
That's all!

. . . .

ROSE: A maiden, and in tears? Can I do aught to soften thy sorrow? This apple –

MARGARET: No! Tell me, are you mad?

ROSE: I? No! That is, I think not.

MARGARET: That's well! Then you don't love Sir Despard Murgatroyd? All mad girls love him. *I* love him. I'm poor Mad Margaret – Crazy Meg – Poor Peg! He! he! he! he!

ROSE: Thou lovest the bad Baronet of Ruddigore? Oh, horrible – too horrible!

MARGARET: You pity me? Then be my mother! The squirrel had a mother, but she drank and the squirrel fled! Hush! They sing a brave song in our parts – it runs somewhat thus: (*sings*)

> 'The cat and the dog and the little puppee
> Sat down in a – down in a – in a ...'

I forget what they sat down in, but so the song goes! Listen – I've come to pinch her!

ROSE: Mercy, whom?

MARGARET: You mean 'who'.

ROSE: Nay! it is the accusative after the verb.

· · · ·

ROSE: Nay, be pacified, for behold I am pledged to another, and lo, we are to be wedded this very day!

MARGARET: Swear me that! Come to a Commissioner and let me have it an affidavit! *I* once made an affidavit – but it died – it died – it died!

· · · ·

ROSE: When the buds are blossoming,
          Smiling welcome to the spring,
          Lovers choose a wedding day –
          Life is love in merry May!

GIRLS: Spring is green –
                 Summer's rose –

QUARTET: It is sad when summer goes.

MEN: Autumn's gold –
                 Winter's grey –

QUARTET: Winter still is far away –
          Leaves in autumn fade and fall,
          Winter is the end of all.

Spring and summer teem with glee:
Spring and summer, then, for me!
Fal la! etc.

HANNAH: In the spring-time seed is sown:
In the summer grass is mown:
In the autumn you may reap:
Winter is the time for sleep.

GIRLS: Spring is hope –
Summer's joy –

QUARTET: Spring and summer never cloy,

MEN: Autumn, toil –
Winter, rest –

QUARTET: Winter, after all, is best –
Spring and summer pleasure you,
Autumn, aye, and winter too –
Every season has its cheer,
Life is lovely all the year!
Fal la! etc.

. . . .

SIR RODERIC: When the night wind howls in the chimney cowls,
and the bat in the moonlight flies,
And inky clouds, like funeral shrouds, sail over the
midnight skies –
When the footpads quail at the night-bird's wail, and
black dogs bay at the moon,
Then is the spectres' holiday – then is the ghosts'
high-noon!

As the sob of the breeze sweeps over the trees, and the
mists lie low on the fen,
From grey tomb-stones are gathered the bones that
once were women and men,
And away they go, with a mop and a mow, to the
revel that ends too soon,
For cockrow limits our holiday – the dead of the
night's high-noon!

And then each ghost with his ladye-toast to their
churchyard beds takes flight,

With a kiss, perhaps, on her lantern chaps, and a
   grisly grim 'good-night';
Till the welcome knell of the midnight bell rings
   forth its jolliest tune,
And ushers in our next high holiday – the dead of the
   night's high-noon!

. . . .

SIR RODERIC: It is our duty to see that our successors commit their daily
   crimes in a conscientious and workmanlike fashion. It is our duty to
   remind you that you are evading the conditions under which you are
   permitted to exist.

ROBIN: Really, I don't know what you'd have. I've only been a bad
   baronet a week, and I've committed a crime punctually every day.

SIR RODERIC: Let us inquire into this. Monday?

ROBIN: Monday was a Bank Holiday.

SIR RODERIC: True. Tuesday?

ROBIN: On Tuesday I made a false income-tax return.

ALL: Ha! ha!

1ST GHOST: That's nothing.

2ND GHOST: Nothing at all.

3RD GHOST: Everybody does that.

4TH GHOST: It's expected of you.

SIR RODERIC: Wednesday?

ROBIN: On Wednesday I forged a will.

SIR RODERIC: Whose will?

ROBIN: My own.

SIR RODERIC: My good sir, you can't forge your own will!

ROBIN: Can't I, though! I like that! I *did*! Besides, if a man can't forge his
   own will, whose will can he forge?

1ST GHOST: There's something in that.

2ND GHOST: Yes, it seems reasonable.

3RD GHOST: At first sight it does.

4TH GHOST: Fallacy somewhere, I fancy!

ROBIN: A man can do what he likes with his own?

SIR RODERIC: I suppose he can.

ROBIN: Well, then, he can forge his own will, stoopid! On Thursday I
   shot a fox.

1ST GHOST: Hear, hear!

SIR RODERIC: That's better (*addressing Ghosts*). Pass the fox, I think? Yes, pass the fox. Friday?

ROBIN: On Friday I forged a cheque?

SIR RODERIC: Whose cheque.

ROBIN: Old Adam's.

SIR RODERIC: But Old Adam hasn't a banker.

ROBIN: I didn't say I forged his banker – I said I forged his cheque. On Saturday I disinherited my only son.

SIR RODERIC: But you haven't got a son.

ROBIN: No – not yet. I disinherited him in advance, to save time. You see – by this arrangement – he'll be born ready disinherited.

SIR RODERIC: I see. But I don't think you can do that.

ROBIN: My good sir, if I can't disinherit my own unborn son, whose unborn son can I disinherit?

SIR RODERIC: Humph! These arguments sound very well, but I can't help thinking that, if they were reduced to syllogistic form, they wouldn't hold water. Now quite understand us. We are foggy, but we don't permit our fogginess to be presumed upon. Unless you undertake to – well, suppose we say, carry off a lady? (*Addressing Ghosts*) Those who are in favour of his carrying off a lady? (*All hold up their hands except a Bishop.*)

. . . .

DESPARD: I once was a very abandoned person –

MARGARET: Making the most of evil chances.

DESPARD: Nobody could conceive a worse 'un –

MARGARET: Even in all the old romances.

DESPARD: I blush for my wild extravagances,
                              But be so kind
                              To bear in mind,

MARGARET: We were the victims of circumstances!
                              (*Dance*)
                   That is one of our blameless dances. . . .

DESPARD: I've given up all my wild proceedings.

MARGARET: My taste for a wandering life is waning.

DESPARD: Now I'm a dab at penny readings.

MARGARET: They are not remarkably entertaining.

DESPARD: A moderate livelihood we're gaining.

MARGARET: In fact we rule
                  A National School.
DESPARD: The duties are dull, but I'm not complaining.
                  (*Dance*)
                  This sort of thing takes a deal of training!

. . . .

MARGARET: Shall I tell you one of poor Mad Margaret's odd thoughts?
Well, then, when I am lying awake at night, and the pale moonlight
streams through the latticed casement, strange fancies crowd upon
my poor mad brain, and I sometimes think that if we could hit upon
some word for you to use whenever I am about to relapse – some word
that teems with hidden meaning – like 'Basingstoke' – it might
recall me to my saner self. For, after all, I am only Mad Margaret!
Daft Meg! Poor Meg! He! he! he!
DESPARD: Poor child, she wanders! But soft – someone comes –
Margaret – pray recollect yourself – Basingstoke, I beg! Margaret, if
you don't Basingstoke at once, I shall be seriously angry.
MARGARET: Basingstoke it is!
DESPARD: Then make it so.

. . . .

ROBIN: My eyes are fully open to my awful situation –
                  I shall go at once to Roderic and make him an oration.
                  I shall tell him I've recovered my forgotten moral senses,
                  And I don't care twopence-halfpenny for any consequences.
                  Now I do not want to perish by the sword or by the dagger,
                  But a martyr may indulge a little pardonable swagger,
                  And a word or two of compliment my vanity would flatter,
                  But I've got to die to-morrow, so it really doesn't matter!
DESPARD: So it really doesn't matter –
MARGARET: So it really doesn't matter –
ALL: So it really doesn't matter, matter, matter, matter, matter!

. . . .

ALL: Oh, happy the lily
          That's kissed by the bee;
       And, sipping tranquilly,
          Quite happy is he;

And happy the filly
  That neighs in her pride;
But happier than any,
A pound to a penny,
A lover is, when he
  Embraces his bride!

or

The Merryman and His Maid

WITH *Ruddigore* established after its uneasy beginning, Carte waited for news of its successor. None came. The rift between Gilbert and Sullivan was wide open again, with Gilbert pushing his notion of a story full of supernatural effects and magic lozenges, and Sullivan flatly refusing to collaborate on it. The idea for *The Yeomen of the Guard* came to Gilbert from a chance sight of an advertising poster featuring the Tower of London. He examined it in the light of his preference for the supernatural theme, decided that the elements would not combine happily, and decided to write a 'straight' comic opera instead. A much relieved Sullivan heard the new idea with enthusiasm: both saw the dramatic and musical possibilities offered by the Tudor age.

Even so, other quarrels intervened and the work might never have come to completion had not Queen Victoria, enraptured by a Command Performance of Sullivan's oratorio *The Golden Legend*, advised the composer to write a grand opera, because 'you would do it so well'. This was just the challenge for Sullivan, and *Yeomen* emerged as the nearest thing Gilbert and Sullivan ever wrote to opera proper, with starkly dramatic elements of story, pathos, wit without satire, and a magnificent musical score. It was first presented at the Savoy Theatre on 3 October, 1888, and in New York on 17 October that same year.

．　．　．　．

The setting throughout is the Tower of London at some time in the sixteenth century. Phoebe Meryll, daughter of the Sergeant Yeoman of the Guard, works at her spinning wheel on Tower Green. The wheel's whirr accompanies a plaintive song about the sweet pain of love; but it is pain of another kind she feels

when her betrothed comes up to her. Wilfred Shadbolt is head
jailer and assistant tormentor, and no man ever loved his work
more. He is gloatingly looking forward to half-past seven that
evening, when Colonel Fairfax, a gallant soldier convicted of
sorcery, is to be beheaded. Wilfred's anticipation is made all the
more eager by the knowledge that Phoebe, who finds his trade
distasteful, sympathizes with the Colonel. The sooner the latter
is out of the way, the better Wilfred will be pleased.

Phoebe is not the only member of the Tower garrison who
pities Fairfax, though she has more cause than most: he has twice
saved her father's life. Some of the Yeomen have fought under
him, and even Dame Carruthers, the Housekeeper to the Tower,
can feel something for a condemned man, despite her veneration
for the Tower and all it stands for.

> There's a legend on its brow
>   That is eloquent to me,
>   And it tells of duty done and duty doing.
>
> 'The screw may twist and the rack may turn,
> And men may bleed and men may burn,
> O'er London town and its golden hoard
> I keep my silent watch and ward!'

There is one hope left. Leonard Meryll, Phoebe's brother, a
young soldier who has distinguished himself in the field, is due
to arrive to join the Tower warders. He is coming straight from
Windsor, where the Court is, and may carry the Colonel's
hoped-for reprieve with him. Alas, Leonard arrives bearing no
reprieve. Sergeant Meryll comes to a quick decision. Since no one
in the Tower has met his son before, he gives him money and
tells him to go into hiding. Phoebe must purloin the key to
Fairfax's cell from Wilfred Shadbolt, and the Sergeant will
smuggle a suit of Yeoman's uniform to the Colonel, who will
then emerge in the character of the newly arrived Leonard
Meryll.

Colonel Fairfax is being escorted to the cell where he will spend
his last hour with his confessor when he meets Sir Richard

Cholmondeley, the Lieutenant of the Tower, who is amongst those who regret the untimely death of a brave man. Fairfax asks him a boon. He is about to die for no better reason than that an influential kinsman has brought the charge of sorcery against him in order to gain Fairfax's estate, which he stands to inherit if the condemned man dies unmarried. The Colonel's last wish is to thwart this traitor by marrying in the brief time left to him. Any bride will do. She will have nothing to lose: she will be a widow again within an hour, and the Colonel will leave her a hundred crowns. The Lieutenant promises to do his best to find a candidate.

A crowd of citizens flock on to Tower Green in pursuit of a man dressed in motley and a young woman. Jack Point and Elsie Maynard are strolling entertainers and the crowd are challenging them to show their worth, or be flung into the river. The Lieutenant questions them and discovers that Elsie's mother, old Bridget Maynard, who travels with them, is seriously ill and that money is urgently needed to buy her medicine. He puts Fairfax's proposition to Elsie, and after a brief hesitation she agrees. The Lieutenant beckons to Wilfred Shadbolt to blindfold her and lead her off into the Cold Harbour Tower.

Although he has protested that he is not so much of a fool as to marry, Jack Point is more than a little jealous of Elsie's undisclosed husband-to-be. The Lieutenant has some other consolation for him. He has a vacancy for a jester, and Point might do.

LIEUTENANT: I trust you are very careful not to give offence. I have daughters.

POINT: Sir, my jests are most carefully selected, and anything objectionable is expunged. If your honour pleases, I will try them first on your honour's chaplain.

LIEUTENANT: Can you give me an example? Say that I had sat me down hurriedly on something sharp?

POINT: Sir, I should say that you had sat down on the spur of the moment.

LIEUTENANT: Humph! I don't think much of that. Is that the best you can do?

POINT: It has always been much admired, sir, but we will try again.

LIEUTENANT: Well, then, I am at dinner, and the joint of meat is but half cooked.

POINT: Why, then, sir, I should say that what is *under* done cannot be helped.

LIEUTENANT: I see. I think that manner of thing would be somewhat irritating.

POINT: At first, sir, perhaps; but use is everything, and you would come in time to like it.

LIEUTENANT: We will suppose that I caught you kissing the kitchen wench under my very nose.

POINT: Under *her* very nose, good sir – not under yours! *That* is where *I* would kiss her. Do you take me? Oh, sir, a pretty wit – a pretty, pretty wit!

LIEUTENANT: The maiden comes. Follow me, friend, and we will discuss this matter at length in my library.

POINT: I am your worship's servant. That is to say, I trust I soon shall be. But, before proceeding to a more serious topic, can you tell me, sir, why a cook's brain-pan is like an overwound clock?

LIEUTENANT: A truce to this fooling – follow me.

POINT: Just my luck; my best conundrum wasted!

Somewhat dazed, Elsie returns, wearing a wedding ring and envying the lot of women unlike herself who have time to enjoy being married before they are widowed. As she leaves the Green, Wilfred enters, followed by Phoebe and Sergeant Meryll. It takes only moments for Phoebe to abstract the bunch of keys from Wilfred's belt and pass it to her father, who hurries off unnoticed to the Tower. To keep Wilfred's attention occupied, Phoebe teases him with the prospect of their marrying. He laps it up, and within a few minutes Sergeant Meryll is able to tiptoe back and return the keys without their absence ever having been realized.

Once Wilfred has gone, overcome by such wooing, Sergeant Meryll leads on Colonel Fairfax, disguised as a Yeoman. The Yeomen of the Guard assemble and greet the supposed Leonard Meryll. Anxious to cut the reception short, he tries to persuade them that his deeds have been much exaggerated, but this only results in a longer recital of them by the admiring men. More dangerously embarrassing is the arrival of Phoebe and Wilfred.

Phoebe rushes to Fairfax and greets him as her brother Leonard, but Fairfax does not know her and has to be saved from giving himself away. Wilfred introduces himself as Phoebe's betrothed and commends her to her supposed brother's care. Fairfax is only too pleased to accept this charge, and contrives to steal a few kisses on the strength of it.

The brief gaiety within the grim old Tower is interrupted by the tolling of the bell of St Peter's. A crowd gathers silently and watches the block set in place and the masked Headsman take his stance. The Lieutenant dispatches three Yeomen, one of them Fairfax, to fetch the prisoner. Within moments they come hurrying back to report that they had found the cell gratings open and the prisoner gone. The Lieutenant orders Wilfred's arrest and a general search, and the populace scatter in all directions. Concerned by the news for different reasons from the rest are Jack Point and Elsie Maynard.

ELSIE: What have I done! Oh, woe is me!
      I am his wife, and he is free!
POINT: Oh, woe is *you*? Your anguish sink!
      Oh, woe is *me*, I rather think!
      Oh, woe is *me*, I rather think!
      Yes, woe is *me*, I rather think!
         Whate'er betide
         You are his bride,
         And I am left
         Alone – bereft!

Tower Green empties, save for Elsie fainting in Fairfax's arms, and the gaunt, immobile figure of the Headsman silhouetted against the darkening sky.

Two days have elapsed. Tower Green is bathed in moonlight but there is plenty of activity still. Dame Carruthers and a crowd of women are taunting the shamefaced Yeomen for letting their prisoner escape and failing to recapture him. The men are only too glad to hurry away to resume their search. Jack Point, clearly in low spirits, wanders on, studying a huge volume of *The Merrie Jestes of Hugh Ambrose* in a despairing effort to stimulate his wit and please his new master. He is accosted by Wilfred Shadbolt and has the small satisfaction of poking some fun at one even more miserable than himself. But Wilfred is preoccupied with an ambition outside the realms of dungeon and torture-chamber: he fancies himself as a professional jester. When he asks Point to help him become one, Jack brightens. He tells Wilfred of the secret marriage between Colonel Fairfax and his Elsie, and promises that if Wilfred will swear that he has shot Fairfax and seen him drown in the river, thus freeing Elsie formally from her marriage bond, Point will transform a mere assistant tormentor into 'the very Archbishop of jesters'.

POINT: I will teach thee all my original songs, my self-constructed riddles, my own ingenious paradoxes; nay, more, I will reveal to thee the source whence I get them. Now, what sayest thou?

WILFRED: Why, if it be but a lie thou wantest of me, I hold it cheap enough, and I say yes, it is a bargain!

In better spirits, they dance off together. Their place on the Green is taken by Fairfax, still disguised as Leonard Meryll. He is relieved enough to have escaped death, but cannot bring himself to slip away from the Tower to freedom. What holds him back is the thought of his unknown bride, to whom he feels fettered still. Sergeant Meryll sees him and they discuss Elsie Maynard, whom Fairfax had carried to the old Sergeant's house after she had fainted at the news of his escape. Dame Carruthers has been nursing her there, to the Sergeant's discomfort, for the formidable housekeeper has been after him to marry her for long enough. Dame Carruthers and her niece Kate join the two men, and Kate reveals that in her delirium Elsie had babbled about having been married to a stranger and mentioned the sum of a hundred crowns. At last, Fairfax knows the identity of his bride. When the others have left, and he sees Elsie herself approaching, he decides to question her, in the character of Leonard Meryll, and find out what she really feels about her lost husband.

FAIRFAX: A fig for this Fairfax! Be mine – he will never know – he dares not show himself; and if he dare, what art thou to him? Fly with

M

me, Elsie – we will be married to-morrow, and thou shalt be the happiest wife in England!

ELSIE: Master Leonard! I am amazed! Is it thus that brave soldiers speak to poor girls? Oh! for shame, for shame! I am wed – not the less because I love not my husband. I am a wife, sir, and I have a duty, and – oh, sir! thy words terrify me – they are not honest – they are wicked words, and unworthy thy great and brave heart! Oh, shame upon thee! shame upon thee!

She has given him his proof, and he is on the point of admitting that he had been testing her when a shot is heard and Tower Green is quickly thronged once more. Wilfred stumbles on to blurt out – with the help of Point – his tale of having spotted Fairfax escaping to the Thames, of having wrestled with him, and then of shooting him with an arquebus, so that

WILFRED: Like a stone I saw him sinking –
POINT: I should say a lump of lead.

The Lieutenant of the Tower orders the river to be dragged for the body and the populace cheer Wilfred as a hero. Point consoles the weeping Elsie that she has lost nothing but a pestilent fellow with 'a face to fright the headsman himself and make him strike awry'. Fairfax and Phoebe are listening and Fairfax promises himself to pay the jester out for these remarks. When he hears Point clumsily trying to woo Elsie he offers him a demonstration of how it should be done; but he goes too far for Phoebe, who fancies Fairfax for herself.

PHOEBE: And I helped that man to escape, and I've kept his secret, and pretended that I was his dearly loving sister, and done everything I could think of to make folk believe I *was* his loving sister, and this is his gratitude!

In her jealous fury she blurts out to Wilfred Shadbolt that she loves Leonard Meryll, who has now shown that he loves another. Even the dull Wilfred is able to perceive that, since Leonard Meryll is Phoebe's brother, there must be something amiss in this.

She realizes that she has unwittingly given away the deception, and Wilfred recognizes that she must know that his story of having shot Fairfax is a lie. There is only one solution – a bargain: his silence for hers. She is even prepared to marry him to keep his mouth shut.

PHOEBE: Thou art a very brute – but even brutes must marry, I suppose.
WILFRED: My beloved!
PHOEBE: Ugh!

The real Leonard Meryll hurries up with the news that Colonel Fairfax's reprieve has arrived, having been held back by his malicious relative until after the date of his intended execution. Even so, lips must remain sealed about the conspiracy to free him, and Dame Carruthers knows too much about Sergeant Meryll's complicity in Fairfax's escape for his comfort. He, too, sees that marriage is the price he must pay for safety.

SERGEANT MERYLL: Ghastly, ghastly!
> When man, sorrowful,
> Firstly, lastly,
> > Of to-morrow full,
> > > After tarrying,
> > > Yields to harrying –
> > > Goes a-marrying.
> > Ghastly, ghastly!

Only one thing needs to be cleared up. Elsie is prepared, after all, to accept 'Leonard Meryll' as husband, though with a sad heart. Until the last possible moment, Fairfax maintains the deception, then dramatically reveals his true identity. She is overcome with joy and general rejoicing prevails. Only Jack Point is left out. After a pathetic attempt to win back Elsie by reminding her of their song of the Merryman and his Maid, he crumples at her feet in what, according to individual interpretations of his fate, is insensibility or death.

Quotations

PHOEBE: When maiden loves, she sits and sighs,
    She wanders to and fro;
Unbidden tear-drops fill her eyes,
And to all questions she replies
    With a sad 'heigho!'
'Tis but a little word – 'heigho!'
So soft, 'tis scarcely heard – 'heigho!'
    An idle breath –
    Yet life and death
May hang upon a maid's 'heighho!'

. . . .

PHOEBE: Are the birds all caged? The wild beasts all littered down? All the locks, chains, bolts and bars in good order? Is the Little Ease sufficiently uncomfortable? The racks, pincers, and thumbscrews all ready for work? Ugh! you brute!

WILFRED: These allusions to my professional duties are in doubtful taste. I didn't become a head-jailer because I like head-jailing. I didn't become an assistant-tormentor because I like assistant-tormenting.

. . . .

FAIRFAX: Is life a boon?
    If so, it must befall
    That Death, whene'er he call,
Must call too soon.
    Though fourscore years he give,
    Yet one would pray to live
Another moon!
    What kind of plaint have I,
    Who perish in July?
    I might have had to die,
Perchance, in June!

Is life a thorn?
    Then count it not a whit!
    Man is well done with it;

> Soon as he's born
>   He should all means essay
>   To put the plague away;
> And I, war-worn,
>   Poor captured fugitive,
>   My life most gladly give –
>   I might have had to live
> Another morn!

.   .   .   .

POINT: I've wisdom from the East and from the West,
     That's subject to no academic rule;
You may find it in the jeering of a jest,
     Or distil it from the folly of a fool.
I can teach you with a quip, if I've a mind;
     I can trick you into learning with a laugh;
Oh, winnow all my folly, and you'll find
     A grain or two of truth among the chaff!

I can set a braggart quailing with a quip,
     The upstart I can wither with a whim;
He may wear a merry laugh upon his lip,
     But his laughter has an echo that is grim!
When they're offered to the world in merry guise,
     Unpleasant truths are swallowed with a will –
For he who'd make his fellow-creatures wise
     Should always gild the philosophic pill!

.   .   .   .

CHORUS (*to tolling accompaniment*):
          The prisoner comes to meet his doom:
               The block, the headsman, and the tomb.
               The funeral bell begins to toll –
               May Heaven have mercy on his soul!

.   .   .   .

POINT: Oh! a private buffoon is a light-hearted loon,
     If you listen to popular rumour;
From the morn to the night he's so joyous and bright,
     And he bubbles with wit and good humour!

He's so quaint and so terse, both in prose and in verse;
  Yet though people forgive his transgression,
There are one or two rules that all family fools
  Must observe, if they love their profession.
          There are one or two rules,
            Half a dozen, maybe,
          That all family fools,
            Of whatever degree,
  Must observe, if they love their profession.
If you wish to succeed as a jester, you'll need
  To consider each person's auricular:
What is all right for B would quite scandalize C
  (For C is so very particular);
And D may be dull, and E's very thick skull
  Is as empty of brains as a ladle;
While F is F sharp, and will cry with a carp
  That he's known your best joke from his cradle!
          When your humour they flout,
            You can't let yourself go;
          And it *does* put you out
            When a person says, 'Oh,
  I have known that old joke from my cradle!'

If your master is surly, from getting up early
  (And tempers are short in the morning),
An inopportune joke is enough to provoke
  Him to give you, at once, a month's warning.
Then if you refrain, he is at you again,
  For he likes to get value for money;
He'll ask then and there, with an insolent stare,
  'If you know that you're paid to be funny?'
          It adds to the tasks
            Of a merryman's place,
          When your principal asks,
            With a scowl on his face,
  If you know that you're paid to be funny?

Comes a Bishop, maybe, or a solemn D.D.
  Oh, beware of his anger provoking!

Better not pull his hair – don't stick pins in his chair;
　　He don't understand practical joking.
If the jests that you crack have an orthodox smack,
　　You may get a bland smile from these sages;
But should they, by chance, be imported from France,
　　Half-a-crown is stopped out of your wages!
　　　　　　　It's a general rule,
　　　　　　　　　Though your zeal it may quench,
　　　　　　　　If the family fool
　　　　　　　　　Tells a joke that's too French,
　　Half-a-crown is stopped out of his wages!

Though your head it may rack with a bilious attack,
　　And your senses with toothache you're losing,
Don't be mopy and flat – they don't fine you for that,
　　If you're properly quaint and amusing!
Though your wife ran away with a soldier that day,
　　And took with her your trifle of money;
Bless your heart, they don't mind – they're exceedingly kind –
　　They don't blame you – as long as you're funny!
　　　　　　　It's a comfort to feel,
　　　　　　　　　If your partner should flit,
　　　　　　　　Though *you* suffer a deal,
　　　　　　　　　They don't mind it a bit –
　　They don't blame you – so long as you're funny!

．　　．　　．　　．

FAIRFAX, SERGEANT MERYLL,
DAME CARRUTHERS AND KATE:
　　　　　　Strange adventure! Maiden wedded
　　　　　　　　To a groom she's never seen –
　　　　　　　　　　Never, never, never seen!
　　　　　　Groom about to be beheaded,
　　　　　　　　In an hour on Tower Green!
　　　　　　　　　　Tower, Tower, Tower Green!
　　　　　　Groom in dreary dungeon lying,
　　　　　　Groom as good as dead, or dying,
　　　　　　For a pretty maiden sighing –

Pretty maid of seventeen!
Seven – seven – seventeen!

.   .   .   .

FAIRFAX: A man who would woo a fair maid
Should 'prentice himself to the trade,
And study all day,
In methodical way,
How to flatter, cajole, and persuade;
He should 'prentice himself at fourteen,
And practise from morning to e'en;
And when he's of age,
If he will, I'll engage,
He may capture the heart of a queen!
ALL: It is purely a matter of skill,
Which all may attain if they will:
But every Jack,
He must study the knack
If he wants to make sure of his Jill!

.   .   .   .

POINT: I have a song to sing, O!
ALL: Sing me your song O!
POINT: It is sung to the moon
By a love-lorn loon,
Who fled from the mocking throng, O!
It's the song of a merryman, moping mum,
Whose soul was sad, and whose glance was glum,
Who sipped no sup, and who craved no crumb,
As he sighed for the love of a ladye!
ALL: Heighdy! heighdy!
Misery me, lackadaydee!
He sipped no sup, and he craved no crumb,
As he sighed for the love of a ladye!

or
The King of Barataria

CLASS-DISTINCTION, which had been the object of Gilbert's satire a decade earlier, was again his chosen target in *The Gondoliers*. Apart from its connotations in the world at large, the subject held special significance for himself and Sullivan in 1889. More disagreement had followed in the wake of *The Yeomen of the Guard*, with Sullivan pressing for their next work to be even more serious in intent, and Gilbert realistically pointing out that public reaction to *The Yeomen* advised otherwise. Then Sullivan returned to his old charges that his music was being subordinated to the librettist's demands. Again it was Gilbert who, without yielding an inch of his own position, averted the threatening storm by insisting that they must work together as Master and Master, without distinction between the value of their individual contributions. It pacified Sullivan who, fortunately, was able to sublimate his more earnest yearnings in writing the romantic opera *Ivanhoe*, to words by Julian Sturgis, for Carte's new opera house in Shaftesbury Avenue, while getting on with *The Gondoliers* for the Savoy. Just how much, if any, of their situation *vis-à-vis* one another Gilbert deliberately reflected in his libretto cannot be known; but if all the parallels are coincidental, there are many of them.

Whatever the hidden significance, as pure entertainment *The Gondoliers* has remained not far behind *The Mikado* in popularity. Its first night – 7 December, 1889 – was a triumph, the story and dialogue delighting its audience and the music proving to be amongst the gayest and cleverest Sullivan would ever write, with not a hint in it of the physical agonies – his kidney trouble again – exhaustion and race against time with which he had coped throughout its composition. A company recruited in America, with some British principals, opened the New York presentation on 7 January, 1890.

. . . .

The year is 1750. Outside the Ducal Palace in Venice a group of eligible maidens manufacture rose bouquets and explain to the blooms that they are all sighing for the love of two young men 'so peerless in their beauty that they shame the summer skies'. To some loitering gondoliers who arrive they explain more particularly that the adored ones are the brothers Marco and Giuseppe Palmieri, who are about to arrive to select brides from among their two dozen devotees. The gondoliers protest that they, too, love the girls passionately, but are coolly told that their pick must be had from those left after Marco and Giuseppe have made their choice. Thanks to their carefree nature, the gondoliers can respond cheerfully that

> Jealousy yellow,
> Unfortunate fellow,
> We drown in the shimmering blue, tra-la!

and join the girls in welcoming the brothers as they step ashore from their gondola.

The selection of brides proceeds speedily, if arbitrarily, by the simple means of Marco and Giuseppe having themselves blind-folded, promising to marry the first two girls they catch. These prove to be Gianetta and Tessa. The remaining girls pair off with the waiting gondoliers and all dance merrily away, thus missing the arrival of another gondola.

The passengers who now step ashore are a strutting Castilian hidalgo, the Duke of Plaza-Toro, his Duchess, their daughter Casilda, and a solitary attendant, Luiz, who carries a side-drum. Their resplendent dress is shabby and they are jaded with travel.

DUKE: From the sunny Spanish shore,
      The Duke of Plaza-Tor' –
DUCHESS: And His Grace's Duchess true –
CASILDA: And His Grace's daughter, too –

LUIZ:	And His Grace's private drum
	To Venetia's shores have come:
ALL:	If ever, ever, ever
	They get back to Spain
	They will never, never, never
	Cross the sea again.

Peeved by the absence of a ceremonial reception, the Duke sends Luiz into the Ducal Palace to demand audience with the Grand Inquisitor. In his absence, Casilda is told by her parents a twenty-year-old secret: when she was a baby she had been married by proxy to the then infant son and heir of the immeasurably wealthy King of Barataria. But, the Duke elaborates, 'Shortly after the ceremony that misguided monarch abandoned the creed of his forefathers, and became a Wesleyan Methodist of the most bigoted and persecuting type. The Grand Inquisitor, determined that the innovation should not be perpetuated in Barataria, caused your smiling and unconscious husband to be stolen and conveyed to Venice. A fortnight since the Methodist Monarch and all his Wesleyan court were killed in an insurrection, and we are here to ascertain the whereabouts of your husband, and to hail you, our daughter, as Her Majesty, the reigning Queen of Barataria!'

Luiz has returned and the Duke and Duchess stride off into the Palace. Luiz and Casilda leap into an embrace, but she tells him what she has learned and declares that henceforward their love, 'so full of life, is but a silent, solemn memory'.

The Duke and Duchess return with the Grand Inquisitor, Don Alhambra, who, for a change in his career, is the one to have to confess. His admission is that having brought the infant prince to Venice, he had put him into the care of a highly respectable gondolier, who had agreed to bring him up alongside his own baby son. Unfortunately

> Owing, I'm much disposed to fear,
> > To his terrible taste for tippling,
> That highly respectable gondolier
> Could never declare with a mind sincere

> Which of the two was his offspring dear,
> And which the Royal stripling!

Both children are now grown up into the trade of gondolier. Only one person seems likely to be able to identify the one from the other, and that is Inez – Luiz's mother, as it happens – who had been the infant prince's nurse and is now married to a brigand in the mountains near Cordova. Luiz and an escort are sent to fetch her thence to solve the mix-up under encouragement of 'the persuasive influence of the torture chamber'.

To Don Alhambra's dismay, Marco and Giuseppe enter with their newly-wedded brides. He tells them that they are not real brothers, but that one is the King of Barataria. Since that country is in a state of insurrection, it is essential for the King to assert his sovereignty at once; but until it has been determined which of them is which, they must occupy the throne together 'as one individual'. The lure of a crown overcoming their republican convictions, they agree and prepare to leave with their wives for Barataria. The Grand Inquisitor stays them: women are not admitted for the time being. Again, the notion of becoming a monarch proves supreme, and Marco and Giuseppe promise that one of the brides shall soon be a 'right-down regular Royal Queen'. A vessel is hauled alongside the quay. Marco, Giuseppe and the rest of the gondoliers go aboard, and

> Away we go to an island fair,
> We know not where, we don't much care,
> Wherever that isle may be.

As good Republicans, Marco and Giuseppe lose no time in reorganizing the Baratarian Court on egalitarian principles, themselves happily sharing in every kind of household and State duty.

> Oh, philosophers may sing
> Of the troubles of a King;
> Yet the duties are delightful, and the privileges great;
> But the privilege and pleasure
> That we treasure beyond measure
> Is to run on little errands for the Ministers of State.

Their only cause for discontentment is that they miss their wives; and this is soon remedied by the arrival of those ladies, together with all the other gondoliers' brides. As Tessa explains: 'After you left we felt very dull and mopey, and the days crawled by, and you never wrote; so at last I said to Gianetta, "I can't stand this any longer; those two poor monarchs haven't got anyone to mend their stockings or sew on their buttons or patch their clothes – at least, I hope they haven't – let us all pack up a change and go and see how they're getting on." And she said, "Done", and they all said, "Done"; and we asked old Giacopo to lend us his boat, and *he* said, "Done"; and we've crossed the sea, and, thank goodness, *that's* done; and here we are. . . .'

A spasm of general rejoicing is cut short by the arrival of the Grand Inquisitor. Don Alhambra discloses that whichever of the temporarily joint monarchs proves to be the sole king is already married since infancy to Casilda, who will be arriving with her parents, the Duke and Duchess of Plaza-Toro, in half an hour to claim her husband. The implications are beyond the company's mental capacities, despite Giuseppe's suggestion that two husbands to three wives simply equals two-thirds of a husband to each wife. Casilda, when she arrives, proves sympathetic, confessing that she, too, is in love, and has no wish to resume the proxy marriage of her infancy.

There seems to be no solution; but Inez, the Prince's former nurse, now arrives to provide one.

> The Royal Prince was by the King entrusted
> To my fond care, ere I grew old and crusted;
> When traitors came to steal his son reputed,
> My own small boy I deftly substituted!
> The villains fell into the trap completely –
> I hid the Prince away – still sleeping sweetly:
> I called him 'son' with pardonable slyness –
> His name, Luiz! Behold his Royal Highness!

Which half of the temporary king, then, is really Inez's son is never stated: presumably the question is overlooked in the rejoicing which prevails. Casilda is already married to Luiz, whom she loves, and who is rightful King of Barataria. Giuseppe and Tessa, Marco and Gianetta, and all the rest of the gondoliers and their brides are free to return to their former way of life, uninhibited by the demands of 'royalizing'.

Quotations

MARCO AND GIUSEPPE: Buon' giorno, signorine!
GIRLS: Gondolieri carissimi!
                     Siamo contadine!
MARCO AND GIUSEPPE: Servitori umilissimi!
  (*bowing*)   Per chi questi fiori –
                     Questi fiori bellissimi?
GIRLS: Per voi, bei signori,
                     O eccellentissimi!

.   .   .   .

MARCO AND GIUSEPPE: We're called *gondolieri*
                    But that's a vagary,
                    It's quite honorary
                         The trade that we ply.
                    For gallantry noted
                    Since we were short-coated,
                    To beauty devoted,
                         Giuseppe ⎫
                         Are Marco ⎬ and I;
                    When morning is breaking,
                    Our couches forsaking,
                    To greet their awaking
                         With carols we come.
                    At summer day's nooning,
                    When weary lagooning,
                    Our mandolins tuning,
                         We lazily thrum.
                    When vespers are ringing,
                    To hope ever clinging,

> With songs of our singing
> > A vigil we keep,
> When daylight is fading
> Enwrapt in night's shading,
> With soft serenading
> > We sing them to sleep.

. . . .

GIRLS: My papa he keeps three horses,
> Black and white, and dapple grey, sir;
Turn three times, then take your courses,
> Catch whichever girl you may, sir!

. . . .

DUKE (*To* LUIZ): Where are the halberdiers who were to have had the honour of meeting us here, that our visit to the Grand Inquisitor might be made in becoming state?

LUIZ: Your Grace, the halberdiers are mercenary people who stipulated for a trifle on account.

DUKE: How tiresome! Well, let us hope the Grand Inquisitor is a blind gentleman. And the band who were to have had the honour of escorting us? I see no band!

LUIZ: Your Grace, the band are sordid persons who required to be paid in advance.

DUCHESS: That's so like a band!

. . . .

DUKE: My child, the Duke of Plaza-Toro does not follow fashions – he leads them. He always leads everybody. When he was in the army he led his regiment. He occasionally led them into action. He invariably led them out of it.

> In enterprise of martial kind,
> > When there was any fighting,
> He led his regiment from behind –
> > He found it less exciting.
> But when away his regiment ran,
> > His place was at the fore, O –
> > That celebrated,

                        Cultivated
                        Underrated,
                        Nobleman,
                    The Duke of Plaza-Toro!

                        .   .   .   .

DON ALHAMBRA: I stole the Prince, and I brought him here,
                    And left him gaily prattling
                With a highly respectable gondolier,
                Who promised the Royal babe to rear,
                And teach him the trade of a timoneer
                    With his own beloved bratling . . .

                    . . . Time sped, and when at the end of a year
                    I sought that infant cherished
                That highly respectable gondolier
                Was lying a corpse on his humble bier –
                I dropped a Grand Inquisitor's tear –
                    That gondolier had perished.

                    A taste for drink, combined with gout,
                        Had doubled him up for ever.
                    Of *that* there is no manner of doubt –
                    No probable, possible shadow of doubt –
                    No possible doubt whatever.

                        .   .   .   .

ALL: Try we life-long, we can never
            Straighten out life's tangled skein,
            Why should we, in vain endeavour,
                Guess and guess and guess again?
LUIZ: Life's a pudding full of plums,
DUCHESS: Care's a canker that benumbs.
ALL: Life's a pudding full of plums,
                Care's a canker that benumbs.
            Wherefore waste our elocution
            On impossible solution?
            Life's a pleasant institution,
                Let us take it as it comes!

            Set aside the dull enigma,
                We shall guess it all too soon;
            Failure brings no kind of stigma –
                Dance we to another tune!
LUIZ: String the lyre and fill the cup,
DUCHESS: Lest on sorrow we should sup.
ALL: String the lyre and fill the cup,
                Lest on sorrow we should sup.
            Hop and skip to Fancy's fiddle,
            Hands across and down the middle –
            Life's perhaps the only riddle
                That we shrink from giving up!

                        . . . .

TESSA: When a merry maiden marries,
            Sorrow goes and pleasure tarries;
                Every sound becomes a song,
                All is right, and nothing's wrong!
            From to-day and ever after
            Let our tears be tears of laughter.
                Every sigh that finds a vent
                Be a sigh of sweet content!
            When you marry, merry maiden,
            Then the air with love is laden;
                Every flower is a rose,
                    Every goose becomes a swan,
                Every kind of trouble goes
                    Where the last year's snows have gone!

                        . . . .

GIANETTA: You men can never understand
                    That heart and hand
                Cannot be separated when
                    We go a-yearning;
            You see, you've only women's eyes
                    To idolize
            And only women's hearts, poor men,
                    To set *you* burning!

                        . . . .

N

GIANETTA: Then one of us will be a Queen,
   And sit on a golden throne,
    With a crown instead
    Of a hat on her head,
   And diamonds all her own!
  With a beautiful robe of gold and green,
   I've always understood;
    I wonder whether
    She'd wear a feather?...
   I rather think she should!

ALL: Oh, 'tis a glorious thing, I ween,
   To be a regular Royal Queen!
   No half-and-half affair, I mean,
   But a right-down regular Royal Queen!

     . . . .

MARCO: For every one who feels inclined,
   Some post we undertake to find
    Congenial with his frame of mind -
    And all shall equal be.

GIUSEPPE: The Chancellor in his peruke –
   The Earl, the Marquis, and the Dook,
   The Groom, the Butler, and the Cook –
    They all shall equal be.

MARCO: The Aristocrat who banks with Coutts –
   The Aristocrat who hunts and shoots –
   The Aristocrat who cleans our boots –
    They all shall equal be!

     . . . .

GIUSEPPE: Rising early in the morning,
    We proceed to light the fire,
   Then our Majesty adorning
    In its workaday attire,
     We embark without delay
     On the duties of the day.

  First, we polish off some batches
  Of political dispatches,
    And foreign politicians circumvent;

Then, if business isn't heavy,
We may hold a Royal *levee*,
    Or ratify some Acts of Parliament.
Then we probably review the household troops –
With the usual 'Shalloo humps!' and 'Shallo hoops!'
Or receive with ceremonial and state
An interesting Eastern potentate.
    After that we generally
    Go and dress our private *valet* –
(It's a rather nervous duty – he's a touchy little man) –
    Write some letters literary
    For our private secretary –
He is shaky in his spelling, so we help him if we can.
    Then, in view of cravings inner,
    We go down and order dinner;
Then we polish the Regalia and the Coronation plate –
    Spend an hour in titivating
    All our Gentlemen-in-Waiting;
Or we run on little errands for the Ministers of State.

                . . . .

MARCO: Take a pair of sparkling eyes,
        Hidden, ever and anon,
            In a merciful eclipse –
    Do not heed their mild surprise –
        Having passed the Rubicon,
            Take a pair of rosy lips;
    Take a figure trimly planned –
        Such as admiration whets –
            (Be particular in this);
    Take a tender little hand,
        Fringed with dainty fingerettes,
            Press it – in parenthesis; –
    Ah! Take all these, you lucky man –
    Take and keep them, if you can!

                . . . .

CHORUS: Dance a cachucha, fandango, bolero,
        Xeres we'll drink – Manzanilla, Montero –

Wine, when it runs in abundance, enhances
The reckless delight of that wildest of dances!
    To the pretty pitter-pitter-patter,
    And the clitter-clitter-clitter-clatter –
        Clitter – clitter – clatter,
        Pitter – pitter – patter,
    Patter, patter, patter, patter, we'll dance.
Old Xeres we'll drink – Manzanilla, Montero;
For wine, when it runs in abundance, enhances
The reckless delight of that wildest of dances!

       • • • •

DON ALHAMBRA: There lived a King, as I've been told,
        In the wonder-working days of old,
        When hearts were twice as good as gold,
           And twenty times as mellow.
        Good-temper triumphed in his face,
        And in his heart he found a place
        For all the erring human race
           And every wretched fellow.
        When he had Rhenish wine to drink
        It made him very sad to think
        That some, at junket or at jink,
           Must be content with toddy. . . .
        He wished all men as rich as he
        (And he was rich as rich could be),
        So to the top of every tree
           Promoted everybody.

MARCO AND GIUSEPPE:
        Now, that's the kind of King for me
        He wished all men as rich as he,
        So to the top of every tree
           Promoted everybody.

DON ALHAMBRA: Lord Chancellors were cheap as sprats,
        And Bishops in their shovel hats
        Were plentiful as tabby cats –
           In point of fact, too many.
         Ambassadors cropped up like hay,
        Prime Ministers and such as they

> Grew like asparagus in May,
>   And Dukes were three a penny.
> On every side Field-Marshals gleamed,
> Small beer were Lords-Lieutenant deemed,
> With Admirals the ocean teemed
>   All round his wide dominions.

MARCO AND GIUSEPPE:
>   With Admirals all round his wide dominions. . . .

DON ALHAMBRA: That King, although no one denies
>   His heart was of abnormal size,
>   Yet he'd have acted otherwise
>   If he had been acuter.
>   The end is easily foretold,
>   When every blessed thing you hold
>   Is made of silver, or of gold,
>   You long for simple pewter.
>   When you have nothing else to wear
>   But cloth of gold and satins rare,
>   For cloth of gold you cease to care –
>   Up goes the price of shoddy.

MARCO AND GIUSEPPE:
>   Of shoddy, up goes the price of shoddy.

DON ALHAMBRA: In short, whoever you may be,
>   To this conclusion you'll agree,
>   When ever one is somebodee,
>   Then no one's anybody!

. . . .

DUKE: And now, my child, prepare to receive the husband to whom you were united under such interesting and romantic circumstances.

CASILDA: But which is it? There are two of them!

DUKE: It is true that at present His Majesty is a double gentleman; but as soon as the circumstances of his marriage are ascertained, he will, *ipso facto*, boil down to a single gentleman – thus presenting a unique example of an individual who becomes a single man and a married man by the same operation.

DUCHESS: I have known instances in which the characteristics of both conditions existed concurrently in the same individual.

DUKE: Ah, he couldn't have been a Plaza-Toro.
DUCHESS: Oh! couldn't he, though!

. . . .

DUKE: Small titles and orders
           For Mayors and Recorders
             I get – and they're highly delighted –
DUCHESS: They're highly delighted!
DUKE: M.P.s baronetted,
           Sham Colonels gazetted,
             And second-rate Aldermen knighted –
DUCHESS: Yes, Aldermen knighted.
DUKE: Foundation-stone laying
           I find very paying:
             It adds a large sum to my makings –
DUCHESS: Large sums to his makings.
DUKE: At charity dinners
           The best of speech-spinners,
             I get ten per cent on the takings –
DUCHESS: One-tenth of the takings.
DUCHESS: I present any lady
           Whose conduct is shady
             Or smacking of doubtful propriety –
DUKE: Doubtful propriety.
DUCHESS: When Virtue would quash her,
           I take and whitewash her,
             And launch her in first-rate society –
DUKE: First-rate society!
DUCHESS: I recommend acres
           Of clumsy dressmakers –
             Their fit and their finishing touches –
DUKE: Their finishing touches.
DUCHESS: A sum in addition
           They pay for permission
             To say that they make for the Duchess –
DUKE: They make for the Duchess!
DUKE: Those pressing prevailers,
           The ready-made tailors,
             Quote me as their great double-barrel –

DUCHESS: Their great double-barrel.
DUKE: I allow them to do so,
              Though Robinson Crusoe
                  Would jib at their wearing apparel –
DUCHESS: Such wearing apparel!
DUKE: I sit, by selection,
              Upon the direction
                  Of several Companies bubble –
DUCHESS: All Companies bubble!
DUKE: As soon as they're floated
              I'm freely bank-noted –
                  I'm pretty well paid for my trouble –
DUCHESS: He's paid for his trouble!
DUCHESS: At middle-class party
              I play at *écarté* –
                  And I'm by no means a beginner –
DUKE: She's not a beginner.
DUCHESS: To one of my station
              The remuneration –
                  Five guineas a night and my dinner –
DUKE: And wine with her dinner.
DUCHESS: I write letters blatant
              On medicines patent –
                  And use any other you mustn't –
DUKE: Believe me, you mustn't –
DUCHESS: And vow my complexion
              Derives its perfection
                  From somebody's soap – which it doesn't –
DUKE: It certainly doesn't!
DUKE: We're ready as witness
              To any one's fitness
                  To fill any place or preferment –
DUCHESS: A place or preferment –
DUCHESS: We're often in waiting
              At junket or *fêting*,
                  And sometimes attend an interment –
DUKE: We enjoy an interment.
BOTH: In short, if you'd kindle
              The spark of a swindle,

Lure simpletons into your clutches –
Yes; into your clutches.
Or hoodwink a debtor,
You cannot do better
DUCHESS: Than trot out a Duke or a Duchess –
DUKE: A Duke or a Duchess!

or

The Flowers of Progress

NEARLY four years elapsed between the opening night of *The Gondoliers* and the rise of the Savoy Theatre curtain on another Gilbert and Sullivan work. They were unhappy years for all three partners. Sullivan, as usual, was suffering the pains of bodily sickness and professional frustration. Carte was preoccupied with building his Royal English Opera House, at the junction of Shaftesbury Avenue and Charing Cross Road, where he proposed 'to establish English Grand Opera'. Gilbert declined the honour of collaborating with Sullivan in a serious opera with which to open it. He was brooding increasingly upon the amount of expenses being deducted by Carte before the annual share-out of income. The discovery that Carte had spent money on replacing worn carpets in the theatre foyer proved the last straw for Gilbert, whose protest led to the 'carpet quarrel' which so soured relationships between himself on the one side and Sullivan and Carte on the other that it seemed that the partnership was ended for good, and that, in Gilbert's threat, their united works would be heard in public no more.

The Royal English Opera House opened triumphantly on 31 January, 1891 with *Ivanhoe*, a grand opera by Sullivan to a libretto by Julian Sturgis. Despite its ecstatic welcome, and a run of 155 performances, it failed to achieve its purpose and the Opera House (now the Palace Theatre) was relinquished by Carte after an unsuccessful attempt to save it with a French operetta. The partnership seemed indeed ended. Works by other hands were being presented at the Savoy. Gilbert and Cellier's *The Mountebanks* was put on at the Lyric Theatre, and Grundy and Sullivan's *Haddon Hall* achieved over 200 performances at the Savoy. Then yet another reconciliation took place. Gilbert handed Sullivan a new synopsis; Sullivan took it away to the south of France: the result was *Utopia Limited*, which ran for 245 performances at the Savoy from 7 October, 1893. Ironically, in view of Gilbert's views on expenditure, it was the most lavishly mounted of any of their works, and also the most demanding of individual talent from its performers. Perhaps largely for these reasons – although the libretto makes poor reading today, compared with most of the others – it has been ignored since, except by ambitious amateurs. It opened in America on 26 March, 1894, and although it soon failed it has occasionally been revived in that country by amateurs.

. . . .

'IN lazy languor – motionless' a group of maidens bask in a se a side palm grove in the tropical paradise of Utopia. Their dreamy murmurings are interrupted by the arrival of Calynx, the Vice-Chamberlain, to report that King Paramount's eldest daughter, Zara, is returning at last from five years' study in England, with a Girton degree and a head full of notions for raising Utopia to world-wide pre-eminence. When the maidens comment lazily that life is pleasant enough without needing anglicization, he retorts:

England has made herself what she is because, in that favoured land, every one has to think for himself. Here we have no need to think, because our monarch anticipates all our wants, and our political opinions are formed for us by the journals to which we subscribe. Oh, think how much more brilliant this dialogue would have been, if we had been accustomed to exercise our reflective powers! They say that in England the conversation of the very meanest is a coruscation of impromptu epigram!

The day's calm is further disturbed by the arrival of Tarara, swearing horribly in Utopian, a language which has already been supplanted, at the King's command, by English. Tarara's post is Public Exploder, whose function is to blow up the King with dynamite should he ever be instructed to do so by Scaphio and Phantis, the two Wise Men, who watch the King day and night for any political or moral indiscretion. If this should occur,

Tarara becomes King and a new Public Exploder is appointed:
as Calynx puts it, 'Despotism tempered by Dynamite provides,
on the whole, the most satisfactory description of ruler – an auto-
crat who dares not abuse his autocratic power'. Tarara's present
agitation is due to his having found a copy of a publication
entitled *Palace Peeper*, containing details of abominable immorali-
ties on the part of King Paramount, despite which no order has
come through from the Wise Men for His Majesty's dynamiting.

The truth, we learn from Scaphio and Phantis themselves, is
that the King is a slave in their hands. They have but to denounce
him and he will be destroyed; and to make their blackmail
doubly effective, they have forced him to write the untrue articles
about his misdeeds in the *Palace Peeper*, as well as to satirize
himself in a comic opera. Although his agents promptly buy up
every copy of the publication as it appears, there is the danger of
the odd one escaping suppression. Phantis, who is 55 years old,
is racked with love for the Princess Zara, but doubts whether she
will return his interest after being five years in 'a land where
every youth is as a Greek god'. He asks Scaphio, who is 11 years
his senior but has never been in love, to exert joint influence with
him upon the King to make Zara marry Phantis. Scaphio agrees.

Having ascertained that his subjects are in favour of Utopia's
adopting the English influence which Zara is about to import,
King Paramount exhibits his two younger daughters, the twins
Nekaya and Kalyba, who have been educated at home by a
stately English governess, Lady Sophy.

NEKAYA AND KALYBA:
> Although of native maids the cream,
> We're brought up on the English scheme –
>> The best of all
>> For great and small
>> Who modesty adore.

NEKAYA: For English girls are good as gold,
> Extremely modest (so we're told),
> Demurely coy – divinely cold –

KALYBA: And we are that – and more.

KALYBA: To please papa, who argues thus –
All girls should mould themselves on us
    Because we are
    By furlongs far
      The best of all the bunch,
We show ourselves to loud applause
From ten to four without a pause –
Which is an awkward time because
      It cuts into our lunch.

Lady Sophy is one of the two people – the Princess Zara being the other – into whose hands the King hopes no copy of the *Palace Peeper* will ever fall. Unfortunately, Tarara has given Lady Sophy one. She faces the King with the scandalous accusations contained in it, which he denies. Aware that he wishes her to accept his love, she demands that he have their writer put to death first, which, of course, he is in no position to do. He resorts to procrastination.

I – I am waiting until a punishment is discovered that will exactly meet the enormity of the case. I am in constant communication with the Mikado of Japan, who is a leading authority on such points; and, moreover, I have the ground plans and sectional elevations of several capital punishments in my desk at this moment.

She does not believe him, and repudiates him for his 'conduct shady'.

A march tune rings out and the entire Utopian Court assemble, to herald the arrival of Princess Zara, escorted by Captain Fitzbattleaxe, of the First Life Guards, and four troopers, who have escorted her from England. The elderly Scaphio, who has never seen her before, is immediately stricken by her beauty, and confesses to Phantis after the assembly has dispersed that instead of helping him to gain the Princess's hand, he will henceforth be his rival for it. The Princess and Captain Fitzbattleaxe, who, it is apparent, have fallen in love during their voyage, discover the Wise Men quarrelling.

ZARA: Dear me. I'm afraid we are interrupting a *tête-à-tête*.

SCAPHIO: No, no. You come very appropriately. To be brief, we – we love you – this man and I – madly – passionately!

ZARA: Sir!

SCAPHIO: And we don't know how we are to settle which of us is to marry you.

FITZBATTLEAXE: Zara, this is very awkward.

SCAPHIO: I – I am paralysed by the singular radiance of your extraordinary loveliness. I know I am incoherent. I never was like this before – it shall not occur again. I – shall be fluent, presently.

ZARA (*aside*): Oh, dear, Captain Fitzbattleaxe, what *is* to be done?

FITZBATTLEAXE (*aside*): Leave it to me – I'll manage it. (*Aloud*) It's a common situation. Why not settle it in the English fashion?

BOTH: The English fashion? What is that?

FITZBATTLEAXE: It's very simple. In England, when two gentlemen are in love with the same lady, and until it is settled which gentleman is to blow out the brains of the other, it is provided, by the Rival Admirers' Clauses Consolidation Act, that the lady shall be entrusted to an officer of Household Cavalry as stakeholder, who is bound to hand her over to the survivor (on the Tontine principle) in a good condition of substantial and decorative repair.

Zara and Fitzbattleaxe reassure one another in whispers that they are on safe ground: it is unlikely that either of her ageing adorers will blow out the other's brains or risk having it done to himself.

For the first time since her arrival, Zara and her father have the chance to converse privately. To his dismay, she promptly produces the *Palace Peeper*, which Lady Sophy has given her. He admits to being the helpless tool of his two Wise Men. She is able to comfort him with the news that at present 'washing their hands after their journey' are 'six Representatives of the principal causes that have tended to make England the powerful, happy, and blameless country which the consensus of European civilization has declared it to be'. If he will place himself unreservedly in their hands, they will reorganize Utopia in a way that will enable him to defy his persecutors. The King orders his Court to reassemble immediately, and Zara proceeds to introduce the six imported 'Flowers of Progress': Sir Bailey Barre, Q.C.; Captain

Fitzbattleaxe; Lord Dramaleigh, Lord High Chamberlain; Mr Blushington, a County Councillor; Mr Goldbury, a company promoter; and Captain Sir Edward Corcoran, K.C.B., of the Royal Navy. Each makes a declaration of his principles, and the Utopians innocently hail them.

> Ye wanderers from a mighty State,
> Oh, teach us how to legislate –
> Your lightest word will carry weight
>   In our attentive ears.
> Oh, teach the natives of this land
> (Who are not quick to understand)
> How to work off their social and
>   Political arrears!

CAPT. FITZBATTLEAXE: Increase your army!
LORD DRAMALEIGH: Purify your Court!
CAPT. CORCORAN: Get up your steam and cut your canvas short!
SIR BAILEY BARRE: To speak on both sides teach your sluggish
                      brains!
MR BLUSHINGTON: Widen your thoroughfares, and flush your
                      drains!
MR GOLDBURY: Utopia's much too big for one small head –
                      I'll float it as a Company Limited!

The King is especially impressed by this last piece of advice and after Mr Goldbury has obliged with fuller details he declares that he will go down to posterity as the first sovereign in Christendom who registered his country under the Joint Stock Company's Act of Sixty-Two. The Utopians obediently rejoice, except for Scaphio, Phantis and Tarara, who mutter threats of what will happen to King Paramount if he goes against their wishes.

One night some time later, Captain Fitzbattleaxe serenades Zara in the Palace throne room. His emotion is so great that he cannot sing properly. Zara soothes him and they discuss the beneficial changes which have been wrought in Utopia by the Flowers of Progress. Fitzbattleaxe and Captain Corcoran have remodelled the army and navy. Mr Goldbury has made every man, woman and child a Limited Liability Company. English dress fashions have been introduced, and when the King enters it is in the uniform of a British Field-Marshal. He has come to preside over his first cabinet meeting, at which all the Flowers of Progress are present, seated in a row like the Christy Minstrels. They chorus their approval of the King's progress report:

> It really is surprising
> What a thorough Anglicizing
> We have brought about – Utopia's quite another land.

A splendid Drawing-Room follows, at which the King and the Princess receive all the Court ladies in a travesty of English ceremonial. At its end, Scaphio and Phantis, robed and wigged as judges, buttonhole the King to complain that the English-men's innovations have brought disaster to their personal schemes to provide for their old age. Their Matrimonial Agency is at a standstill, their Cheap Sherry business bankrupt, their Army Clothing contracts paralysed: all largely because when they send in their bills their customers plead liability limited to a declared capital of eighteenpence, and apply to be dealt with under the Winding-up Act. The King replies offhandedly that they must submit a list of any grievances to the Secretary of Utopia Limited for consideration at the Board's next monthly meeting. When the Wise Men threaten to have him dynamited for such defiance, he points out that since he is now a Limited Company, he can be wound up, but not blown up. Dismayed, Scaphio and Phantis find Tarara and invite him to join them in concocting a plot to overthrow the King and his English advisers. After much whisper-ing they hit upon a scheme.

> At last a capital plan we've got;
> We won't say how and we won't say what:
> It's safe in my noddle –
> Now off we will toddle,
> And slyly develop this capital plot!

They are soon back with the inflamed populace and general cries of 'Down with the Flowers of Progress'. The popular complaint is that Utopian life has been made dull by the efficiency instituted by the Englishmen, so that members of professions whose traditional reliance is upon others' inefficiency – doctors and lawyers, for example – are starving. The King asks Zara's advice. She confesses that there must be some element of English government that they have forgotten to introduce which would settle the situation. Sir Bailey Barre reminds her what it is – Government by Party, guaranteed to reduce any orderly system to chaos. The King declares that Utopia shall immediately become a Limited Monarchy, instead of a Monarchy Limited, and that Government by Party shall prevail. Scaphio and Phantis are arrested, and Zara and the King – who has now been accepted by Lady Sophy after confessing that his reported misdeeds were his own invention – sing Great Britain's praise.

ZARA: There's a little group of isles beyond the wave –
  So tiny, you might almost wonder where it is –
  That nation is the bravest of the brave,
   And cowards are the rarest of all rarities.
  The proudest nations kneel at her command;
   She terrifies all foreign-born rapscallions;
  And holds the peace of Europe in her hand
   With half a score invincible battalions!

ALL: Such, at least, is the tale
   Which is borne on the gale,
    From the island which dwells in the sea.
   Let us hope, for her sake,
   That she makes no mistake –
    That she's all she professes to be!

KING: Oh, may we copy all her maxims wise,
   And imitate her virtues and her charities;
  And may we, by degrees, acclimatize
   Her Parliamentary peculiarities!
  By doing so, we shall, in course of time
   Regenerate completely our entire land –
  Great Britain is that monarchy sublime,
   To which some add (but others do not) Ireland.

Quotations

LADY SOPHY:　　　　Bold-faced ranger
　　　　　　　　　(Perfect stranger)
　　　Meets two well-behaved young ladies.
　　　　　　　　　He's attractive,
　　　　　　　　　Young and active –
　　　Each a little bit afraid is.
　　　　　　　　　Youth advances,
　　　　　　　　　At his glances
　　　To their danger they awaken;
　　　　　　　　　They repel him
　　　　　　　　　As they tell him
　　　He is very much mistaken.
　　　Though they speak to him politely,
　　　Please observe they're sneering slightly,
　　　Just to show he's acting vainly.
　　　This is Virtue saying plainly,
　　　　　　　'Go away, young bachelor,
　　　　　　　We are not what you take us for!'
　　　When addressed impertinently,
　　　English ladies answer gently,
　　　　　　　'Go away, young bachelor,
　　　　　　　We are not what you take us for!'

　　　　　　　　　As he gazes,
　　　　　　　　　Hat he raises,
　　　Enters into conversation.
　　　　　　　　　Makes excuses –
　　　　　　　　　This produces
　　　Interesting agitation.
　　　　　　　　　He, with daring,
　　　　　　　　　Undespairing,
　　　Gives his card – his rank discloses.
　　　　　　　　　Little heeding
　　　　　　　　　This proceeding,
　　　They turn up their little noses.
　　　Pray observe this lesson vital –

o

When a man of rank and title
His position first discloses,
Always cock your little noses.
　　When at home, let all the class
　　Try this in the looking-glass.
English girls of well-bred notions
Shun all unrehearsed emotions.
　　English girls of highest class
　　Practise them before the glass.

. . . .

KING: Captain Fitzbattleaxe –

FITZBATTLEAXE: Sir.

KING: Your Troopers appear to be receiving a troublesome amount of attention from those young ladies. I know how strict you English soldiers are, and I should be extremely distressed if anything occurred to shock their puritanical British sensitiveness.

FITZBATTLEAXE: Oh, I don't think there's any chance of that.

KING: You think not? They won't be offended?

FITZBATTLEAXE: Oh no! They are quite hardened to it. They get a good deal of that sort of thing, standing sentry at the Horse Guards.

KING: It's English, is it?

FITZBATTLEAXE: It's particularly English.

. . . .

ZARA (*looking at cartoon*): Why do they represent you with such a big nose?

KING: Eh? Yes, it *is* a big one! Why, the fact is that, in the cartoons of a comic paper, the size of your nose always varies inversely as the square of your popularity. It's the rule.

. . . .

MR GOLDBURY: Some seven men form an Association
　　　　(If possible, all Peers and Baronets),
　　　They start off with a public declaration
　　　　To what extent they mean to pay their debts.
　　　That's called their Capital: if they are wary
　　　　They will not quote it at a sum immense.

The figure's immaterial – it may vary
    From eighteen million down to eighteenpence.
    I should put it rather low;
    The good sense of doing so
Will be evident at once to any debtor.
    When it's left to you to say
    What amount you mean to pay,
Why, the lower you can put it at, the better.

They then proceed to trade with all who'll trust 'em,
    Quite irrespective of their capital
(It's shady, but it's sanctified by custom);
    Bank, Railway, Loan, or Panama Canal.
You can't embark on trading too tremendous –
    It's strictly fair, and based on common sense –
If you succeed, your profits are stupendous –
    And if you fail, pop goes your eighteenpence.
        Make the money-spinner spin!
        For you only stand to win,
And you'll never with dishonesty be twitted,
        For nobody can know,
        To a million or so,
To what extent your capital's committed!
If you come to grief, and creditors are craving
    (For nothing that is planned by mortal head
Is certain in this Vale of Sorrow – saving
    That one's Liability is Limited) –
Do you suppose that signifies perdition?
    If so you're but a monetary dunce –
You merely file a Winding-up Petition,
    And start another Company at once!
        Though a Rothschild you may be
        In your own capacity,
    As a Company you've come to utter sorrow –
        But the Liquidators say,
        'Never mind – you needn't pay,'
So you start another Company to-morrow!

. . . .

FITZBATTLEAXE: A tenor, all singers above
(This doesn't admit of a question),
Should keep himself quiet,
Attend to his diet
And carefully nurse his digestion;
But when he is madly in love
It's certain to tell on his singing –
You can't do chromatics
With proper emphatics
When anguish your bosom is wringing!
When distracted with worries in plenty,
And his pulse is a hundred and twenty,
And his fluttering bosom the slave of mistrust is,
A tenor can't do himself justice.

. . . .

PHANTIS: Are you aware that the Lord Chamberlain, who has his own views as to the best means of elevating the national drama, has declined to license any play that is not in blank verse and three hundred years old – as in England?

. . . .

GOLDBURY: Are you really under the impression that English girls are so ridiculously demure? Why, an English girl of the highest type is the best, the most beautiful, the bravest, and the brightest creature that Heaven has conferred upon this world of ours. She is frank, open-hearted, and fearless, and never shows in so favourable a light as when she gives her own blameless impulses full play!

NEKAYA AND KALYBA: Oh, you shocking story!

GOLDBURY: Not at all. I'm speaking the strict truth. I'll tell you all about her.

A wonderful joy our eyes to bless,
In her magnificent comeliness,
Is an English girl of eleven stone two,
And five foot ten in her dancing shoe!
She follows the hounds, and on she pounds –
The 'field' tails off and the muffs diminish –

Over the hedges and brooks she bounds
  Straight as a crow, from find to finish.
At cricket, her kin will lose or win –
  She and her maids, on grass and clover,
Eleven maids out – eleven maids in –
  And perhaps an occasional 'maiden over'!

Go search the world and search the sea,
Then come you home and sing with me
There's no such gold and no such pearl
As a bright and beautiful English girl!

With a ten-mile spin she stretches her limbs,
She golfs, she punts, she rows, she swims –
She plays, she sings, she dances, too,
From ten or eleven till all is blue!
  At ball or drum, till small hours come
    (Chaperon's fan conceals her yawning)
  She'll waltz away like a teetotum,
    And never go home till daylight's dawning.

  Lawn-tennis may share her favours fair –
    Her eyes a-dance and her cheeks a-glowing –
  Down comes her hair, but what does she care?
    It's all her own and it's worth the showing!
      Go search the world, etc.

Her soul is sweet as the ocean air,
For prudery knows no haven there;
To find mock-modesty, please apply
To the conscious blush and the downcast eye.
  Rich in the things contentment brings,
    In every pure enjoyment wealthy,
  Blithe as a beautiful bird she sings.
    For body and mind are hale and healthy.
  Her eyes they thrill with right goodwill –
    Her heart is light as a floating feather –
  As pure and bright as the mountains rill
    That leaps and laughs in the Highland heather!
      Go search the world, etc.

. . . .

ZARA: Government by Party! Introduce that great and glorious element – at once the bulwark and foundation of England's greatness – and all will be well! No political measures will endure, because one Party will assuredly undo all that the other Party has done; and while grouse is to be shot, and foxes worried to death, the legislative action of the country will be at a standstill. Then there will be sickness in plenty, endless lawsuits, crowded jails, interminable confusion in the Army and Navy, and, in short, general and unexampled prosperity!

THE GRAND DUKE

or

The Statutory Duel

BY the time *Utopia Limited* had been running for three months, Carte was writing to warn Gilbert that its time was nigh, and urging him to get on with another 'frankly comic' piece, such as was clearly demanded by a public revelling in the frothy, tuneful musical comedies at the Gaiety and other theatres. Gilbert was unable to respond; he seems to have known that his rich vein of humour had petered out. Sullivan, too, was re-working old material into *The Chieftain* for Carte to present at the Savoy. It failed, and the contrasting success of a revival of *The Mikado* made the public's attitude doubly plain.

Carte's hoped-for new piece from the old partners materialized at last in 1896 when, on 7 March, he was able to present *The Grand Duke*. Neither partner's heart had been in the work and it achieved the shortest run of any of their works – 123 performances. It had its rewarding moments, but they were too few, and what fell between fell very flat indeed, dragging the piece into well-merited oblivion. It has never received a full professional production in New York.

The Grand Duke was the last collaboration between W. S. Gilbert and Arthur Sullivan. The only cheerful footnote one can append to an account of it is that the revival of *The Mikado*, with which Carte replaced it on the day after its closure, ran for 226 performances and demonstrated emphatically that the great partnership owed nothing to transitory fashion and had nothing to fear from current decline.

. . . .

IN the year 1750, in the market square of Speisesaal, capital of the Grand Duchy of Pfennig Halbpfennig, members of the local theatrical company are seated at a number of tables, enjoying a feast, the reason for which they soon make apparent.

> Here they come, the couple plighted –
>   On life's journey gaily start them.
> Soon to be for aye united,
>   Till divorce or death do part them.

The happy couple are Ludwig, leading comedian of the company, and Lisa, their soubrette. They are not yet united, however. The Grand Duke Rudolph has called a convocation of all the clergy in the town to settle the details of his approaching marriage with the rich Baroness von Krakenfeldt, and no parson will be available to marry Ludwig and Lisa before six o'clock that evening. Since the curtain must go up on the company's revival of *Troilus and Cressida* at seven, the wedding feast is having to be eaten in anticipation.

There is more to these actors and actresses than meets the eye. All are members of a conspiracy to depose the Grand Duke on the following day, and to vote their manager, Ernest Dummkopf, on to the throne in his place. This has nothing to do with affection for Ernest: he has ensured their support by promising to ennoble every man of them, arrange unlimited credit for every lady at the Court Milliner's, and pay all their salaries weekly in advance.

Ernest Dummkopf is in love with his leading comedienne, Julia Jellicoe, who is English, beautiful and haughty, but she has treated all his protestations with contempt. Now she is in a dilemma. If he becomes Grand Duke, she, under the terms of her contract as leading lady, will no doubt be expected to become Grand Duchess, and therefore his wife. This had not occurred to him, and he makes sure that she will not stint herself in the role.

ERNEST: But, considering your strong personal dislike to me and your persistent rejection of my repeated offers, won't you find it difficult to throw yourself into the part with all the impassioned enthusiasm that the character seems to demand? Remember, it's a strongly emotional part, involving long and repeated scenes of rapture, tenderness, adoration, devotion – all in luxuriant excess, and all of the most demonstrative description.

JULIA: My good sir, throughout my career I have made it a rule never to allow private feeling to interfere with my professional duties. You may be quite sure that (however distasteful the part may be) if I undertake it, I shall consider myself professionally bound to throw myself into it with all the ardour at my command.

ERNEST (*aside – with effusion*): I'm the happiest fellow alive! (*Aloud*) Now – would you have any objection – to – to give me some idea – if it's only a mere sketch – as to how you would play it? It would be really interesting – to me – to know your conception of – of – the part of my wife.

Her answers are all that he could hope for and he faces his future joyously, until an agitated Ludwig rushes up to admit that he has unwittingly betrayed the conspiracy. The plotters' secret sign of identification is the eating of a sausage roll; and Ludwig, seeing a stranger eating sausage rolls with relish, had chatted freely to him about the scheme before discovering that he was talking to the Grand Duke's private detective, who simply happened to like sausage rolls. It must be only a matter of time before the entire troupe is arrested, but Dr Tannhäuser, a notary acting as legal adviser to the conspiracy, is able to suggest a way of making the Grand Duke believe that the plot has collapsed. Ernest and Ludwig must fight a Statutory Duel, an old Pfennig Halbpfennig means of settling disputes under which the two combatants draw playing cards and the higher wins. The loser is then regarded as dead, losing all his civil rights and continuing to exist merely as a non-being, while the winner takes over the loser's position, functions and responsibilities. Dr Tannhäuser's idea is that whichever of Ernest or Ludwig 'survives' will go to the Grand Duke, denounce his 'dead' opponent as leader of the conspiracy, and gain a free pardon for himself for having turned King's Evidence. Fortuitously, the Act instituting Statutory Duels has only one more day to run before the expiry of the hundred years which terminate all Pfennig Halbpfennig laws

unless they are renewed; so that the loser of the duel will only
have to endure twenty-four hours in limbo before resuming his
normal identity. Having legally died once, he will not be liable
for arrest, and the whole situation will be saved.

The two men promptly fight their duel. Ernest draws a king,
but Ludwig's card is an ace. The conspirators dance gaily away,
and an unhappy-looking figure takes their place. This is the
Grand Duke Rudolph himself, weak and ill-looking from poor
diet, dressed in shabby clothes but ablaze with orders and decora-
tions. His most noted characteristic is his meanness, and he is
entertaining misgivings.

RUDOLPH: I hope I'm not doing a foolish thing in getting married. After
all, it's a poor heart that never rejoices, and this wedding of mine is the
first little treat I've allowed myself since my christening. Besides,
Caroline's income is very considerable, and as her ideas of economy are
quite on a par with mine, it ought to turn out well. Bless her tough old
heart, she's a mean little darling!

He gives orders to his Court officials about the wedding
arrangements, for which the populace will have to provide all
the food and entertainment, and they go about their duties,
leaving him to receive the Baroness von Krakenfeldt. She brings
him his detective's report, wrapped in a newspaper in which she
chances to see a biography of Rudolph, revealing that he had
been betrothed in infancy to the Princess of Monte Carlo. He
reassures her: the Prince of Monte Carlo is bankrupt and has
been unable to leave his house for years, for fear of arrest. Rudolph
has ignored his repeated pleas to advance him enough money to
send his daughter to Pfennig Halbpfennig, and tomorrow at two
the Princess comes of age, at which moment the betrothal
becomes, by agreement, void. At that same time, so as to ensure
getting as much marriage as he can for his money, Rudolph will
marry the Baroness.

With this little matter cleared up and the Baroness gone, the
Grand Duke turns to his detective's report and reads that there
is a conspiracy afoot, but that the detective had been too con-

vulsed with laughter to arrest the conspirator who had unwittingly chosen to confide in him. The cowardly Rudolph, convinced that the plot will succeed, bursts into tears and sinks to the ground, where he is found by Ludwig, come to report the 'death' of Ernest and the collapse of the conspiracy. Before Ludwig can make his announcement, the Grand Duke tells him that he is looking for some cheap and painless method of putting an end to an existence which has become insupportable. In a flash, Ludwig sees his chance to save himself and his colleagues for a certainty. He persuades Rudolph to fight a Statutory Duel with him in front of the populace, which Ludwig shall be sure to win. The Grand Duke will be able to disappear from public life long enough for the plot to be carried out unsuccessfully, and then can resume his office without fear. Only ensuring that Ludwig will not spend any of his money while temporarily reigning in his place, Rudolph agrees and they quarrel impressively in front of the people. They challenge each other to a duel, and when offered a pack of cards to draw from contrive to produce cards of their own from their sleeves – a king from Rudolph's, an ace from Ludwig's. So Rudolph is deposed for twenty-four hours and Ludwig is Grand Duke for a day – but he has other ideas about that.

LUDWIG: For instance, this measure (his ancestor drew it),
      This law against duels – to-morrow will die –
    The Duke will revive, and you'll certainly rue it –
      He'll give you 'what for' and he'll let you know why!
    But in twenty-four hours there's time to renew it –
    With a century's life I've the right to imbue it –
    It's easy to do – and, by Jingo, I'll do it!
    (*signing paper, which* NOTARY *presents*)
    It's done! Till I perish your Monarch am I!

He announces that that very afternoon he will announce the Court appointments of his fellow players, in precedence of professional position. This brings Julia Jellicoe forward with the now familiar claim that, as leading lady, she must reluctantly take on the role of Grand Duchess. Ludwig's betrothed, Lisa, protests, but Julia insists on going through with the 'repulsive part'. In any case, she reminds Lisa

> You couldn't play it, darling!
> It's 'leading business', pet,
> And you're but a soubrette.

Ludwig is sorry, but preoccupied with entering into his own new role. Lisa can only retire in tears.

One innovation Ludwig determines upon is 'to revive the classic memories of Athens at its best'. This is a particularly convenient period to choose, for the theatrical company already possesses all the right costumes for its presentation of *Troilus and Cressida*. It is in these that the actors and actresses assemble in the entrance hall of the Grand Ducal Palace next morning to hail the return of Ludwig and Julia from their marriage ceremony, in phrases appropriate to their garb.

> As before you we defile,
>   Eloia! Eloia!
> Pray you, gentles, do not smile
> If we shout, in classic style,
>   Eloia!
> Ludwig and his Julia true
> Wedded are each other to –
> So we sing, till all is blue,
>   Eloia! Eloia!
>   Opoponax! Eloia!

Ludwig is left alone with his bride to discuss the precise manner in which she shall tackle the role; but not for long. An insistent visitor is announced. It is the Baroness von Krakenfeldt, come to call on the Grand Duke Rudolph. When the circumstances of the Statutory Duel are explained to her by Ludwig, who adds that he has renewed the Act for another hundred years, thus debarring Rudolph from reclaiming his throne, the Baroness reminds him that in winning the duel Ludwig automatically took over all Rudolph's responsibilities – and these include her. He must marry her at once, and the fact that he has just married someone else is beside the point: the Baroness has the law on her side. She bears him off to their wedding.

Ernest Dummkopf comes wandering disconsolately on to the scene. He encounters Lisa and Julia in turn, but both recoil from him in horror: he is, legally speaking, a ghost. He begs Julia to defy the law and marry him, but she cannot see her way to doing it. They are interrupted by the return of the wedding party, whose festivities are halted in turn by a herald announcing the arrival of none less than the Prince of Monte Carlo, who, having employed his enforced incarceration in inventing the game of roulette, at which he has since made a fortune, has paid off all his debts and brought his daughter, in the nick of time, to marry the Grand Duke Rudolph. The Prince mistakes Ludwig for Rudolph, but the latter explains that the man he is seeking had died the day before of 'a pack-of-cardiac infection', the victim of a Statutory Duel, and that he, Ludwig, has assumed his title and other responsibilities. In that case, the Prince of Monte Carlo is quick to observe, the responsibilities include his daughter, to whom the former Grand Duke had been engaged for twenty years, so that her claim to be Grand Duchess overtops all others. He pushes her into Ludwig's arms, and the populace joyously prepare for yet another wedding.

This situation is suddenly settled by the entry of Dr Tann-häuser. He denounces Ludwig as an impostor. On referring to the wording of the Act regulating Statutory Duels, he has discovered that, instead of ranking as the highest card in the pack, the Ace invariably counts lowest; and the duel which recently took place is null and void, because Ludwig was legally dead when he fought Randolph. Rudolph returns and accepts the Princess of Monte Carlo, Julia consents to marry Ernest, and Ludwig and Lisa are united at last.

Quotations

LUDWIG: By the mystic regulation
  Of our dark Association,
  Ere you open conversation
   With another kindred soul,
   You must eat a sausage-roll!

ALL: You must eat a sausage-roll!

LUDWIG: If, in turn, he eats another,
  That's a sign that he's a brother –
  Each may fully trust the other.
   It is quaint and it is droll,
   But it's bilious on the whole.

ALL: Very bilious on the whole.

LUDWIG: It's a greasy kind of pasty,
  Which, perhaps, a judgement hasty
  Might consider rather tasty:
   Once (to speak without disguise)
   It found favour in our eyes.

ALL: It found favour in our eyes.

LUDWIG: But when you've been six months feeding
  (As we have) on this exceeding
  Bilious food, it's no ill-breeding
   If at these repulsive pies
   Our offended gorges rise!

     . . . .

ERNEST: Were I a king in very truth,
  And had a son – a guileless youth –
   In probable succession;
  To teach him patience, teach him tact,
  How promptly in a fix to act,
  He should adopt, in point of fact,
   A manager's profession.
  To that condition he should stoop
   (Despite a too fond mother),

With eight or ten 'stars' in his troupe,
All jealous of each other!

. . . .

LUDWIG, LISA, NOTARY, ERNEST, JULIA:
Strange the views some people hold!
Two young fellows quarrel –
Then they fight, for both are bold –
Rage of both is uncontrolled –
Both are stretched out, stark and cold!
Prithee, where's the moral?
Ding dong! Ding dong!
There's an end to further action,
And this barbarous transaction
Is described as 'satisfaction'!
Ha! ha! ha! ha! satisfaction!
Ding dong! Ding dong!
Each is laid in churchyard mould –
Strange the views some people hold!
Better than the method old,
Which was coarse and cruel,
Is the plan that we've extolled.
Sing thy virtues manifold
(Better than refined gold),
Statutory Duel!
Sing song! Sing song!
Sword or pistol neither uses –
Playing card he lightly chooses,
And the loser simply loses!
Ha! ha! ha! ha! simply loses.
Sing song! Sing song!
Some prefer the churchyard mould!
Strange the views some people hold!

. . . .

BARONESS: I once gave an evening party
(A sandwich and cut-orange ball),
But my guests had such appetites hearty
That I couldn't enjoy it, enjoy it at all!
I made a heroic endeavour

To look unconcerned, but in vain,
And I vow'd that I never – oh never –
    Would ask anybody again!
But there's a distinction decided –
    A difference truly immense –
When the wine that you drink is provided, provided,
    At somebody else's expense.
So bumpers – aye, ever so many –
    The cost we may safely ignore!
For the wine doesn't cost us a penny,
    Tho' it's Pommery seventy-four!

Index of First Lines

ACT TWO   'Tis twelve, I think

Why, where be oi, and what be oi a doin'
(If you'll marry me, I'll dig for you and rake for you!)

Dear friends, take pity on my lot
(You very, very plain old man)

Oh joy! oh joy!

Thou hast the power thy vaunted love

I rejoice that it's decided
(She will tend him, nurse him, mend him)

Hate me! I drop my H's – have through life!

Engaged! To a maiden fair
(Oh, agony, rage, despair!)

Oh, my voice is sad and low
(She's engaged to So-and-so!)

Oh, joyous boon! oh, mad delight!

Alas! that lovers thus should meet
(Oh, pity, pity me!)

Or I or he
   Must die!

Now to the banquet we press

H.M.S. *PINAFORE*

ACT ONE   We sail the ocean blue

For I'm called Little Buttercup – dear Little Buttercup

The Nightingale
   Sighed for the moon's bright ray

A maiden fair to see

I am the Captain of the *Pinafore*
(What, never?)

THE PIRATES OF PENZANCE

ACT ONE   Pour, oh, pour the pirate sherry

When Frederic was a little lad he proved so brave
  and daring

Oh, better far to live and die
(For I am a Pirate King)

You told me you were fair as gold!

Climbing over rocky mountain

Oh, is there not one maiden breast

Poor wandering one!

What ought we to do
(How beautifully blue the sky)

Here's a first-rate opportunity
(To get married with impunity)

I am the very model of a modern Major-General

Although our dark career
(Hail, Poetry, thou heaven-born maid!)

ACT TWO   Oh, dry the glistening tear

When the foeman bares his steel,
  Tarantara! Tarantara!

When you had left our pirate fold
(A paradox, a paradox)

Away, away! my heart's on fire
(To-night he dies)

Stay, Frederic, stay!

Ah, leave me not to pine alone

When a felon's not engaged in his employment
(When constabulary duty's to be done)

Come, walk up, and purchase with avidity

I hear the soft note of the echoing voice

Oh, list while we a love confess

ACT TWO   Silvered is the raven hair

Gentle Jane was good as gold

A magnet hung in a hardware shop
(A Silver Churn)

Love is a plaintive song

So go to him and say to him
(Sing 'Booh to you')

It's clear that mediaeval art alone retains its zest
(You hold yourself like this)

If Saphir I choose to marry
(In that case unprecedented)

When I go out of door
(A most intense young man)

After much debate internal
(Nobody be Bunthorne's bride!)

IOLANTHE

ACT ONE   Tripping hither, tripping thither
(We are dainty little fairies)

Welcome to our hearts again,
Iolanthe! Iolanthe!

Fare thee well, attractive stranger

None shall part us from each other
(Thou the tree and I the flower)

Loudly let the trumpet bray!
(Bow, bow, ye lower middle classes!

The Law is the true embodiment

When Britain really ruled the waves

In vain to us you plead –
Don't go!

Oh, foolish fay
(Oh, Captain Shaw!)

Though p'r'aps I may incur your blame
(In Friendship's name!)

When you're lying awake with a dismal headache

If you go in
You're sure to win
(Faint heart never won fair lady!)

If we're weak enough to tarry

He loves! If in the bygone years

Soon as we may
(Every one is now a fairy)

PRINCESS IDA

ACT ONE   Search throughout the panorama

Now hearken to my strict command
On every hand, on every hand

Ida was a twelvemonth old
Twenty years ago!

We are warriors three,
Sons of Gama, Rex

If you give me your attention, I will tell you what I
   am
(Yet everybody says I'm such a disagreeable man!)

Perhaps if you address the lady

Expressive glances
(Oh, dainty triolet!)

Whene'er I poke sarcastic joke
(Nothing whatever to grumble at!)

When anger spreads his wing
(Oh, I love the jolly rattle
Of an ordeal by battle)

This helmet, I suppose
(So off that helmet goes!)

With joy abiding

THE MIKADO

ACT ONE   If you want to know who we are,
We are gentlemen of Japan

A wandering minstrel I

Our great Mikado, virtuous man
(And I am right,
And you are right)

Young man, despair
(And the brass will crash)

Behold the Lord High Executioner!

Taken from the county jail

As some day it may happen that a victim must be
found,
I've got a little list – I've got a little list

Comes a train of little ladies

Three little maids from school are we

So please you, Sir, we much regret
If we have failed in etiquette

Were you not to Ko-Ko plighted

My brain it teems
(To sit in solemn silence in a dull, dark dock)

RUDDIGORE

ACT ONE   Fair is Rose as bright May-day

Sir Rupert Murgatroyd
His leisure and his riches

If somebody there chanced to be
(It's contrary to etiquette!)

I know a youth who loves a little maid –
Hey, but his face is a sight for to see!

From the briny sea
Comes young Richard, all victorious!

I shipped, d'ye see, in a Revenue sloop
(Which paralysed the Parley-voo)

My boy, you may take it from me
(If you wish in the world to advance)

The battle's roar is over

If well his suit has sped,
Oh, may they soon be wed!

In sailing o'er life's ocean wide
(My heart says, to this maiden strike)

Cheerily carols the lark
Over the cot
(Mad Margaret! Poor Peg!)

To a garden full of posies

Welcome, gentry,
For your entry
(When thoroughly tired
Of being admired)

Oh, why am I moody and sad?

You understand?
(For duty, duty must be done)

(Sing hey,
Lackaday!)

Having been a wicked baronet a week.
Once again a modest livelihood I seek

For happy the lily
That's kissed by the bee

THE YEOMEN OF THE GUARD

ACT ONE   When maiden loves, she sits and sighs

Tower Warders,
Under orders

When our gallant Norman foes
(The screw may twist and the rack may turn)

Alas! I waver to and fro!
Dark danger hangs upon the deed!

Is life a boon?

Here's a man of jollity

I have a song to sing, O!
(Heighdy! heighdy!
Misery me, lackadaydee!)

How say you, maiden, will you wed
A man about to lose his head?

I've jibe and joke
And quip and crank
(Oh, winnow all my folly, and you'll find
A grain or two of truth among the chaff!)

'Tis done! I am a bride!

Were I thy bride

Oh, Sergeant Meryll, is it true?

To thy fraternal care
Thy sister I commend

The prisoner comes to meet his doom

THE GONDOLIERS

ACT ONE

List and learn, ye dainty roses

For the merriest fellows are we, tra la

Buon' giorno, signorine!

We're called *gondolieri*

From the sunny Spanish shore,
The Duke of Plaza-Tor'
(If ever, ever, ever,
They get back to Spain)

In enterprise of martial kind
(The Duke of Plaza-Toro!)

Ah, well-beloved

There was a time
(Oh, bury, bury – let the grave close o'er)

I stole the Prince, and brought him here
(No probable, possible shadow of doubt)

Try we life-long, we can never
(Life's perhaps the only riddle
That we shrink from giving up!)

Bridegroom and bride!

When a merry maiden marries

Kind sir, you cannot have the heart
Our lives to part

Then one of us will be a Queen,
And sit on a golden throne
(A right-down regular Royal Queen!)

Replying, we sing
As one individual

For everyone who feels inclined
(And all shall equal be)

Q

UTOPIA LIMITED

ACT ONE   In lazy langour – motionless

O make way for the Wise Men!

Let all your doubts take wing

Quaff the nectar – cull the roses

A King of autocratic power we

Although of native maids the cream,
We're brought up on the English scheme

Bold-faced ranger
(Perfect stranger)

First you're born – and I'll be bound you
Find a dozen strangers round you

Subjected to your heavenly gaze

Oh, maiden, rich
In Girton lore

Five years have flown since I took wing
(And we are her escort – First Life Guards!)

Ah! gallant soldier, brave and true

It's understood, I think, all round

Oh, admirable art!
Oh, neatly-planned intention!

When Britain sounds the trump of war
(And Europe trembles)

What these may be, Utopians all,
Perhaps you'll hardly guess –
They're types of England's physical
And moral cleanliness

A Company Promoter this, with special education

THE GRAND DUKE

By the mystic regulation
Of our dark Association

Were I a king in very truth,
And had a son – a guileless youth –
In probable succession

How would I play this part –
The Grand Duke's Bride?

Ten minutes since I met a chap
Who bowed an easy salutation

About a century since,
The code of the duello
To sudden death
For want of breath
Sent many a strapping fellow

Strange the views some people hold!

A pattern to professors of monarchical autonomy,
I don't indulge in levity or compromising *bonhomie*

As o'er our penny roll we sing

When you find you're a broken-down critter

Come hither, all you people

Big bombs, small bombs, great guns and little ones!

Oh, a Monarch who boasts intellectual graces
Can do, if he likes, a good deal in a day

Ah, pity me, my comrades true,
Who love, as well I know you do,
This gentle child

Oh, listen to me, dear

The die is cast,
My hope has perished!

Sing hey, the jolly jinks of Pfenning Halbpfennig!

ACT TWO   As before you we defile,
Eloia! Eloia!

A Gilbertian Glossary

ABUDAH CHESTS: *Our Abudah chests, each containing a patent Hag*
(Mr Wells, *Sorcerer*).
Abudah is a hag-haunted merchant of Baghdad in James
Ridley's *Tales of the Genii* (1765).

ACELDAMA: *Oh, to be wafted away*
From this black Aceldama of sorrow (Bunthorne,
Patience).
A scene of bloodshed; originally the 'field of blood' near
Jerusalem purchased with the bribe Judas took for betraying
Christ.

AMARANTHINE ASPHODEL: *Quivering on a maranthine asphodel*
(Bunthorne, *Patience*).
Fadeless daffodil.

ANCIENT BAILEY: *And every day my voice was heard*
At the Sessions or Ancient Bailey (Judge, *Trial*).
The Old Bailey is London's Central Criminal Court.

AQUINAS, THOMAS: Referred to in Colonel Calverley's 'Heavy
Dragoon' song (*Patience*). Italian Dominican Friar (1226–74)
from whose principles much of the teaching of the Catholic
Church is derived.

BACKWARDATION: see CONTANGO.

BANK HOLIDAY: *A steady and stolid-y, jolly Bank Holiday*
Every-day young man (Bunthorne and Grosvenor,
Patience).
The Bank Holiday Act of 1871, initiated by Sir John Lubbock
(later Lord Avebury, 1834–1913), created four special closing
days for British banks which were also adopted as public
holidays.

BARING: *The shares are a penny, and ever so many are taken by Rothschild and Baring* (Lord Chancellor, *Iolanthe*).
The great financial house of Baring was established in London in 1770. Its head when *Iolanthe* first appeared was Edward Charles Baring (1828–97), later Baron Revelstoke.

BEADLE OF BURLINGTON: Referred to in Colonel Calverley's 'Heavy Dragoon' song (*Patience*). The stately beadle who ensured decorum in the Burlington Arcade, off Piccadilly. This privately-owned arcade of superior shops is still supervised by uniformed beadles, who combine helpfulness to its users with security duties and the suppression of misbehaviour.

BELGRAVE SQUARE: *Hearts just as pure and fair*
                  May beat in Belgrave Square
                  As in the lowly air
                  Of Seven Dials (Lord Tolloller, *Iolanthe*).
Belgrave Square, near Hyde Park Corner, now much occupied by foreign diplomatic establishments, was one of the most superior London residential districts of Victorian times, as Seven Dials, in Holborn, near Shaftesbury Avenue, was one of the least reputable.

BELGRAVIAN AIRIES: *Serving fairies –*
                   Stars of proud Belgravian airies (Chorus, *Utopia*).
The below-pavement areas adjoining the serving quarters of the grand houses of Belgravia (see BELGRAVE SQUARE) where housemaids exchanged badinage with tradesmen and stole furtive kisses with their admirers.

BISMARCK: *Genius of Bismarck devising a plan* (Colonel Calverley, *Patience*).
Prince Otto Eduard Leopold von Bismarck (1815–98), the 'Iron Chancellor', had been chancellor of the first German Reich for ten years when *Patience* appeared.

BLUE-AND-WHITE: *A Japanese young man,*
      A blue-and-white young man,
      Francesca da Rimini, miminy, piminy,
      Je-ne-sais-quoi young man! (Bunthorne,
      Patience).

Japanese art was one of the passions of the aesthetes whom *Patience* satirizes, as were blue-and-white ceramics. Francesca da Rimini was a girl living in 13th-century Ravenna whose tragic story fascinated the Pre-Raphaelites.

BLUNDERBORE: *Blood must be the best and bravest in England, or it's not good enough for the old Blunderbore* (Phoebe, *Yeomen*).
Phoebe is likening the Tower of London to Blunderbore, the giant in *Jack the Giant-killer*, whom Jack killed by scuttling his boat.

BOLERO: See CACHUCHA.

BOMBAZINE: *A servile usher then, in crumpled bands and rusty bombazine* (Strephon, *Iolanthe*).
The material, usually black, of which legal and clerical gowns are made. Bands are the strips of white material hanging from the neck.

BOTTICELLIAN: *How Botticellian! How Fra Angelican! Oh, Art, we thank thee for this boon!* (Saphir, *Patience*).
Sandro Botticelli (1444–1510) and Fra Angelico (1387–1455), two of the greatest Florentine painters, were much admired by the nineteenth-century English aesthetes.

BOUCICAULT: *The pathos of Paddy, as rendered by Boucicault* (Colonel Calverley, *Patience*).
Dion Boucicault (1822–90) was a prolific Irish-born playwright, many of whose works had sentimental Irish themes.

BOWDLERIZED: *If you'd climb the Helicon,*
      You should read Anacreon,
      Ovid's Metamorphoses,
      Likewise Aristophanes,
      And the works of Juvenal:

> *These are worth attention, all;*
> *But, if you will be advised,*
> *You will get them Bowdlerized!* (Psyche, *Ida*).

Thomas Bowdler (1754–1825) published editions of Shakespeare's works and Gibbon's *Decline and Fall of the Roman Empire* from which 'those words are omitted which cannot with propriety be read aloud in a family'.

BUMBOAT: Little Buttercup, in *H.M.S. Pinafore*, is a bumboat woman, i.e. a purveyor, by small boat, of provisions to vessels lying offshore.

CACHUCHA: *Dance a cachucha, fandango, bolero* (Chorus, *Gondoliers*).
Spanish dances of different measures.

CAESAR or HANNIBAL: *The genius strategic of Caesar or Hannibal* (Colonel Calverley, *Patience*).
Gaius Julius Caesar (*c.* 101–44 B.C.), Roman general, and Hannibal (247–183 B.C.), Carthaginian general.

CALOMEL: *All can be set right with calomel* (Bunthorne, *Patience*).
A purgative medicine.

CAMBERWELL: *Camberwell became a bower,*
> *Peckham an Arcadian Vale* (Counsel for the Plaintiff, *Trial*).
Both Camberwell and Peckham were thickly populated London districts by the time these words were first sung, and quite the opposite of blissfully rural, as implied by 'Arcadian'.

CARACTACUS: *Every detail of Caractacus's uniform* (Major-General Stanley, *Pirates*).
British general who resisted the Romans but was defeated and taken to Rome as a public exhibit. He died there *c.* A.D. 54.

CARADOC: *I know our mythic history, King Arthur's and Sir Caradoc's* (Major-General Stanley, *Pirates*).
Sir Caradoc was one of the knights of King Arthur's Round Table in British legend.

CATCHY-CATCHIES: *Men are grown-up catchy-catchies* (Captain Corcoran, *Pinafore*).
An affectionate term for babies.

CHANCERY LANE: *A Chancery Lane young man,*
                    A Somerset House young man,
                    A very delectable, highly respectable,
                    Threepenny-bus young man (Grosvenor,
                    Patience).
Chancery Lane is a thoroughfare in the heart of legal London, with Somerset House, used by Government departments, near by. The implication is that a young man employed in the neighbourhood would be of the steady, respectable sort, able to afford to travel to work in an omnibus, rather than walk.

CHASSEPÔT: See MAUSER.

CLASSICAL MONDAY POPS: Referred to in the Mikado's song 'My object all sublime', and in *Patience*. A series of popular classical concerts held in the St James's Hall which stood in Piccadilly where the Piccadilly Hotel is now. The hall had a room 139 ft. long and 60 ft. high and two smaller ones. Ballad concerts were presented on Saturday afternoons and 'Pops' on Monday evenings during the winter season from 1858, instituted by William Chappell (1809–88).

COLOCYNTH: *Something poetic lurks,*
           Even in colocynth and calomel (Bunthorne, *Patience*).
A colocynth is a bitter-apple, and, like calomel, has purgative properties.

COMMON PLEAS: See EXCHEQUER, COURT OF.

COMPANY LIMITED: See JOINT STOCK COMPANY'S ACT.

CONIES: *I've chickens and conies, and pretty polonies* (Little Buttercup, *Pinafore*).
Conies are rabbits.

CONTADINE: Gianetta, Tessa and their friends in *Gondoliers* are contadine, or country-girls.

CONTANGO: *A Company Promoter this, with special education,*
Which teaches what Contango means and also Backward-
ation (Zara, *Utopia*).
These are Stock Exchange terms of opposite meaning, relating to settlement of accounts for purchase of stock.

CRICHTON: *Though clever as clever can be –*
A Crichton of early romance – (Robin, *Ruddigore*).
A scholastic paragon. James Crichton (1560–*c.* 1582), dubbed 'The Admirable Crichton', graduated as a Master of Arts at the age of 15, spoke a dozen languages, and was also an expert fencer.

CROWN: *Wouldst thou earn a hundred crowns?* (Cholmondeley, *Yeomen*).
A gold coin, first minted in the period of this work and worth five shillings.

DAPHNEPHORIC: See PANDAEAN.

DECEASED WIFE'S SISTER: *He shall prick that annual blister,*
Marriage with deceased wife's sister
(Queen, *Iolanthe*).
A measure often and hotly debated in the British Parliament in Victorian times culminated, in 1907, in the Deceased Wife's Sister Marriage Act, permitting a man so to marry, but enabling objecting clergymen to refuse to officiate.

DEFOE, DANIEL: Referred to in Colonel Calverley's 'Heavy Dragoon' song (*Patience*). Born 1660 and died 1731, he published his best-known work, *Robinson Crusoe*, in 1719.

DELLA CRUSCAN: *You are not Della Cruscan* (Saphir, *Patience*).
A group of affected English poets living in late eighteenth-century Florence called themselves the Della Cruscan School, after the Accademia della Crusca, a sixteenth-century Florentine institute dedicated to purifying the Italian language.

DICKENS AND THACKERAY: *Narrative powers of Dickens and Thackeray* (Colonel Calverley, *Patience*).

The novelists Charles Dickens (1812–70) and William Make-peace Thackeray (1811–63). Gilbert knew their works well, and one may feel sure that they – or Dickens, at least – would have revelled in the Gilbert and Sullivan operettas, had they lived to see them.

DIMITY: *Pray observe the magnanimity*
       We display to lace and dimity! (Chorus, *Pirates*).
A cotton cloth with raised thread patterns.

DIVORCE: See EXCHEQUER, COURT OF.

D'ORSAY: *The dash of a D'Orsay, divested of quackery* (Colonel Calverley, *Patience*).
Alfred Guillaume Gabriel, Count D'Orsay (1801–52), born in Paris, was known as the 'last of the dandies' during the latter half of his life, spent in London. 'Quackery' is used here in its rarer meaning of dandyism or affectation.

DOUBLE-FIRST: *O make way for the Wise Men!*
       They are prizemen –
       Double-first in the world's university! (Chorus, *Utopia*).
Formerly a first-class degree in both classics and mathematics from Cambridge University, a double-first is now a combination of any two first-class degrees there.

DOW, GERARD: *I can tell undoubted Raphaels from Gerard Dows and Zoffanies* (Major-General Stanley, *Pirates*).
The painters Raphael (Raffaello Santi) 1483–1520; Gerard Dow (or Dou) 1613–80; and John Zoffany (1725–1810).

EARLY ENGLISH: *You are not even Early English. Oh, be Early English, ere it is too late!* (Saphir, *Patience*).
The ideal period of architecture of the Pre-Raphaelites, i.e from the twelfth to the fourteenth century.

ÉCARTÉ: *At middle-class party*
       I play at écarté – (Duchess of Plaza-Toro, *Gondoliers*).
A card game for two players, of French origin.

ELECTUARY: *The old woman is a-bed with fever, and we have come here to pick up some silver to buy an electuary for her* (Point, *Yeomen*).

A medicine sweetened with honey or syrup to enable it to be licked, rather than swallowed hastily.

ELISION: *With greater precision*
      (*Without the elision*),
      Sir Ruthven Murgatroyd (Robin, *Ruddigore*).

Elision is the dropping of a vowel, consonant, or syllable in pronunciation – for example 'can't' in place of 'cannot'. The name Ruthven, with the elision, is pronounced Rivven.

EMEUTES: *For when threatened with emeutes,*
      Tarantara! tarantara!
      And your heart is in your boots,
      Tarantara! (Sergeant of Police, *Pirates*).

Brawls – from the French.

EMPYREAN: *You are not Empyrean* (Saphir, *Patience*).
Celestial.

EQUITY DRAFTSMAN: *Allow me, as an old Equity draftsman, to make a suggestion* (Lord Chancellor, *Iolanthe*).

English equity law derives from decisions in the Court of Chancery; thus, an equity draftsman is one who drafts equity laws into their precise form.

ÉTUI: *Here is an* étui *dropped by one of them* (Melissa, *Ida*).
A small case for sewing equipment.

EXCHEQUER, COURT OF:
  Or assume that the witnesses summoned in force
  In Exchequer, Queen's Bench, Common Pleas, or Divorce,
  Have perjured themselves as a matter of course . . .
    (Lord Chancellor, *Iolanthe*)

London Courts of Justice. They had been reorganized, though, a few years before *Iolanthe* was written.

FANDANGO: See CACHUCHA.

FIELDING: *The humour of Fielding (which sounds contradictory)* (Colonel Calverley, *Patience*).

Henry Fielding (1707–54) wrote the humorous novel *Tom Jones*, 1749, but was also a fierce attacker of crime and social evils. The reference is more likely to his half-brother, Sir John Fielding (d. 1780), the blind Bow Street magistrate, who published a collection of laws relating to breaches of the peace in London and attempted, in 1773, to get the *Beggar's Opera* suppressed. It has been suggested also that this reference relates to the lack of amusement to be derived from fielding in a cricket match.

FILDES: *Who knows but we may count among our intellectual chickens,*
Like you, an Earl of Thackeray and p'raps a Duke of Dickens –
Lord Fildes and Viscount Millais (when they come) we'll welcome sweetly (King Paramount, *Utopia*).

Sir Luke Fildes (1844–1927) and Sir John Everett Millais (1829–96) were eminent English artists of the Victorian age, but neither was ennobled, any more than were Dickens (*q.v.*) and Thackeray (*q.v.*). King Paramount is demonstrating here his limited knowledge of the England he is so enthusiastic to copy in all things.

FRA ANGELICAN: See BOTTICELLIAN.

FRIDAY NIGHTS: *He shall end the cherished rights*
You enjoy on Friday nights (Fairy Queen, *Iolanthe*).

The night, in Parliament, on which private Members may introduce Bills, as distinct from those sponsored by their Parties.

FROGS OF ARISTOPHANES: *I know the croaking chorus from the* Frogs *of* Aristophanes (Major-General Stanley, *Pirates*).

One of the best-known comedies of Aristophanes (c. 448–c. 388 B.C.), the greatest of the ancient comic poets.

GARNET, SIR: *Skill of Sir Garnet in thrashing a cannibal* (Colonel Calverley, *Patience*).

Field-marshal Garnet Joseph, Viscount Wolseley (1833–1913), commander of several successful military expeditions against recalcitrant African leaders.

GASK AND GASK: See SWAN AND EDGAR.

GERMAN BANDS: . . . *German bands*
From music stands
Played Wagner imperfectly – (King Gama, *Ida*).
Bands of musicians of varying ability were a common feature of Victorian streets and public places. The more brassy and noisy of them tended to be German, and their playing infuriated such seekers of peace and quiet as Charles Dickens, who abandoned the Kent coastal resort of Broadstairs as a holiday place because of their prevalence.

GIDEON CRAWLE: *Gideon Crawle, it won't do* (Robin, *Ruddigore*). This is a surviving reference back to a now-omitted exchange between Robin and Old Adam in which it was stated that a bad Bart's 'vally-de-sham' (valet de chambre) was automatically named something like Gideon Crawle in the type of melodrama which Gilbert was satirizing.

GILLOWS: *Everything that isn't old, from Gillows* (Josephine, *Pinafore*).
A leading Oxford Street furnishing store, now Waring and Gillows.

GIRTON: *At Girton all is wheat, and idle chaff is never heard within its walls* (Zara, *Utopia*).
The first women's college in Cambridge University, founded at Hitchin in 1869, transferred to Girton, Cambridge, in 1873.

GROSVENOR GALLERY: *A greenery-yallery, Grosvenor Gallery,*
Foot-in-the-grave young man (Bunthorne, *Patience*).
The gallery was founded by Sir Coutts Lindsay (1824–1913) at 135 New Bond Street in 1877 for the exhibition of pictures, but was subsequently annexed into the adjoining Grosvenor

Club. It was much used by the Pre-Raphaelites and the aesthetes, in whose pictures intense greens and yellows often feature.

GUIZOT: Referred to in Colonel Calverley's 'Heavy Dragoon' song (*Patience*). François Pierre Guillaume Guizot (1787–1874), French writer, educational reformer and statesman, whose policies, while chief adviser to King Louis-Philippe, helped to precipitate the revolution which caused that monarch to abdicate in 1848.

GURNEYS: *At length I became as rich as the Gurneys* (Judge, *Trial*). A contemporary London banking family, of Norfolk origins.

HANNIBAL: See CAESAR or HANNIBAL.

HEAVY DRAGOON: *If you want a receipt for that popular mystery,*
　　　　　　Known to the world as a Heavy Dragoon
(Colonel Calverley, *Patience*).
An imaginary prescription: the satirical antithesis of the nimble light dragoon, or light cavalry.

HELIOGABALUS: *I quote in elegiacs all the crimes of Heliogabalus* (Major-General Stanley, *Pirates*).
Born in A.D. 204, Heliogabalus became Emperor of Rome soon after the murder of Caracalla (217) and made himself infamous by gluttony and debauchery. He was murdered in 222. There is a further reference by Tarara (*Utopia Limited*): *His Majesty is one of the most Heliogabalian profligates that ever disgraced an autocratic throne.*

HESSIANS: *A lover's professions,*
　　　　　When uttered in Hessians,
　　　　　Are eloquent everywhere! (Colonel Calverley, *Patience*).
High boots with decorative tassels, first worn by cavalry of the German state of Hesse and adopted by other armies.

HIGHLOWS: *Highlows pass as patent leathers* (Little Buttercup, *Pinafore*).

R

Victorian equivalent of the modern laced ankle boots, and
therefore totally unlike patent leather shoes.

HOPS: *Suburban hops* (Grosvenor, *Patience*).
Dances at local halls, as opposed to society balls.

HORACE: See MORRIS.

HOUSEHOLD CAVALRY: See LIFE GUARDS.

HOWELL AND JAMES: *A Howell and James young man* (Grosvenor, *Patience*).
A leading draper in Regent Street.

HURDY-GURDS: *Grinning herds*
Of hurdy-gurds
Retired apologising (King Gama, *Ida*).
The hurdy-gurdy was a familiar musical instrument in Victorian streets, not to be confused with the barrel-organ, which
is often given its name. It was portable, slung from the player's
neck, and played by turning a handle with one hand and
fingering keys with the other.

IN BANC: *May each decree*
As statute rank
And never be
Reversed in banc (Chorus, *Trial*).
i.e. by a Court of Appeal.

JACKY: *I've snuff and tobaccy, and excellent jacky* (Little Buttercup, *Pinafore*).
Plug tobacco.

JINK: See TODDY.

JOINT STOCK COMPANY'S ACT:
We'll go down to Posterity renowned
As the first Sovereign in Christendom
Who registered his Crown and Country under
The Joint Stock Company's Act of Sixty-two
(King Paramount, *Utopia*).

Act of 1862, since somewhat modified, to limit a company's liability to its creditors to the amount of its declared capital, hence the expression 'limited company'.

JORUM: *None so knowing as he*
At brewing a jorum of tea (Chorus, *Sorcerer*).
Properly, a drinking vessel of the punchbowl type, but here denoting a large teapotful.

JULLIEN: *The science of Jullien, the eminent musico* (Colonel Calverley, *Patience*).
Louis Antoine Jullien, or Julien (1812–60), sometime organizer and conductor of concerts and opera at Drury Lane, would be well remembered by audiences at *Patience*, twenty-one years after his death, for his eccentricities and a still-popular series of dances, *British Army Quadrilles*.

JUNKET: See TODDY.

K.C.B.: Knight Commander of the Order of the Bath, the second grade of Britain's second oldest order of chivalry. It is held by Sir Marmaduke Pointdextre (*Sorcerer*), Sir Joseph Porter (*Pinafore*), and Sir Edward Corcoran (*Utopia*).

KIRTLE: *It was of this Fairfax she spake, and he is her husband, or I'll swallow my kirtle* (Dame Carruthers, *Yeomen*).
A tunic, chemise or long petticoat with elaborate trimmings, at its most conspicuous in the Tudor age.

LEWIS AND ALLENBY: See SWAN AND EDGAR.

LIFE GUARDS: *And we are her escort – First Life Guards!* (Troopers, *Utopia*).
The British sovereign's personal escort, which enjoys precedence over all other regiments. They and the Royal Horse Guards (The Blues) comprise the Household Cavalry.

LITTLE EASE: *Is the Little Ease sufficiently uncomfortable?* (Phoebe, *Yeomen*).
A cell so small that the prisoner could neither lie down in it nor stand.

LOUISE, MADAME: *We're Madame Louise young girls* (Girls, *Patience*).
A fashionable Regent Street milliner.

MACAULAY: *Wit of Macaulay, who wrote of Queen Anne* (Colonel Calverley, *Patience*).
The historian Thomas Babington Macaulay (1800–59) 'wrote of Queen Anne' in his *History of England from the Accession of James II*, the first volumes of which appeared in 1848. 'Wit' here means intelligence, for Macaulay's writing was anything but witty in the other sense, though his love of paradox and his biting assertion of his own opinions would have been admired by Gilbert.

MAMELON: *When I know what is meant by 'mamelon' and 'ravelin'* (Major-General Stanley, *Pirates*).
These are archaic military terms relating to earth-works.

MANFRED: *Little of Manfred (but not very much of him)* (Colonel Calverley, *Patience*).
The hero of Byron's play of that name.

MANZANILLA: See XERES.

MARAVEDI: *He who shies*
    At such a prize
    Is not worth a maravedi (Lord Tolloller, *Iolanthe*).
A Spanish copper coin of the Victorian period, of infinitesimal value.

MAUSER: *When I can tell at sight a Mauser rifle from a javelin* (Major-General Stanley, *Pirates*).
The efficient rifle developed for the Prussian Army in 1871 and widely adopted by other armies. Originally this line referred to a 'chassepôt rifle', the earlier firearm of the French Army.

MAXIM GUN: *And how the Saxon and the Celt*
    Their Europe-shaking blows have dealt
    With Maxim gun and Nordenfeldt (Captain Corcoran, *Utopia*).

The Maxim and Nordenfeldt were types of quick-firing gun for use on land and sea, respectively.

MEPHISTO: *Force of Mephisto pronouncing a ban* (Colonel Calverley *Patience*).
The demon of Goethe's *Faust*.

MICAWBER: Referred to in Colonel Calverley's 'Heavy Dragoon' song (*Patience*). Wilkins Micawber was David Copperfield's landlord and mentor in Charles Dickens's novel, and one of the most familiar of all Dickens's characters.

MIDSHIPMITE: Tom Tucker, in *Pinafore*, is described as a midshipmite. This is not an actual naval term, but an affectionate reference to the extreme youth of many midshipmen in the old Royal Navy, sometimes as young as 11. A midshipman ranks above cadet and immediately below the lowest commissioned rank, sub-lieutenant.

MILLAIS: See FILDES.

MIYA SAMA: *Miya sama, miya sama,*
On n'm-ma no mayé ni
Pira-Pira suru no wa
Nan gia na
Toko tonyaré tonyaré na? (Chorus, *Mikado*).
This was the war song of the Imperial Army of Japan, composed in 1868. Except for the first four lines, Gilbert reproduced its sound, rather than its sense. It means:
'O my Prince, O my Prince,
'What is that fluttering in the wind
Before your Imperial horse?
Do you not know that that is a royal brocade flag,
Signifying our intention to defeat our enemies?'

MONTERO: See XERES.

MOP AND MOW: *Away they go, with a mop and a mow, to the revel that ends too soon* (Sir Roderic, *Ruddigore*).
A leering grimace.

MORRIS: *As a poet, I'm tender and quaint –*
I've passion and fervour and grace –
From Ovid and Horace
To Swinburne and Morris,
They all of them take a back place (Robin, *Ruddigore*).

As opposed to the ancient poets Publius Ovidius Naso (43 B.C.–A.D. 17) and Quintus Horatius Flaccus (65–8 B.C.), Algernon Charles Swinburne (1837–1909) and William Morris (1834–96) were as 'modern' as anyone Gilbert could have chosen to name; though *Ruddigore* is set quite some years before either of the latter was born.

MYSTICAL GERMANS: . . . *mystical Germans*
Who preach from ten till four (Mikado).

The Victorians would sit through marathon sermons, often without daring to leave their seats for fear they would immediately be taken by others. Theology and philosophy were frequently combined in these immense and intense dissertations, delivered often by divines from Germany, France and elsewhere.

NATIONAL SCHOOL: *In fact we rule*
A National School (Mad Margaret, *Ruddigore*).

The Elementary Education Act of 1870 established elementary schools, financed by the ratepayers, throughout England, to supplement the privately owned establishments which had supplied the only primary education hitherto available. These were called National Schools.

NELSON: *Pluck of Lord Nelson on board of the* Victory (Colonel Calverley, *Patience*).

Horatio, Viscount Nelson (1758–1805), Britain's greatest admiral, and victor at Trafalgar in his flagship H.M.S. *Victory*, 21 October, 1805. He fought the battle with great audacity, and also displayed his customary personal 'pluck', pacing the quarter-deck in full uniform and wearing all his orders as an inspiration to his men, until he was shot down by a marksman in the French ship *Redoubtable* alongside *Victory*.

NORDENFELDT: See MAXIM GUN.

OBOLOI: *I'll pay 'em (if they'll back me) all in* oboloi *and* drachmae (Ludwig, *Utopia*).
Units of Athenian currency, of small value.

ODALISQUE: *Grace of an Odalisque on a divan* (Colonel Calverley, *Patience*).
A female member of a harem.

ONE TREE HILL: *Hate me! I often roll down One Tree Hill!* (Mr Wells, *Sorcerer*).
A steep grassy hill below Greenwich Observatory, down which children and other young people delighted to roll, unmindful of dignity.

O NI! BIKKURI SHAKKURI TO!
    KATISHA: *In vain you interrupt with this tornado!*
        He is the only son of your –
        CHORUS: *O ni! bikkuri shakkuri to!* (*Mikado*)
This ejaculation, used to interrupt Katisha's disclosure of Nanki-Poo's identity, means the equivalent of today's 'We don't wish to know that!'

OTTO: *Breathing concentrated otto!*
    An existence à la Watteau (Counsel for the Plaintiff, *Trial*).
Otto is another term for attar, a perfumed oil derived from rose petals. Counsel is picturing his client's expectations of carefree bliss.

OVID: See MORRIS.

P. & O.: *A keener hand at scuttling a Cunarder or cutting out a P. & O. never shipped a handspike* (Pirate King, *Pirates*).
Like Cunard, Pacific and Orient was a leading shipping line by the time *Pirates* was produced.

PADDINGTON POLLAKY: *The keen penetration of Paddington Pollaky* (Colonel Calverley, *Patience*).

A noted contemporary detective, operating from the Paddington Police Office. He died in 1918.

PAGET: *Coolness of Paget about to trepan* (Colonel Calverley, *Patience*).

Sir James Paget (1814–99), one of the most noted surgeons in Victorian Britain, had been elected President of the Royal College of Surgeons in 1875, six years before *Patience* appeared.

PANDAEAN: *Gaily pipe Pandaean pleasure,*
     With a Daphnephoric bound (Chorus, *Patience*).

The god Pan personifies nature. Daphne, in mythology, evaded Apollo's amorous pursuit by being changed into a laurel, so a feature of the Daphnephoric festival at Thebes in Apollo's honour was the capering of a laurel-carrying youth.

PARLIAMENTARY TRAINS: *The idiot who, in railway carriages,*
          Scribbles on window-panes,
          We only suffer
          To ride on a buffer
          In Parliamentary trains (Mikado,
               Mikado).

The cheapest form of Victorian railway transportation – one penny a mile – these trains covered routes prescribed by an Act of Parliament, stopping at every station, making for journeys that were frustratingly slow and tediously uncomfortable. To ride on a buffer – i.e. the coupling between two coaches - implies the extreme of discomfort.

PECKHAM: See CAMBERWELL.

PEVERIL: *Peak-haunting Peveril* (Colonel Calverley, *Patience*).
Sir Geoffrey Peveril, called 'Peveril of the Peak', the cavalier hero of Sir Walter Scott's novel of that title.

PIANO-ORGANIST: One of the public nuisances referred to in Ko-Ko's song 'I've got a little list' (*Mikado*). The street piano, much in evidence in Victorian London, was sometimes known as a piano-organ because – though not the same instrument – it resembled a barrel-organ in operation.

PICKFORD: *He's a Parliamentary Pickford – he carries everything!* (Lord Mountararat, *Iolanthe*).

A punning reference to Strephon's fairy-aided ability to carry Parliamentary measures as he wishes them to go. Pickfords was – and still is, though now nationalized – a leading firm of carriers and removers.

POCKET BOROUGH: *I grew so rich that I was sent*
        By a pocket borough into Parliament (Sir Joseph
        Porter, *Pinafore*).

Until the Reform Act of 1832 influential worthies in districts of small population had the Parliamentary borough 'in their pocket', and could get whom they wished elected. The Queen of the Fairies in *Iolanthe* ('I've a borough or two at my disposal') makes Strephon a Member of Parliament by this means.

QUEEN'S BENCH: See EXCHEQUER, COURT OF.

RAPHAEL: See DOW, GERARD.

RAVELIN: See MAMELON.

RICHARDSON'S SHOW: Referred to in Colonel Calverley's 'Heavy Dragoon' song (*Patience*). A familiar attraction at Victorian fairs, as described by Charles Dickens in 'Greenwich Fair' (*Sketches by Boz*): 'This immense booth ... where you have a melo-drama (with three murders and a ghost), a pantomime, a comic song, an overture, and some incidental music, all done in five-and-twenty minutes.'

RODERICK: *Swagger of Roderick, heading his clan* (Colonel Calverley, *Patience*).

Roderick Dhu, the outlaw leader defeated by the Saxon Fitz-James in Sir Walter Scott's major narrative poem *The Lady of the Lake* (1810).

ROSHERVILLE: *Hate me! I sometimes go to Rosherville!* (Mr Wells, *Sorcerer*).

Rosherville Gardens, near Gravesend, was one of several pleasure haunts of Victorian Londoners. They were notorious
for the number of prostitutes who used them to ply their
trade.

SACHEVERELL, DOCTOR: Referred to in Colonel Calverley's
'Heavy Dragoon' song (*Patience*). Dr Henry Sacheverell
(1674–1724), impeached before the House of Lords for political
sermons which he preached at Derby and St Paul's, London,
in 1709. He was suspended from preaching for three
years, but as a result of much popular feeling being excited in
his favour, he gained widespread sympathy and eventual
reward.

SALLY LUNN: *Now for the muffin and toast,*
Now for the gay Sally Lunn! (Chorus, *Sorcerer*).
A tea-cake, originated by Sally Lunn, a Bath pastry-cook, who
sold them from a basket in the streets there in the late eighteenth century.

SEVEN DIALS: See BELGRAVE SQUARE.

SEWELL AND CROSS: See SWAN AND EDGAR.

SHALLOO HUMPS: *Then we probably review the household troops –*
With the usual 'Shalloo humps!' and 'Shalloo
hoops!' (Giuseppe, *Gondoliers*).
Drill sergeants' mutilations of words in shouting orders.

SHAW, CAPTAIN: *Oh, Captain Shaw!*
Type of true love kept under!
Could thy Brigade
With cold cascade
Quench my great love, I wonder! (Queen of the
Fairies, *Iolanthe*).
Sir Eyre Massey Shaw, K.C.B. (1830–1908) was chief of the
London Fire Brigade 1861–91. He was a keen theatre-goer
and was present at the first night of *Iolanthe*.

SILLERY: *Expressive glances*
Shall be our lances,
And pops of Sillery
Our light artillery (Hilarion, Cyril and Florian, *Ida*).

Sillery is a champagne-producing town. The three young princes propose to overcome Castle Adamant and its female occupants with nothing more violent than charm and the discharge of champagne corks.

SODOR AND MAN: *Style of the Bishop of Sodor and Man* (Colonel Calverley, *Patience*).

The style of this Anglican bishopric is impressive but illogical, for Sodor embraces the Hebrides and other isles west of Scotland, while the Isle of Man lies off Lancashire.

SOMERSET HOUSE: See CHANCERY LANE.

SOUTH KENSINGTON: *Red and Yellow! Primary colours! Oh, South Kensington!* (Jane, *Patience*).

South Kensington was the site of the leading art schools of the time. The juxtaposition of these primary colours would have occasioned much anguish there.

STRANGER, THE: *Flavour of Hamlet – the Stranger, a touch of him* (Colonel Calverley, *Patience*).

The Stranger was a popular tragedy by Benjamin Thompson from the German of August Kotzebue, first performed in London in 1798 and often revived. It was played again not long before Gilbert wrote *Patience*.

SWAN AND EDGAR:

Let old associations all dissolve,
Let Swan secede from Edgar – Gask from Gask,
Sewell from Cross – Lewis from Allenby!
In other words – let Chaos come again! (Princess, *Ida*).

These are all names of leading London firms patronized by fashionable ladies for dress-making materials.

SWINBURNE: See MORRIS.

TENNYSON: See TUPPER and TENNYSON.

THACKERAY: See DICKENS and THACKERAY.

TIES PAY THE DEALER: *And you're playing round games, and he calls you bad names when you tell him that 'ties pay the dealer'* (Lord Chancellor, *Iolanthe*).

In gambling games, for example *Vingt-et-Un* (also known as Pontoon or Blackjack), a player generally loses to the dealer, who holds the 'bank', if his hand is lower than, or even equal to, i.e. ties with, the dealer's.

TIMONEER: *And teach him the trade of a timoneer* (Don Alhambra, *Gondoliers*).

A helmsman.

TODDY: *When he had Rhenish wine to drink*
    It made him very sad to think
    That some, at junket or at jink,
    Must be content with toddy (Don Alhambra, *Gondoliers*).

Spirits mixed with sugar and hot water: a much less appropriate form of drink than Rhenish wine for the sort of gay feast which the terms junket and jink (high jinks) imply.

TOILET CLUB: *He grew moustachios, and he took his tub,*
    And he paid a guinea to a toilet club (Psyche, *Ida*).

An exclusive gentlemen's hairdressing establishment.

TOKO: *For yam I should get toko* (Yum-Yum, *Mikado*).

Toko was a Victorian schoolboy's expression for punishment, in the form of a thrashing or 'bread and scrape', i.e. bread with the thinnest coating of butter. In other words, instead of yam (the sweet potato, or something sweet) I should get something nasty.

TONTINE: The lady shall be entrusted to an officer of Household Cavalry as stakeholder, who is bound to hand her over to the survivor (on the Tontine principle) (Fitzbattleaxe, *Utopia*).

A principle, generally of financial application, under which the last surviving member of a group of subscribers gets the whole amount.

TROLLOPE, ANTHONY: Referred to in Colonel Calverley's

'Heavy Dragoon' song (*Patience*). Prolific novelist (1815–82), his best-known works are the Barchester series.

TUPPER AND TENNYSON: Referred to in Colonel Calverley's 'Heavy Dragoon' song (*Patience*). Martin Tupper (1810–89) was author of the tremendously successful *Proverbial Philosophy* (1838–67). Alfred, Lord Tennyson (1809–92) was Poet Laureate from 1850 until his death. Gilbert based *Princess Ida* on Tennyson's *The Princess*.

TUSSAUD, MADAME: *The amateur tenor, whose vocal villainies*
    All desire to shirk,
    Shall, during off-hours,
    Exhibit his powers
    To Madame Tussaud's waxwork (Mikado, Mikado).

Marie Tussaud (1760–1850) was born in Berne, learned wax modelling in Paris where she modelled many heads of Revolutionary victims, and brought her craft to London in 1802. In 1884, the year before *The Mikado*, her exhibition had moved from the premises it had occupied in Baker Street since 1833 to a building on the present site in Marylebone Road.

VICTOR EMMANUEL: Referred to in Colonel Calverley's 'Heavy Dragoon' song (*Patience*). Victor Emmanuel II (1820–78), King of Sardinia, became unified Italy's first king.

WARD: *And every one who'd marry a Ward*
    Must come to me for my accord (Lord Chancellor, *Iolanthe*).
A minor under legal guardianship, in this case of the Court of Chancery.

WATERFORD, LORD: *A smack of Lord Waterford, reckless and rollicky* (Colonel Calverley, *Patience*).
Most likely Henry Beresford, 3rd Marquis of Waterford (1811–59), eccentric and noted practical joker. He was killed while hunting.

WATERLOO HOUSE: *Waterloo House young man* (Grosvenor, *Patience*).

A leading drapery firm, Messrs Halling, Pearce and Stone, occupied Waterloo House, Cockspur Street.

WATTS, DR: *She'll scarcely suffer Dr Watts's hymns* (King Gama, *Ida*).

Isaac Watts (1674–1748) wrote hundreds of hymns, among them the well-known 'When I survey the wondrous Cross' and 'O God, our help in ages past'.

XERES: *Xeres we'll drink – Manzanilla, Montero* (Chorus, *Gondoliers*).

Spanish wines, of which the first two are sherries.

YEOMEN OF THE GUARD: In Henry VIII's time this personal, dismounted bodyguard to the sovereign was stationed in the Tower of London; but the guards in Tudor garb familiar to visitors to the Tower today are Yeomen Warders, a different corps, whose duties are confined to the Tower itself. The term 'Beefeaters', commonly applied to both, seems to have originated from their well-fed appearance at a time when few common folk could afford to eat beef.

ZOFFANY: See DOW, GERARD.

Discography

It would be impossible to compile a definitive Gilbert and Sullivan discography. Virtually complete recordings of many of the works were being sold as long ago as 1907 and countless others have followed, not to mention hundreds of recordings of selections, potpourris and individual songs and overtures. I have confined my list to recordings of 'complete' works, or substantial selections of 'highlights', that are currently available on long-playing or extended-play discs, or were so recently deleted from the catalogues that they are still often to be found on sale. Ardent collectors who wish to seek out the earlier 78 r.p.m. records should try to see a copy of *The D'Oyly Carte Opera Company in Gilbert and Sullivan Operas* by Cyril Rollins and R. John Witts (Michael Joseph, London), which, unfortunately, is as hard to find as are many of the records listed in its discography.

I have also omitted record numbers and the names of the companies publishing them. This is because the numbering system throughout the world is undergoing radical changes; and because so many leading record publishers are now conglomerates that it takes an expert to identify which label belongs to which group. Also, records originated under one label are published under others in other countries, or as budget offers. Any good record dealer will be able to identify the issues listed here by reference to the title, artists and conductor. In case of utter frustration, I shall be pleased to give what help I can to any reader caring to write to me through Drake Publishers Inc.

. . . .

TRIAL BY JURY

Reed, Hood, Round, Sandford, Adams, Raffell, D'Oyly Carte Chorus; Royal Opera House Orchestra, Covent Garden, cond. Godfrey. (1 l.p., inc. on reverse side excerpts from *Utopia*, q.v.)

Watson, Flynn, Harding, Osborn, Rands, Harris, D'Oyly Carte Chorus; orchestra cond. Godfrey. (1 l.p.)

Sheffield, Lawson, Oldham, Hosking, Baker, D'Oyly Carte Chorus. (A one-side reissue of the 78 r.p.m. recording, coupled on 2 l.ps. with a reissue of the 78 r.p.m. *Pinafore* – see below.)

Baker, Morison, Lewis, Cameron, Brannigan, Turgeon; Pro Arte Orchestra and Glyndebourne Festival Chorus, cond. Sargent. (Coupled with *Pinafore*, q.v.).

SORCERER

Without dialogue: Adams, Palmer, Styler, Riley, Reed, Masterson, Allister, Hood, D'Oyly Carte Chorus; Royal Philharmonic Orchestra, cond. Godfrey. (2 l.ps.)

Without dialogue: Griffiths, Skitch, Adams, Pratt, Drummond-Grant, Harding, Dixon, Dean, D'Oyly Carte Chorus; New Symphony Orchestra of London, cond. Godfrey (2 l.ps.)

Highlights: Skitch, Harding, Morgan, Drummond-Grant, Pratt, Griffiths, Dixon, D'Oyly Carte Chorus; New Symphony Orchestra, cond. Godfrey. (1 l.p. with *Pinafore* highlights on reverse.)

PINAFORE

With dialogue: Reed, Wales, Lawlor, Palmer, Mason, Masterson, Ayldon, Jackson, Ellison, D'Oyly Carte Chorus; Royal Philharmonic Orchestra, cond. James Walker. (2 l.ps.)

With dialogue: Reed, Skitch, Round, Adams, Cook, Wilson-Hyde, Hindmarsh, Wright, Knight, D'Oyly Carte Chorus; New Symphony Orchestra, cond. Godfrey. (2 l.ps.)

Without dialogue: Green, Rands, Osborn, Fancourt, Walker, Flynn, Halman, Harding, D'Oyly Carte Chorus; orchestra cond. Godfrey. (2 l.ps.)

Without dialogue: Lytton, Baker, Goulding, Fancourt, Granville, Robertson, Griffin, Briercliffe, Lewis, D'Oyly Carte Chorus; (2 l.ps. comprising a reissue of the 78 r.p.m. recording on three sides, coupled with the 78 r.p.m. recording of *Trial*, q.v.).

Without dialogue: Baker, Cameron, Lewis, Brannigan, Milligan, Morison, Thomas, Sinclair; Pro Arte Orchestra and Glyndebourne Festival Chorus, cond. Sargent. (2 l.ps. coupled with *Trial*, q.v.)

Highlights from the above version. (1 l.p.)

Excerpts from the above version. (1 l.p.)

Highlights: Osborn, Rands, Green, Gillingham, Harding, Walker, D'Oyly Carte Chorus; orchestra cond. Godfrey. (1 l.p. with *Sorcerer* highlights on reverse.)

Highlights: Stephens, Landis, Downie, Camburn, Sammes, Wilson-Hyde; The Mike Sammes Singers and Orchestra, cond. Gregory. (1 l.p.)

Excerpts: Skitch, Reed, Hindmarsh; New Symphony Orchestra, cond. Godfrey. (1 e.p.)

PIRATES

With dialogue: Reed, Adams, Cook, Potter, Brannigan, Masterson, Allister, Wales, Maisey, Palmer, D'Oyly Carte Chorus; Royal Philharmonic Orchestra, cond. Godfrey. (2 l.ps.)

Without dialogue: Pratt, Adams, Short, Sandford, Hindmarsh, Dixon, Martin, Drummond-Grant, D'Oyly Carte Chorus; New Symphony Orchestra, cond. Godfrey. (2 l.ps.)

Without dialogue: Green, Evans, Goodier, Emmanuel, Shelley, Newman, Avis, Howe, Richards; orchestra and chorus cond. Alan Ward. (2 l.ps.)

Highlights: Baker, Milligan, Cameron, Lewis, Brannigan, Morison, Harper, Thomas, Sinclair; Pro Arte Orchestra and Glyndebourne Festival Chorus, cond. Sargent. (2 l.ps.)

Highlights: Baker, Oldham, Fancourt, Lewis, Granville, Dixon, Robertson, D'Oyly Carte Chorus; orchestra cond. Sargent. (An abridged version, on 1 l.p., from the version issued on 78 r.p.m. discs.)

Highlights: Stephens, Landis, Downie, Heard, Wilson-Hyde, Sammes; Mike Sammes Singers and Orchestra, cond. Gregory. (1 l.p.)

PATIENCE

With dialogue: Adams, Cartier, Potter, Reed, Sandford, Sansom, Newman, Lloyd-Jones, Toye, Knight, D'Oyly Carte Chorus; New Symphony Orchestra, cond. Godfrey. (2 l.ps.)

Without dialogue: Adams, Round, Pratt, Sandford, Styler, Grundy, Hindmarsh, Dixon, Toye, Drummond-Grant, D'Oyly Carte Chorus; New Symphony Orchestra, cond. Godfrey. (2 l.ps.)

Without dialogue: Fancourt, Pratt, Griffiths, Green, Styler, Dean, Drummond-Grant, Halman, Harding, Mitchell, D'Oyly Carte Chorus; orchestra cond. Godfrey. (2 l.ps.)

IOLANTHE

With dialogue: Reed, Adams, Round, Sandford, Styler, Knight, Newman, Sansom, D'Oyly Carte Chorus; Section of Grenadier Guards Band and New Symphony Orchestra, cond. Godfrey. (2 l.ps.)

Without dialogue: Green, Thornton, Osborn, Morgan, Styler, Halman, Drummond-Grant, Hill, Dean, Mitchell, D'Oyly Carte Chorus; orchestra cond. Godfrey. (2 l.ps.)

Baker, Wallace, Young, Brannigan, Cameron, Sinclair, Thomas, Cantelo, Harper, Morison; Pro Arte Orchestra and Glyndebourne Festival Chorus, cond. Sargent. (2 l.ps.)

Highlights from the above version. (1 l.p.)

Highlights: Green, Morgan, Thornton, Osborn, Mitchell, D'Oyly Carte Chorus; orchestra cond. Godfrey. (1 l.p. with *Gondoliers* on reverse.)

Excerpts: Reed, Adams, Sansom, Round, Sandford, D'Oyly Carte Chorus; Section of Grenadier Guards Band and New Symphony Orchestra, cond. Godfrey. (1 e.p.)

Highlights: Thomas, Landis, Curtis, Sammes, Camburn; Mike Sammes Singers and Orchestra, cond. Gregory. (1 l.p.)

Excerpts: Shilling, Harwood, Kern, Green; Sadler's Wells Chorus and Orchestra, cond. Faris. (1 l.p.)

PRINCESS IDA

Without dialogue: Sandford, Potter, Palmer, Skitch, Reed, Adams, Raffell, Cook, Harwood, Hood, Masterson, D'Oyly Carte Chorus; Royal Philharmonic Orchestra, cond. Sargent. (2 l.ps.)

Without dialogue: Pratt, Dixon, Harding, Morey, Sladen, Round, Osborn, Skitch, Drummond-Grant, Morgan, Adams, Banks, Hill, D'Oyly Carte Chorus; New Symphony Orchestra, cond. Godfrey. (2 l.ps.)

Highlights: Sandford, Potter, Adams, Raffell, Cook, Reed, Masterson, Hood, Harwood, Palmer, Skitch, D'Oyly Carte Chorus; Royal Philharmonic Orchestra, cond. Sargent. (1 l.p.)

MIKADO

Without dialogue: Adams, Round, Pratt, Sandford, Styler, Grundy, Hindmarsh, Dixon, Toye, Drummond-Grant, D'Oyly Carte Chorus; New Symphony Orchestra, cond. Godfrey. (2 l.ps.)

Without dialogue: Fancourt, Osborn, Green, Watson, Styler, Flynn, Mitchell, Gillingham, Wright, Halman, D'Oyly Carte Chorus; orchestra cond. Godfrey. (2 l.ps.)

Without dialogue: Wakefield, Heddle-Nash, Revill, Holmes; Sadler's Wells Chorus and Orchestra, cond. Faris. (2 l.ps.)

Without dialogue: Brannigan, Lewis, Evans, Wallace, Morison, Thomas Pro Arte Orchestra and Glyndebourne Festival Chorus, cond. Sargent. (2 l.ps.)

Highlights from the above version. (1 l.p.)

Highlights: Stephens, Curtis, Camburn, Landis, Wilson-Hyde, Heard, Sammes; Mike Sammes Singers and Orchestra, cond. Gregory. (1 l.p.)

Excerpts: Fancourt, Flynn, Granville, Green, Oldham, Rands, D'Oyly Carte Chorus; orchestra cond. Godfrey. (1 l.p. comprising excerpts from the 78 r.p.m.)

Excerpts: Hindmarsh, Dixon, Toye, Round, Pratt, D'Oyly Cart Chorus; New Symphony Orchestra, cond. Godfrey. (1 e.p.)

RUDDIGORE

Without dialogue: Reed, Round, Sandford, Hindmarsh, Allister, Knight, Adams, Riley, Sansom, D'Oyly Carte Chorus; Royal Opera House Orchestra, cond. Godfrey. (2 l.ps.)

Without dialogue: Green, Osborn, Watson, Flynn, Fancourt, Mitchell, Drummond-Grant, Halman, Thurlow, D'Oyly Carte Chorus; orchestra cond. Godfrey. (2 l.ps.)

Highlights: Halman, Green, Mitchell, Osborn, Flynn, Fancourt, Watson, Drummond-Grant, D'Oyly Carte Chorus; orchestra cond. Godfrey. (1 l.p., *Yeomen* on reverse.)

YEOMEN

Without dialogue: Raffell, Potter, Adams, Palmer, Reed, Sandford, Lawler, Harwood, Hood, Knight, Eales, D'Oyly Carte Chorus; Royal Philharmonic Orchestra, cond. Sargent. (2 l.ps.)

Without dialogue: Harris, Osborn, Fancourt, Griffiths, Green, Watson, Sanders, Harding, Halman, Thurlow, Drummond-Grant, D'Oyly Carte Chorus; New Symphony Orchestra, cond. Godfrey. (2 l.ps.)

Without dialogue: Dowling, Lewis, Carol-Case, Young, Brannigan, Cameron, Morison, Thomas, Sinclair, Hume; Pro Arte Orchestra and Glyndebourne Festival Chorus, cond. Sargent. (2 l.ps.)

Highlights from the above version. (1 l.p.)

Highlights: Hood, Lawlor, Potter, Reed, Harwood, Raffell, Knight, Sandford, Adams, Eales, D'Oyly Carte Chorus; Royal Philharmonic Orchestra, cond. Sargent. (1 l.p.)

Highlights: Drummond-Grant, Osborn, Green, Harding, Fancourt, Halman, Thurlow, D'Oyly Carte Chorus; orchestra cond. Godfrey. (1 l.p. with *Ruddigore* on reverse.)

Highlights: Thomas, Cole, Landis, Camburn; Mike Sammes Singers and Orchestra, cond. Gregory. (1 l.p.)

Excerpts: Harwood, Reed, Hood, Potter, D'Oyly Carte Chorus; Royal Philharmonic Orchestra, cond. Sargent. (1 e.p.)

GONDOLIERS

With dialogue: Reed, Skitch, Sandford, Round, Styler, Wakeham, Cook, Knight, Toye, Sansom, Wright, Bradshaw, Jones, Gill, Roach, D'Oyly Carte Chorus; New Symphony Orchestra, cond. Godfrey. (3 l.ps. with *Cox & Box* on side 6).

Without dialogue: Green, Goodier, Watson, Osborn, Styler, Sanders,

Hancock, Flynn, Youngman, Halman, Mitchell, Harding, Dean, Walsh, Wright, Fane, D'Oyly Carte Chorus; orchestra cond. Godfrey. (2 l.ps.)

Without dialogue: Evans, Young, Brannigan, Lewis, Cameron, Sinclair, Morison, Thomas, Watts; Pro Arte Orchestra and Glyndebourne Festival Chorus, cond. Sargent. (2 l.ps.)

Highlights from the above version. (1 l.p.)

Highlights: Osborn, Styler, Green, Halman, Mitchell, Goodier, Watson, Dean, Harding, Walsh, D'Oyly Carte Chorus; orchestra cond. Godfrey. (2 l.ps.)

Highlights: M. Thomas, I. Thomas, Curtis, Camburn, Sammes, Wilson-Hyde; Mike Sammes Singers and Orchestra, cond. Gregory. (1 l.p.)

Excerpts: Wakeham, Round, Styler, Reed, Knight, Toye, Skitch, Sandford, Wright, D'Oyly Carte Chorus; New Symphony Orchestra, cond. Godfrey. (1 e.p.)

UTOPIA

Excerpts: Reed, Sandford, Hood, Round, Allister, Adams, Raffell, D'Oyly Carte Chorus, Royal Opera House Orchestra, cond. Godfrey. (1 l.p., these excerpts occupying part of the reverse side, preceded by *Trial.*)

MISCELLANEOUS

COX AND BOX (by Sullivan and Burnand). Riordan, Styler, Adams. New Symphony Orchestra, cond. Godfrey. (Side 6 of the 3 l.p. D'Oyly Carte Company's *Gondoliers* – see above.)

D'OYLY CARTE SPECTACULAR. Excerpts from *Pinafore, Pirates, Mikado, Ruddigore.* D'Oyly Carte Soloists and Chorus; Royal Philharmonic Orchestra, cond. Sargent. (1 l.p.)

GILBERT AND SULLIVAN CHORUSES. Excerpts from *Iolanthe, Pirates, Pinafore, Ruddigore, Mikado, Trial, Patience, Yeomen, Ida, Sorcerer, Gondoliers.* D'Oyly Carte Soloists and Chorus; Royal Philharmonic Orchestra, cond. Walker. (1 l.p.)

CHORUSES FROM THE SAVOY OPERAS. Excerpts from *Pinafore, Iolanthe, Mikado, Pirates, Yeomen, Trial, Patience, Gondoliers, Ruddigore.* D'Oyly Carte Chorus and Orchestra, cond. Godfrey. (1 l.p.)

WORLD OF GILBERT AND SULLIVAN, THE. Excerpts from *Pinafore, Ruddigore, Ida, Gondoliers, Patience, Mikado, Iolanthe, Yeomen, Sorcerer, Pirates*. Green, Gillingham, Osborn, Pratt, Mitchell, Halman, Styler, Goodier, Harding, Drummond-Grant, Watson, D'Oyly Carte Chorus; orchestra cond. Godfrey. (1 l.p.)

WORLD OF GILBERT AND SULLIVAN, THE, Vol. I. Excerpts from *Pinafore, Ida, Mikado, Gondoliers, Patience*. Reed, Wright, Knight, Hindmarsh, Skitch, Adams, Raffell, Cook, Round, Dixon, Toye, Pratt, Styler, D'Oyly Carte Chorus; New Symphony Orchestra, cond. Godfrey and Royal Philharmonic Orchestra, cond. Sargent. (1 l.p.)

WORLD OF GILBERT AND SULLIVAN, THE, Vol. II. Excerpts from *Yeomen, Iolanthe, Pirates, Ruddigore*. Lawlor, Hood, Reed, Harwood, Toye, Wales, Adams, Round, Brannigan, Masterson, Allister, Potter, Hindmarsh, Sandford, D'Oyly Carte Chorus; Royal Philharmonic Orchestra, New Symphony Orchestra, Royal Opera House Orchestra, cond. Sargent and Godfrey. (1 l.p.)

WORLD OF GILBERT AND SULLIVAN, THE, Vol. III. Excerpts from *Gondoliers, Trial, Ruddigore, Iolanthe, Mikado, Sorcerer, Patience*. Reed, Knight, Toye, Skitch, Sandford, Wakeham, Sansom, Round, Wright, Styler, Hindmarsh, Pratt, Drummond-Grant, Dixon, Palmer, Newman, D'Oyly Carte Chorus; various orchestras, cond. Godfrey. (1 l.p.)

THE BEST OF GILBERT AND SULLIVAN. Excerpts from *Mikado, Pirates, Pinafore, Iolanthe, Gondoliers, Patience*. Allister, Clarke, Glover, Adams, Cartier, Fleet, Howlett, Raffel, Riley, Sandford, Beecham Choral Society; Royal Philharmonic Orchestra, cond. Walker. (3 l.ps.) published by Reader's Digest Association, but not available through retailers. One side each devoted to the excerpts.)

BALLADS, SONGS AND SNATCHES, Vol. I. Excerpts from *Yeomen, Mikado, Trial, Ida, Gondoliers, Ruddigore, Pirates, Iolanthe, Sorcerer, Pinafore*. D'Oyly Carte Chorus and Orchestra, cond. Godfrey. (1 l.p.)

BALLADS, SONGS AND SNATCHES, Vol. II. Excerpts from *Ida, Gondoliers, Mikado, Pinafore, Pirates, Yeomen, Ruddigore, Patience, Trial, Sorcerer*. D'Oyly Carte Chorus and Orchestra, cond. Godfrey. (1 l.p.)

SONGS AND SNATCHES. Excerpts from *Gondoliers, Iolanthe, Ruddigore, Yeomen*. D'Oyly Carte Chorus; Royal Philharmonic Orchestra, cond. Walker. (1 l.p.)

PINEAPPLE POLL. The arrangement by Charles Mackerras of music from the Gilbert and Sullivan operas and other pieces by Sullivan for John Cranko's ballet with this title (first performance Sadler's Wells Theatre Ballet, March 1951); based on 'The Bumboat Woman's Story' from *Bab Ballads*. Royal Philharmonic Orchestra, cond. Mackerras. (1 l.p.)

A Selected Bibliography

TEXTS

Libretti of the Savoy Operas have been published singly by Chappell & Co. Ltd. Collected editions of the libretti have been published by Macmillan & Co., Corgi Books, and Oxford University Press (World Classics edition, two volumes).

The following books contain the texts of various works by Gilbert, together with extensive historical and critical introductions by the editors:

Reginald Allen, *The First Night Gilbert and Sullivan* (Heritage Press, New York, 1958)

James Ellis, *The Bab Ballads* (Oxford University Press, London, 1970)

Terence Rees, *Thespis: A Gilbert & Sullivan Enigma* (Dillon's University Bookshop, London, 1964)

Jane W. Stedman, *Gilbert Before Sullivan: Six Comic Plays* (Routledge & Kegan Paul, London, 1969)

BIBLIOGRAPHIES

Reginald Allen, *W. S. Gilbert: An Anniversary Survey* (The Bibliographical Society of the University of Virginia, Charlottesville, 1963)

Townley Searle, *Sir William Schwenck Gilbert* (Alexander-Ouseley Ltd., London, 1931)

PICTORIAL COLLECTIONS

Raymond Mander and Joe Mitchenson, *Gilbert and Sullivan: A Picture History* (Vista Books, London, 1962)

Roger Wood, *A D'Oyly Carte Album* (Adam and Charles Black, London, 1953)

BIOGRAPHIES, CRITICAL WORKS, ETC.

Leslie Baily, *The Gilbert and Sullivan Book*. Revised edition. (Spring Books, London, 1966)

Edith A. Browne, *W. S. Gilbert*. Stars of the Stage Series. (John Lane, London, 1907)

François Cellier and Cunningham Bridgeman, *Gilbert, Sullivan and D'Oyly Carte* (Sir Isaac Pitman & Sons Ltd., London, 1914)

William Cox-Ife, *Training the Gilbert and Sullivan Chorus* (Chappell & Co. Ltd., London, 1954)

William Cox-Ife, *How to Sing Both Gilbert and Sullivan* (Chappell & Co. Ltd., London, 1961)

Sidney Dark and Rowland Grey, *W. S. Gilbert: His Life and Letters* (Methuen & Co. Ltd., London, 1923)

W. A. Darlington, *The World of Gilbert and Sullivan* (Peter Nevill Limited, London, 1951)

Thomas F. Dunhill, *Sullivan's Comic Operas* (Edward Arnold & Co., London, 1928)

Percy Fitzgerald, *The Savoy Opera and the Savoyards* (Chatto & Windus, London, 1894)

Isaac Goldberg, *The Story of Gilbert and Sullivan* (John Murray, London, 1929)

Gervase Hughes, *The Music of Arthur Sullivan* (Macmillan & Co. Ltd., London, 1960)

Arthur Jacobs, *Gilbert and Sullivan* (Max Parrish & Co. Limited, London, 1951)

John Bush Jones (Ed), *W. S. Gilbert: A Century of Scholarship and Commentary* (New York University Press, 1970)

Hesketh Pearson, *Gilbert: His Life and Strife* (Methuen & Co. Ltd., London, 1957)

Cyril Rollins and R. John Witts, *The D'Oyly Carte Opera Company in Gilbert and Sullivan Opera: A Record of Productions 1875–1961* (Michael Joseph, London, 1962). Two supplements update this work to 1972.

Herbert Sullivan and Newman Flower, *Sir Arthur Sullivan* (Cassell & Company Ltd., London, 1927)

Audrey Williamson, *Gilbert and Sullivan Opera* (Rockliff, London, 1953)

Percy H. Young, *Sir Arthur Sullivan* (J. M. Dent & Sons Ltd, London, 1971)

Gilbert & Sullivan Journal issued by the Gilbert & Sullivan Society to its members.

REMINISCENCES OF FORMER SAVOYARDS

The following works are not histories of Gilbert and Sullivan performances, but are the anecdotal memoirs of members of the D'Oyly Carte Company and therefore particularly interesting for their revelations of the players' personalities.

Rutland Barrington, *Rutland Barrington by Himself* (Grant Richards, London, 1908)

Rutland Barrington, *More Rutland Barrington* (Grant Richards, London, 1911)

Jessie Bond and Ethel MacGeorge, *The Life and Reminiscences of Jessie Bond* (John Lane, London, 1930)

Martyn Green, *Here's a How-de-do* (Max Reinhardt, London, 1952)

George Grossmith, *A Society Clown* (J. W. Arrowsmith, Bristol, 1888)

Winifred Lawson, *A Song to Sing-O* (Michael Joseph, London, 1955)

Henry Lytton, *The Secrets of a Savoyard* (Jarrolds, London, no date)

Henry Lytton, *A Wandering Minstrel* (Jarrolds, London, 1933)

BOOKS ON GILBERT AND SULLIVAN WRITTEN SPECIALLY FOR CHILDREN

Illustrated by Anne and Janet Grahame Johnstone
Told by Martha Mearns, H.M.S. *Pinafore*

Told by Jean Blashfield, *The Pirates of Penzance*

Told by Jean Blashfield, *Iolanthe*

Told by Martha Mearns, *The Yeomen of the Guard*

Told by Jean Blashfield, *The Gondoliers* (Thomas Nelson and Sons Ltd., London, 1966)

Told by Sir W. S. Gilbert, Illustrated by Alice B. Woodward, *The Pinafore Book* (George Bell and Sons, London, 1908)

Told by Sir W. S. Gilbert, Illustrated by Alice B. Woodward, *The Story of The Mikado* (Daniel O'Connor, London)

W. Russell Flint, *Illustrated editions of the Operas by W. S. Gilbert* (George Bell and Sons, London, 1911/1912)

Louis Untermeyer, *The Last Pirate*: Tales from the Gilbert and Sullivan Operas, illustrated by Reginald Birch (Harcourt, Brace and Company, New York, 1934)

Robert Lawrence (adapted) H.M.S. *Pinafore, The Mikado, The Gondoliers (and possibly other Operas)*, illustrated by Sheilah Beckett (Grosset and Dunlap, New York, 1940)

H. W. Reiter and Shepard Chartoe *The Merry Gentlemen of Japan*, illustrated by Philip Gelb (The Bass Publishers, New York, 1935)